LIBERTARIANISM
THE BASICS

Libertarianism: The Basics is an up-to-date and accessible introduction to libertarianism that breaks down abstract philosophical ideas in a fresh way.

Flanigan and Freiman interweave a wide-ranging survey of different libertarian philosophical traditions, with a discussion of libertarian perspectives on various applied topics of contemporary interest. Chapters introduce readers to the major theoretical debates in libertarianism, illustrating these debates through real-world policy case studies that draw on contemporary issues concerning criminal justice reform, immigration policy, national security, the environment, and more.

Ideal for teaching and appropriate for students at all levels, including high school, *Libertarianism: The Basics* will be a go-to-text for anyone who is interested in learning more about political philosophy, applied ethics, philosophy, politics, economics, and public policy. The authors present arguments and ideas through a series of historical and contemporary cases, making the book suitable for all readers who want to learn about cutting-edge libertarian views on matters in both political philosophy and public policy.

Jessica Flanigan is the Richard L. Morrill Chair of Ethics and Democratic Values at the University of Richmond. Her research addresses the ethics of public policy, medicine, and business. Jess is the author of *Pharmaceutical Freedom* (OUP 2017), *Debating Sex Work* (OUP 2019), and *Why It's OK to Have Bad Spelling and Grammar* (Routledge 2025). Jess has also published scholarly articles in *Philosophical Studies*, *Australasian Journal of Philosophy*, *The Journal of Moral Philosophy*, *The Journal of Political Philosophy*, and *The Journal of Business Ethics*. Her research has been featured in media outlets including NPR, *The Washington Post*, *Reason*, *Slate*, and *The Conversation*. At the University of Richmond, she received the Distinguished Educator Award, the Distinguished Scholarship Award, and Faculty Member of the Year. She teaches Leadership Ethics, Medical Ethics, and Critical Thinking.

Christopher Freiman is Professor of General Business in the John Chambers College of Business and Economics at West Virginia University. Previously, he was Associate Professor of Philosophy at William & Mary. Chris is the author of *Unequivocal Justice* and *Why It's OK to Ignore Politics* as well as over 50 articles and chapters on topics including democratic theory, distributive justice, and immigration. His work has appeared in *The Australasian Journal of Philosophy*, *Philosophy and Phenomenological Research*, *Philosophical Studies*, *The Journal of Political Philosophy*, *Social Philosophy and Policy*, *The Journal of Ethics*, *Politics, Philosophy, and Economics*, *The Journal of Ethics and Social Philosophy*, *The Journal of Politics*, and *The Oxford Handbook of Political Philosophy*. Chris's writing has also been featured in a variety of popular outlets, including *The Washington Post*, *Reason*, *Aeon*, and *Inside Higher Education*. At William & Mary, he received an Alumni Fellowship Award for Excellence in Teaching and the Class of 1963 Term Distinguished Associate Professorship of Philosophy.

THE BASICS SERIES

The Basics is a highly successful series of accessible guidebooks which provide an overview of the fundamental principles of a subject area in a jargon-free and undaunting format.

Intended for students approaching a subject for the first time, the books both introduce the essentials of a subject and provide an ideal springboard for further study. With over 50 titles spanning subjects from artificial intelligence (AI) to women's studies, *The Basics* are an ideal starting point for students seeking to understand a subject area.

Each text comes with recommendations for further study and gradually introduces the complexities and nuances within a subject.

BIOPSYCHOLOGY
PHILIP WINN AND MADELEINE GREALY

AMERICAN PHILOSOPHY
NANCY STANLICK

ANCIENT EGYPT
DONALD P. RYAN

ANCIENT NEAR EAST
DANIEL C. SNELL

ANIMAL ETHICS
TONY MILLIGAN

ANTHROPOLOGY
PETER METCALF

ARCHAEOLOGY (SECOND EDITION)
CLIVE GAMBLE

ART HISTORY
GRANT POOKE AND DIANA NEWALL

ARTIFICIAL INTELLIGENCE
KEVIN WARWICK

ATTACHMENT THEORY
RUTH O'SHAUGHNESSY,
KATHERINE BERRY, RUDI DALLOS AND
KAREN BATESON

BEHAVIORAL ECONOMICS
(SECOND EDITION)
PHILIP CORR AND ANKE PLAGNOL

LIBERTARIANISM
JESSICA FLANIGAN AND
CHRISTOPHER FREIMAN

For more information about this series, please visit:
www.routledge.com/The-Basics/book-series/B

LIBERTARIANISM

THE BASICS

JESSICA FLANIGAN AND CHRISTOPHER FREIMAN

Routledge
Taylor & Francis Group

NEW YORK AND LONDON

Designed cover image: 'enjoynz' on Getty Images

First published 2026
by Routledge
605 Third Avenue, New York, NY 10158

and by Routledge
4 Park Square, Milton Park, Abingdon, Oxon, OX14 4RN

Routledge is an imprint of the Taylor & Francis Group, an informa business

ISBN: 978-1-032-21967-7 (hbk)
ISBN: 978-1-032-21962-2 (pbk)
ISBN: 978-1-003-27072-0 (ebk)

DOI: 10.4324/9781003270720

Typeset in Bembo
by Apex CoVantage, LLC

CONTENTS

PREFACE

This book is an introduction to libertarianism as an applied political philosophy. We approach this topic through a series of cases in order to make these ideas accessible to anyone who is interested in ethics and public policy. Philosophical training is not required to engage with the ideas in this book. Through a series of examples and thought experiments, we show that libertarian ideas matter for the decisions that people make every day.

A limitation of this approach is that we cover some of the more philosophical, historical, and empirical aspects of the libertarian tradition quite quickly. Instead of describing abstract theoretical arguments about self-ownership or the value of autonomy, we introduce these ideas by showing how they matter for our judgments about business, environmentalism, medicine, criminal justice, and public policy. Instead of surveying the history of libertarian thought, we focus on a few especially influential historical legal cases and philosophical approaches as a way of illustrating the diversity of libertarian ideas. Instead of reviewing evidence for the long-term collective benefits of a market economy, we describe how markets improve people's everyday lives. Throughout, we suggest further reading and references for readers who are interested in learning more about these aspects of libertarian thought.

Libertarianism is not a single, unified view and libertarians disagree about many of the subjects we discuss in this book. We hope that readers will approach this book with an open mind. This is an invitation to engage with libertarian perspectives on the issues that people care about. Our goal isn't to convince readers that libertarianism is true. Our goal is to show readers that the libertarian perspective matters for the decisions they face in their roles as employees, employers, consumers, patients, friends, and citizens.

THE STATE ISN'T SPECIAL

Here's a one-sentence summary of libertarianism: "The state isn't special." Libertarians argue that public officials are bound by the same moral standards as ordinary citizens. If it would be wrong for your barista to force you to stop smoking for your own good, then so, too, would it be wrong for a senator to force you to stop smoking for your own good. The default assumption is that people aren't wiser or more generous in their political lives than their non-political lives—after all, you're the same person at the ballot box that you are at work, at home, or at the store.

Since the state isn't special, there is a strong moral presumption against state interference in people's lives. Whenever public officials pass and enforce laws, they are using public threats to compel people to change their behavior. In most cases, ordinary people aren't liable to be threatened with violence, even if the person issuing the threats has a fancy title or wears a badge.

In this chapter, we will describe the philosophical foundations of libertarianism. We begin by elaborating on the claim that all law enforcement involves threats of violence. We then consider whether threatening people with violence can sometimes be justified for the sake of the greater good or in cases where public officials are pretty sure they know what's best for you. Next, we ask whether public

DOI: 10.4324/9781003270720-1

officials may justifiably threaten people with violence if a majority of citizens support the passage of a law.

We're not convinced by many of the arguments that purport to justify law enforcement. For instance, some people hold public officials to lower moral standards than everyone else. Others simply assume that governments will work better than markets. But once we recognize that public officials are as flawed and fallible as the rest of us, we can see that the case for governmental solutions to social and economic problems is weaker than we thought.

This isn't to say that libertarian theorists have all the answers. Many difficult questions remain regarding the moral foundations of libertarian theory, the extent of people's natural rights, and the scope of libertarianism. We will preview these questions at the end of this chapter, and we will address some of them in subsequent sections. Yet it is worth emphasizing at this point that these difficult questions are not unique to libertarianism—all theories of justice face similar challenges.

VIOLENCE

In 1646, Richard Overton wrote *An Arrow shot from the Prison of Newgate into the Prerogative Bowels of the Arbitrary House of Lords*, which is one of the earliest published arguments that defends a principle of natural liberty for all citizens. Overton was ahead of his time when he wrote,

> *For by natural birth all men are equally and alike born to like propriety, liberty and freedom; and as we are delivered of God by the hand of nature into this world, every one with a natural, innate freedom and propriety—as it were writ in the table of every man's heart, never to be obliterated—even so are we to live, everyone equally and alike to enjoy his birthright and privilege; even all whereof God by nature has made him free.*

Overton was part of the political movement called the Levellers. The Levellers wrote pamphlets that challenged the existing systems of hereditary rule and religious political authority. They also advocated for religious toleration and popular sovereignty.

Overton was not a libertarian in the contemporary sense, as libertarianism wasn't even a concept at the time. However, Overton's pamphlet articulated the core libertarian idea that public officials do not have any special moral authority, so they are not entitled to tell the rest of us what to do.

More recently, the philosopher Michael Huemer has developed a helpful way of illustrating the idea that no one has more natural authority than anyone else to use threats or violence against other people. This is part of what we mean when we say, "The state isn't special." Here is a modified version of a case that Huemer presents to illustrate this point:

THE NEIGHBORHOOD BUSYBODY

Imagine that your notoriously nosy neighbor, Sam, decides to start a one-man neighborhood watch. Sam patrols the neighborhood to deter burglars and violent people. He also encourages people to pick up their litter and keep their lawns in good repair. In the town square, Sam posts the list of rules he aims to enforce. One day, Sam catches someone who is stealing from parked cars. Sam pulls a gun on the thief and forces him into his basement. Later that month, Sam knocks on your door demanding a fee for his services. If you refuse, he will lock you in his basement with the thief and anyone else who has violated his rules.

If this case strikes you as outrageous, just imagine that Sam was wearing an official-looking mayor sash or a police badge. Would that change the ethics of his conduct? Libertarians say that the symbolic features of state power do nothing to authorize the violence that law enforcement entails. It's only because people are so used to living under state power that we no longer see it for what it is. Huemer's example is compelling because it strips away the rhetorical and traditional trappings of political power to reveal how illusory public officials' claims of authority really are.

This is not to say that no one has the authority to enforce any rules in a society. Rather, whether someone has the authority to enforce a law doesn't depend on whether he occupies an official position of political power. The authority to enforce a law depends on whether the law aligns with the underlying moral facts about whether a person has violated an enforceable moral requirement. So maybe the thief has acted in a way that makes him liable to Sam's threats of violence and incarceration. But unless you consented to live under Sam's rule, you haven't done anything to forfeit your rights against interference when Sam knocks on your door looking to collect.

ASSISTANCE

Public officials not only claim the authority to protect people's rights to life and property, they also redistribute resources. Ostensibly, officials engage in redistribution so that even the worst-off members of a political community can meet their basic needs and participate as equals in collective life. Clearly, they are not always successful at ensuring that everyone in a political community has enough. But even if they were, many libertarians are skeptical that they have the authority to enforce redistributive taxes. Consider another analogy from Michael Huemer:

THE ALTRUISTIC MUGGER

Sarah is convinced that no one in her community should suffer from serious material deprivation when others have far more than they need. So one day she approaches a rich man, Tim. She pulls a gun on Tim and informs him that he will need to go to the ATM and withdraw as much as he can so that she can transfer it to her poor and elderly neighbors. If he refuses then he will be shot or captured and imprisoned, and his property will then be seized by Sarah anyhow.

In this case, let's assume that Sarah is correct that no one should be so poor that they cannot meet their basic needs. Even if she's right about that, she's not entitled to threaten Tim with violence in an effort to get him to support the poor and elderly. Even if Sarah donned a badge and a uniform, and even if a bunch of Tim's neighbors encouraged her to do it, Tim has done nothing to make himself liable to be threatened by Sarah in this way.

This case illustrates a distinction that we'll return to throughout the book, namely the distinction between what's awful and what should be unlawful. It is awful that someone who has far more than they need would refuse to help someone in poverty. But it is less clear that this choice not to help should be unlawful—that is, the sort of thing that would entitle someone to threaten them with violence to force them to do otherwise. It doesn't immediately follow from the fact that something is morally wrong that the state ought to make it illegal. And this general point is uncontroversial; for instance, it's obviously wrong to break off all contact and "ghost" a lifelong friend because they were four minutes late to your party, but few, if any, people would argue that this behavior should be illegal.

There's also something curious about Sarah's focus on her own political community to the exclusion of other communities that are far worse off. Imagine that when Sarah takes Tim's property, she gives it to some middle-class elderly people to top off their retirement income. Someone tells Sarah that she could instead give some of Tim's property to people outside of her political community, and that redistributing resources to them would prevent children under the age of five from dying of malaria. Sarah replies that she is more concerned about people in her own community than children in other countries.

This extension of the case reveals a strange feature of the redistributionist ideology that libertarians typically oppose. Despite their egalitarian rhetoric, people who support wealth or income redistribution in wealthy countries are not motivated by a moral conviction that institutions should be arranged to benefit those who are *truly* worst off. If they were, they would redistribute resources to people living in poorer countries. The United States is so rich that an American at the domestic poverty line is still richer than the vast majority of people alive today. This reveals that redistributionists in rich countries don't apply their egalitarian commitments to everyone equally. Rather, egalitarians are typically nationalists—they prioritize people in their own country even there are if people with more urgent and serious needs elsewhere.

It gets worse though:

ELDERLY TRANSFERS

Sarah seizes Tim's property to pay poor elderly people. She also wants to pay some rich elderly people so that they like her more and will support her plan to pay poor elderly people. So Sarah decides to just transfer Tim's money to anyone who is old, rather than targeting the poorest elderly people in her political community. Sarah actually pays the rich elderly people more money on a monthly basis, and since poorer elderly people don't live as long as richer elderly people Sarah ends up transferring a lot of what she took from Tim to wealthy old people who live nearby. Sarah lies to everyone and tells them that she's actually just paying the old people money that they previously contributed. But Sarah's actually giving them money she took from Tim.

This is how Social Security works in the United States. Public officials tax high-income citizens and redistribute a large portion of those taxes to fund a basic income for old people. Old people who earned more throughout their lives receive a greater share of the universal basic income. Public officials deliberately frame Social Security as a savings account by using terms like "trust fund." But Social Security is funded through general taxation and individual taxpayers lack property claims to any subsequent Social Security payments.

To summarize, libertarians tend to oppose redistribution for three reasons. First, redistribution is usually enforced with threats of violence against people who are not liable to be threatened in these ways. People like Tim are often the most productive members of their communities, and public officials respond to their productive contributions by threatening to imprison them if they don't pay a cut to their fellow citizens. Second, redistributive policies are nationalist—they don't actually benefit the worst-off people in the world; they benefit poor people in rich countries. And third, redistribution is often inefficient and counterproductive even with respect to the goal of helping the worst off-members of one's own political community.

We'll return to debates about redistribution in Chapters 4 and 5.

KNOWLEDGE

Sometimes, people justify political authority on epistemic grounds, meaning that they think that political leaders have the authority to rule over the rest of us because they are smarter, or at least more knowledgeable, than everyone else. We're sure we can all think of political leaders who challenge this assumption, but for now, let's grant it just for the sake of argument. Even if a political leader is smarter and more knowledgeable than the average citizen, it doesn't follow from that fact that she has the authority to tell other people what to do. Consider another analogy:

THE KNOW-IT-ALL STRANGER

Jodie is very smart and knowledgeable. She knows all about what makes people happy and healthy, and she notices that many of her peers are making decisions that seem to make them unhappy and unhealthy. For example, people regularly date people who want different things out of the relationship. People eat sugary and unsatisfying food that is bad for their health in the long run. People drink and smoke and spend a lot of money on frivolous things, going into debt instead of investing in their future. Seeing this, Jodie concludes that she should be in charge of her neighbors' lives. If they followed her advice, they'd be happier and healthier in the long run.

At first glance, one might be skeptical about Jodie's argument that she knows best. After all, Jodie is an expert about health and happiness in general, but each individual is usually the best judge of his or her own overall well-being. Sitting in a recliner while you watch TV won't do as much good for your physical fitness as doing burpees during *The Simpsons*, but it might do more good for your overall well-being or satisfaction with your life. On the other hand, if you're vying for a spot on an NFL roster, you might want to do those burpees. Some people don't value long-term health or even short-term happiness; they care about different things. Jodie can't know the best way to make tradeoffs between different values for every individual person, and a universal policy that applies to everyone in the same way will fail to strike the right balance for everyone.

Political leaders also cannot claim to have authority over their fellow citizens by virtue of their expertise because, in ordinary cases, experts only have the authority to interfere with people who voluntarily consent to let an expert decide. Physicians, mechanics, and accountants are experts about medicine, cars, and taxes, but that fact doesn't entitle them to force their fellow citizens to use allergy medicine, change the oil in their cars, or take a standard deduction.

Many people value experts' opinions, but others would rather decide for themselves, even if that means they get a worse result. Even if your neighbor is a nutritionist and you're not, she doesn't have the right to dictate what you eat for breakfast.

And finally, even if a public official is correct that things would go better for people if they followed experts' advice, it would be a mistake to conclude that people would therefore be better off if the experts were in charge. Imagine that you need to finish an assignment to meet an important deadline. You agree with your smart and informed friends and family members that your life will go better if you sit down and finish the assignment instead of going to the movies. But you might nevertheless also believe that your life would go worse if your friend or family member forced you to finish the assignment, even though you agree it would be good for you to do it.

These examples illustrate the problem with appealing to expertise as a justification for political leadership. Even if political leaders really were experts, that would only mean that they had the authority to advise us. It would not establish that they had the authority to tell the rest of us what to do.

DEMOCRACY

Some people think that public officials have the authority to threaten and incarcerate their fellow citizens because a majority of citizens authorized them to do so. Let's set aside the fact that very few public officials ever have a majority of citizens' expressed support because elections are often close and many people do not or cannot vote. Even if public officials *did* have the support of voters, that support is irrelevant to the question of whether they have the authority to coerce people. Consider another Huemer-inspired analogy which makes a similar point:

THE DEMOCRATIC DINER

You are eating at a roadside diner when the clock strikes 4pm. The hostess asks everyone to vote to choose who shall pay for all the food that will be consumed in the next four hours. You didn't choose to attend a diner that used this procedure, but finding yourself in these circumstances you cast a ballot for everyone to pay for their own food. Unfortunately, you lost, and a majority of the diners voted for you and a few other patrons to get the check for everyone. You try to refuse to pay but the manager tells you that if you don't pay then they will lock you in the storage closet.

For libertarians, every day is a day at the democratic diner. Libertarians who do vote are outvoted every time, and public officials then require them to pay for a bunch of things that they had no desire to pay for!

Imagine that the democratic diner also chose the menu, told you where you could sit, and who you could sit with. Presumably, there are limits to what the majority of the patrons at the diner can force you to do, especially if it would be very costly for you to leave. Proponents of democratic authority are typically quick to point out that there are limits to what a majority can enforce. A racist majority lacks the authority to enforce a policy of segregation. A majority of voters are not entitled to censor minority viewpoints or to prohibit people from practicing a minority religion. A majority of voters are not entitled to force those with two healthy kidneys to give one to those with none. Yet if majorities are constrained by the moral requirement that they respect people's natural rights, then if people also have property rights, these rights set limits on voters' ability to authorize public officials to enforce taxes.

Many proponents of democratic authority agree that public officials should enforce protections for people's basic rights against interference because no one has the authority to coercively impose their vision of the good life on another person. But they also argue that public officials should give everyone a vote because it's an important way of expressing that everyone in a political community is equal. Yet these two conceptions of political equality are in tension. If treating people as equals requires respecting their freedom to decide for themselves, it cannot also require empowering people who happen to be in the majority to interfere with minority groups' and individuals' authority to decide how to spend their time and property. This tension should be resolved in favor of more liberty and less democracy. Having a vote doesn't necessarily confer equal status, especially for those whose votes never make a difference or for people who are always outvoted.

As an illustration of this point, consider the following case, which is adapted from Nozick's *Anarchy, State and Utopia*:

THE TALE OF THE SLAVE

A man is enslaved by a cruel person who requires him to work 5 days a week, not retaining any of the fruits of his labor. One day, the person enslaving him is replaced by a kinder person, who permits the slave to keep half of his wages. Over time, he is also permitted a wider range of occupational choices, as long as he continues to contribute his wages to his enslaver. The enslaver is replaced by a collective, which reduces the slave's mandatory contribution to 2 days' wages per week. One day, the collective tells the slave that he can vote in their decision-making if there is ever a tie. There is never a tie. Eventually, the collective tells the slave that he can vote anyhow, but his vote will never matter.

Nozick asks, at what point is the enslaved man no longer a slave? If it was wrong for the cruel and kind enslavers to force him to work without retaining the fruits of his labor, then so too for the collective. If forcing him to work uncompensated for five days a week was wrong, then forcing him to work uncompensated for two days a week is presumably wrong for the same reasons. There is no sense in which the slave is politically equal to the majority group that coercively seizes 40% of his labor every week, even if he does have the opportunity to cast a meaningless vote.

For these reasons, public officials cannot justify their authority by pointing out that most people in a political community have a right to vote, and so they cannot complain. For one thing, one person's vote almost never affects the outcome when it comes to who is elected or which policies are enforced. It makes sense to argue that someone can't complain when they had the power to change the outcome but didn't exercise that power ("You can't complain about being hungry given that you chose not to grab a snack before leaving."), but not when you can't affect the outcome regardless of what you do. And for another, whether the vote affects the outcome of an election matters far less than whether the outcome is morally better than the alternative.

So while libertarians generally support policies that expand the scope of people's freedom, they are more tepid when it comes to the right to vote. To see why, consider how the right to vote doesn't function in an ordinary person's life in the same way that other liberties do. For most people, if their vote were tossed in an incinerator, their life would go on, basically unchanged. (Imagine that each vote you've cast in previous presidential elections *really was* tossed in an incinerator. Would your life today—or the life of anyone else—be any different than it is?) But if they were prevented from practicing their religion, going to lunch with their friends, quitting their jobs, or speaking their minds, their lives would be much worse off.

A further reason for libertarians' comparative lack of enthusiasm for the right to participate in politics is that it's a right to have a say in telling other people what to do. By contrast, other liberties tend to give you a right against being told what to do—for instance, the right to religious freedom is a right against other people interfering with your decision to practice your religion. In some cases, voters or elected officials exercise their political liberties to enforce policies that restrict people's other liberties such as the freedom to associate or contract. But libertarians believe that no one is entitled to exercise their political freedoms in ways that constrain their fellow citizens' *other* freedoms.

This is not to say that libertarians always reject democratic decision-making. Groups have to use some kind of procedure to decide what to do. In many private groups, it's likely that the members will resolve to make decisions by majority rule or through elected officials and to abide by those decisions. But in political contexts, where people do not consent to follow a majoritarian decision procedure, libertarians generally support democratic institutions only when and to the extent that they make the world fairer, happier, and freer. Democracy is a tool for improving the world, but political participation is not a natural entitlement or a morally valuable practice in its own right.

Some people defend democratic decision-making on instrumental grounds by appealing to the old cliché that two heads are better than one. If so, then wouldn't millions of people voting in an election be about as good as we can do at figuring out how we should live together? This is an empirical intuition. But as many libertarian philosophers and social scientists have pointed out, it's not true. Voters are extremely uninformed about a range of political and economic issues. For example, most American voters cannot answer basic questions about their political representatives, the structure of government, economics, or the national budget. Voters beliefs are also systematically biased, meaning that you are more likely to get the wrong answer to a variety of political and economic questions if you take a vote than if you just flip a coin.

The philosopher Jason Brennan argues that uninformed voters undermine the public good of high-quality governance in the same way that air polluters undermine the public good of clean air. His argument goes like this:

POLLUTING THE POLLS

Any given air polluter doesn't make much of a difference, but collectively air pollution harms everyone who lives in a place where lots of people pollute. If people can refrain from pollution without much personal cost, they therefore have a duty to not pollute. Similarly, any given voter doesn't make much of a difference, but collectively uninformed voters harm everyone who lives in a place where uninformed voters pass bad policies. Uninformed voters can refrain from voting without much personal cost, so uninformed voters should stay home.

It gets worse when we consider that most voters don't even vote on the issues anyhow. Instead, voters choose public officials who will act in ways that reflect their partisan identities. Indeed, liberals will support a conservative policy if they're told a liberal politician endorses it—and the same goes for conservatives and liberal policies. Voters are like fans who support their team through thick and thin. Yet as Rishi Joshi argues, the problem with this kind of voting behavior is that it is very unlikely that one political party is systematically right about dozens of seemingly unrelated issues from tax policy to abortion to gun control to drug policy to immigration, while the other political party is a party of anti-experts who get it all wrong. So when voters defer to their party and a single party controls the government, even if that party is better than the alternative, it's still very likely to be wrong about a lot of issues.

Voters can make these uninformed and biased choices because they don't personally bear the cost of their own votes. You have strong incentives to have accurate beliefs about, for instance, the quality of the medicine you're taking, because if you get things wrong, the results will be harmful for you. But voting decisions aren't like this. When you decide to buy a bottle of medicine, you'll get that medicine. When you decide to vote for a candidate, you may or may not get that candidate—it depends on how millions of other people vote. Even though they are affected by public policy, in the voting booth the main benefit citizens get from choosing one candidate over another is expressive—they are contributing to a collective signal about their values and they are reassuring themselves that they are a certain kind of person. It's a bit like deciding what message you want on your bumper sticker.

Unfortunately, voters' expressive choices do have real consequences for the people who are affected by public policy. When voters choose candidates based on vibes and social identities, they are choosing people who look good, sound good, and make them feel good about themselves rather than asking which candidate is the most likely to pass policies that will respect citizens' rights and improve their well-being.

PUBLIC GOODS

In this chapter, we've argued that the state isn't special—if ordinary people do not have the authority to do something, then public officials lack that authority as well. Some people suggest that, while the state is not morally special, public officials can provide a corrective against market failures that arise in the private sphere:

EVETTE AND THE EV

Evette is debating between buying a more expensive electric vehicle or a cheaper gas vehicle. She realizes that if enough other people drive EVs, she'll have clean air regardless of whether she personally drives an EV, in which case she can go ahead and buy the cheaper gas car. On the other hand, if enough other people are driving a gas car, then she won't have clean air regardless of what she drives, so she figures she might as well go ahead and buy the cheaper gas car in this case, too. In short, she concludes that she should buy the cheaper gas car regardless of what everyone else is doing. But of course other car buyers are thinking the same thing. As a result, too many people are driving gas cars and polluting the atmosphere even though this outcome is bad for everyone. To correct for the failure of the car marketplace to ensure clean air, public officials can impose a carbon tax to disincentivize carbon emissions.

Libertarians reply to this style of argument by pointing out that the same kinds of considerations that cause market failures in the private sphere also cause government failure in the public sphere. The difference is simply that public officials claim the legal authority to be the only people who can use violence, so it's even more difficult to correct for government failures than it is to correct for market failures. Consider:

VAUGHN THE VOTER

Vaughn is deciding whether or not to cast an unbiased, informed vote for the candidate with a stronger environmental record. He realizes that if enough other citizens cast unbiased, informed votes for the candidate with a stronger environmental record, the country will get the candidate that's best for the environment even if he himself doesn't vote for them. If too few other citizens cast unbiased, informed votes for the candidate with the stronger environmental record, the country won't get the candidate that's best for the environment, regardless of how he votes. So, in neither case does Vaughn have the incentive to cast an unbiased, informed vote for the candidate that's best for the environment—and neither do other citizens. As a result, too few citizens cast unbiased, informed voters to secure effective environmental policies, even though this outcome is bad for everyone.

It's important to notice something about the two cases above: the reason why an effective state solution to climate change is out of reach is the same reason why an effective market solution to climate change is out of reach. The contribution of individual car buyers or voters is inconsequential and so they have no incentive to pay the costs of making that contribution. Casting a single vote makes no difference to political outcomes just as driving an individual car makes no difference to environmental outcomes.

Many libertarians are fans of public choice economics, which is roughly the economic analysis of political behavior. The crucial assumption made by public choice theorists is that you're the same person when you're casting a vote as you are when you're buying a car. If you're unwilling to pay higher costs to make an inconsequential contribution to better environmental outcomes, we should assume that you're unwilling to pay higher costs to make an inconsequential contribution to better *political* outcomes, absent some compelling reason to believe otherwise.

Although we're the same people in the marketplace as we are in the voting booth, our incentives in those contexts differ. In particular, voters and consumers have different incentives to acquire information:

MOTORCYCLE

Maude is shopping for a motorcycle. She visits several dealers, reads reviews, checks safety reports, and checks price tags. Maude buys the motorcycle that she believes provides the best value at the lowest price.

Maude's effort to acquire information about the price, safety, and comfort of different motorcycles is costly—it takes time away from other things she could be doing, like lounging at the beach. But Maude realizes that acquiring this information also comes with benefits—it enables her to select the motorcycle that best suits her needs. If she didn't do any research, she could end up with a motorcycle that is too expensive, unsafe, and unreliable. Maude does the research, then, because the benefits exceed the costs.

Just as acquiring information about motorcycles is costly, so too is acquiring information about politicians and policies. It eats up time that could be spent on something else. However, unlike in the motorcycle case, acquiring information about politicians and policies doesn't bring about much, if any, benefit. As noted earlier, you have far more control over consumption outcomes than political outcomes. When you decide to buy a motorcycle, you'll get that motorcycle. Consequently, you benefit from an informed purchase.

But when you decide to vote for the Democrat, you may or may not get the Democrat. Whether or not you get the Democrat depends not on how *you* vote, but on how hundreds of millions of other people vote. The odds of your individual vote actually changing the winner of a presidential election range from around 1 in 10 million to 1 in 200 trillion, depending on where in the United States you live. And it doesn't make sense to pay the costs of casting an informed vote when it has such a small chance of making a difference. In short, you don't benefit from an informed vote.

To further illustrate the point, let's take a pop quiz: Who was the King of England in 1137? (You can take a minute to think.)

The correct answer is Stephen of Blois. Now, we're guessing you didn't know that. And there's no shame in not knowing! It takes time and effort to acquire information and it's not worth your while to pay that cost to acquire information that's of no practical importance. There's simply not much that most of us can do with extensive knowledge of English royal history.

You might reply that in the case of voting, there is *some* (very small) chance that it could be beneficial. But that isn't enough to give you a strong reason to inform your vote. If we told you had a 1 in 60 million chance of getting a surprise call to appear on a trivia show tomorrow and be asked a question about Stephen, King of England, would this possibility be enough to motivate you to crack open a book about English royal history? We doubt it.

Of course, public choice theorists recognize that voters tend to have *some* information. But it's usually information that is easy or entertaining to absorb:

ELECTION SEASON

As presidential campaigns start ramping up, Cindy realizes she'll need to fig-ure out which candidate to vote for. She watches one of the debates, scrolls through her algorithmically-curated social media feeds, and occasionally catches a political advertisement that happens to air during a football game. She casts her vote based on the information she acquires from these sources.

Cindy's process of acquiring political information probably looks familiar. It's pretty cheap to get some superficial information about candidates by watching debates or browsing TikTok. But this isn't the sort of information we need to make truly wise voting decisions. For instance, a campaign ad might tell you what a candidate promises, but we really need to know whether they follow through on their promises or if their promises were even good ones in the first place.

Maybe Smith promises to ban fracking. Well, to start, what *is* fracking? Is it good for the economy? Is it good for the environment? If it's bad for the environment but good for the economy, how should we balance environmental and economic considerations? To competently think these questions through, we need to know at least a little about economics, ecology, and even ethics. But the vast majority of voters don't do this about fracking or anything else because the cost exceeds the benefit.

Now just as motorcycle designers would have a weak incentive to produce good motorcycles if they knew that motorcycle buyers did very little research, politicians have a weak incentive to produce good policy given that voters do very little research. For example, politicians have incentives to produce policies that benefit a special interest group at the expense of the public interest. The typical voter is unmotivated to acquire information about farm subsidies. The costs of those subsidies are spread across millions and millions of people. If an individual voter would become, say, $5 poorer as a result of the subsidies, they have little incentive to learn about candidates' stances on subsidies and cast a vote for the anti-subsidy candidate. The reason is that acquiring that information is costly and the payoff is a 1 in 100 million chance (let's assume) of saving $5. But the benefits of those subsidies are concentrated among a comparatively small group of farmers, meaning each farmer stands to gain handsomely if they're implemented. Consequently, farmers have a strong incentive to support pro-subsidy politicians. So a pro-subsidy politician can get support from farmers without losing support from anyone else, even if the farm subsidies are a bad deal for the country as a whole.

Political economist Samuel DeCanio argues that market decisions tend to be more informed than political decisions for a reason other than incentives too. When buying a motorcycle, the motorcycles you're choosing between actually exist. You can see how much they cost, their safety record, their reliability record, and how other people who've bought them have liked them. But voting decisions are educated guesses. At most, you can make predictions about how a politician will govern based on their track record. But all candidates are making promises about what policies they will actually enact and what the costs and benefits of those policies will be.

DIFFICULT QUESTIONS

In the rest of this book, we'll describe the implications of libertarian political philosophy across a range of cases. But before we jump into a detailed discussion of ethics and public policy, it's worth flagging a few areas where libertarian theory doesn't have clear answers for normative questions about politics. Specifically, libertarianism cannot settle questions in normative ethics about how people should balance the requirement to respect rights against the moral value of promoting good consequences. Libertarianism also doesn't clearly specify the boundaries of people's enforceable rights. Like all moral frameworks, libertarians struggle to balance people's rights against risk and people's rights to engage in risky conduct. And libertarians also disagree about the moral and political status of children.

As Robert Nozick wrote in *Anarchy State and Utopia*, theories of justice (like libertarianism) are models of the conditions for permissible enforcement and punishment. There are other normative questions we can ask though, which don't have anything to do with enforcement and punishment. For example, we can ask whether one choice would be more praiseworthy than another choice, or whether it has more aesthetic value, or whether it is more virtuous. We can also ask about the balance of different moral considerations, for example, when we ask whether a person should ever violate one person's rights for the sake of the greater good. Consider, for example, a famous case that pits two competing moral considerations against each other:

THE TROLLEY PROBLEM

A trolley is speeding towards five people who are stuck on the track. You can turn the switch, and the trolley will kill one person instead of five.

Many people say that it would be better to turn the trolley on the one to save the five. Others claim that turning the trolley on the one would violate his rights, which would be wrong, so it would be morally better to let the trolley hit the five.

We're not here to settle this long-standing debate. Actually, we disagree with each other about the answer! We are bringing up the Trolley Problem to show that there are interesting normative questions that lie outside the scope of political philosophy. Libertarianism can answer questions about whether someone who turned a trolley on the one to save the five (or didn't) should be liable to criminal sanctions, whether the one would have a legal right to shoot you if you tried to turn a trolley against him, and whether the trolley company should be held liable for the deaths they caused. But libertarianism doesn't provide ready answers for the difficult questions of whether and when someone ought to violate rights for the sake of the greater good.

Another long-standing ethical challenge for libertarians relates to the boundaries of people's natural rights. Consider this case:

THE SNEEZE

You are sitting on the subway and another passenger sneezes. Some of their saliva lands on your face.

Libertarians say that you have enforceable rights of bodily integrity. But it's unclear whether those rights include the right against having a small droplet of saliva hit your face. It may not seem like a big deal, but if that droplet is carrying a deadly virus, sneezing on someone starts to sound like a serious violation of their defensive rights. At the same time, imagine that someone sneezes on you and you take their saliva and use the DNA in it to create a useful medical product or clone of them. If they have property rights to their body, it's unclear whether these rights include rights to parts of their body that are no longer attached to the person.

A related boundary problem relates to rights against risk. Consider another case:

THE SHOTGUN BLAST

To celebrate the fourth of July, you fire a shotgun in the air. There is a 0.0001% chance that the blast will injure someone. No one is injured.

Laws that prohibit drunk driving and reckless endangerment reflect the intuition that, if people have bodily rights, those rights also include some rights against being put at risk. Yet every libertarian theory of risk struggles to draw the line between an acceptable and unacceptable level of risk exposure. Part of the problem is that even if people do not have rights to not be exposed to very small risks, in some cases, many small risk impositions can add up to a substantial level of risk. For example, even if one person's car-related air pollution doesn't put anyone at substantial risk of respiratory illness or lung damage, hundreds of thousands of individual commuters might.

Here's a good place to spotlight an important point about the case for libertarianism: many of the standard objections to libertarians are also objections to *any* form of liberalism—that is, a political view that prioritizes the protection of liberties. For instance, left-wing egalitarian liberals also endorse a right of bodily autonomy (think "my body, my choice") and so they too must confront the questions of whether, for instance, this right includes the right against having a small droplet of saliva hit your face or against the risk imposed by a fourth of July celebration or car-related air pollution.

The boundaries of the community of rights-holders are also unclear. Some libertarians think that people's rights begin even before they are born. Some of these pro-life libertarians, therefore, support legal restrictions on women's rights to end their pregnancy on the grounds that fetuses have defensive rights against being killed. Other libertarians think that fetuses are not full rights holders. Either way, libertarians struggle to identify the line when a child becomes the kind of being that has the moral authority to make his own decisions. Consider this legal case:

IN RE CASSANDRA C

Cassandra was a seventeen-year-old cancer patient. Her physicians told her that chemotherapy was required to save her life, but Cassandra wanted to refuse treatment. Cassandra's mother supported her decision, but Cassandra's doctors obtained a court order that required her to undergo chemotherapy against her will.

In this case, Cassandra lacked the legal right to make decisions about her own body. It's not clear that Cassandra lacked a moral right to choose though, since it seems arbitrary to say that Cassandra, and every other teenager, acquires enforceable moral rights against forced treatment on her eighteenth birthday but not one day beforehand. Yet it's unclear where exactly public officials should recognize teenagers' authority to decide for themselves. If public officials can legitimately prohibit a 12-year-old from buying cigarettes from the gas station but not a 22-year-old, when does the moral right to smoke come online? Similar issues arise in discussions of the nature of rights for people with significant intellectual disabilities.

We are not going to answer any of these difficult questions here, though we will return to them as we discuss related cases in the next chapters. We are raising these issues because some critics of libertarianism cite them as if they pose distinctive problems for libertarianism. Here, our aim is just to point out that none of these difficult questions are particularly distinctive to libertarianism. Proponents of any moral theory that includes protections for people's rights will struggle to draw a line between rights holders and non-rights holders. The boundaries of people's rights are difficult to know for all theories of rights, and they may be indeterminate for all these theories as well. Risk is also a challenging problem for all moral theories, including for consequentialists who think that consequences are all that ultimately matter, morally speaking. And proponents of all moral theories should wonder and worry about the normative foundations for their views.

SUMMARY

People often look to the government to solve the conflicts and moral problems that inevitably arise when people live and work together. But the government isn't something that exists outside of the political community. Rather, public officials are simply people within the community who claim that they have the authority to tell everyone else what to do. Libertarians hold that people who work for the government don't actually have that kind of distinctive moral authority. Even if people voted for them and even if they are doing good work, public officials' authority derives from the same moral reasons that apply to the rest of us. Which is to say, public officials have the authority to protect people's rights and enforce policies that improve people's lives, but they do not have the authority to violate people's rights or to impose their vision of the good life on everyone else.

Lastly, libertarians are not naively optimistic about human nature when they argue that people should be left to make their own decisions. Rather, libertarians see all the ways that people can be ignorant, weak-willed, self-interested, and misguided. Public officials are people too. And since everyone is prone to error, it's a good idea to minimize the extent that people can inflict their error-prone decision-making on the rest of us, especially when those decisions are backed by threats and force.

FURTHER READING

- Brennan, Jason. 2009. "Polluting the Polls: When Citizens Should Not Vote." *Australasian Journal of Philosophy* 87 (4): 535–549. https://doi.org/10.1080/00048400802587309.
- Brennan, Jason. 2016. *Against Democracy: New Preface.* Princeton University Press.
- DeCanio, Samuel. 2014. "Democracy, the Market, and the Logic of Social Choice." *American Journal of Political Science* 58 (3): 637–652.
- Freiman, Christopher. 2017. *Unequivocal Justice.* Routledge.
- Huemer, Michael. 2013. *The Problem of Political Authority: An Examination of the Right to Coerce and the Duty to Obey.* 1st edition. Houndmills, Basingstoke, Hampshire and New York: Palgrave Macmillan.
- Huemer, Michael, and Daniel Layman. 2021. *Is Political Authority an Illusion?: A Debate.* Routledge.
- In re Cassandra C. 2015, 112 A. 3d 158. Supreme Court.
- Klosko, George. 1987. "Presumptive Benefit, Fairness, and Political Obligation." *Philosophy & Public Affairs* 16 (3): 241–259.
- Lomasky, Loren E. 1987. *Persons, Rights, and the Moral Community.* Oxford University Press.
- Mill, John Stuart. 1966. *On Liberty.* Edited by John M. Robson. London, UK: Macmillan Education.
- Nozick, Robert. 1974. *Anarchy, State, and Utopia.* Basic Books.
- Overton, Richard. 1646. *An Arrow shot from the Prison of Newgate into the Prerogative Bowels of the Arbitrary House of Lords.*
- Thomson, Judith Jarvis. 1985. "The Trolley Problem." *The Yale Law Journal* 94 (6): 1395. https://doi.org/10.2307/796133.

- Thomson, Judith Jarvis. 1986. *Rights, Restitution, and Risk: Essays, in Moral Theory*. Harvard University Press.
- Thomson, Judith Jarvis. 2008. "Turning the Trolley." *Philosophy & Public Affairs* 36 (4): 359–374. https://doi.org/10.1111/j.1088-4963.2008.00144.x.
- Tullock, Gordon, Gordon Brady, and Arthur Seldon. 2002. *Government Failure: A Primer on Public Choice*. Cato Institute.

2

BODILY RIGHTS

It's uncontroversial that public officials may pass laws against murder, assault, or theft, which stop people from violating others' bodily rights. But what about laws that stop people from hurting themselves? There are many of these paternalistic laws on the books. In most states, you can't ride a motorcycle without a helmet or ride in a car without a seatbelt. You can't shoot heroin even in the privacy of your own home. You can't buy heart medication without a prescription. You can't sell your kidney. You can't duel to the death even if both parties consent to it. But libertarians argue that these paternalistic restrictions aren't justified.

To understand why, let's first sketch the case *for* paternalism. The core argument is straightforward: you should welcome interference with your choices when that interference helps, rather than hinders, your ability to get what you want. Paternalistic laws may help citizens get what they really want by restricting their freedom to make an uninformed choice. For instance, maybe the typical consumer lacks the relevant information about a drug's side effects to make a good choice for herself. The paternalist argues that the state should, therefore, require that she get a prescription from her doctor before she may take the drug.

DOI: 10.4324/9781003270720-2

To be clear, paternalists aren't committed to regulating away every bad choice people might make. Few, if any, paternalists would demand that public officials install cameras in your refrigerator to monitor your kale consumption and authorize a SWAT team to smash through your front door with a battering ram if you aren't eating enough. And the reason is simple: the costs of such a policy likely outweigh the benefits.

The case for paternalism goes wrong in two ways. First, people have the right to make their own decisions about their bodies and their property, even if those decisions turn out to be harmful. After all, it's your bank account, your body, and your life—as we suggested earlier, that your nutritionist neighbor knows more about cholesterol than you do doesn't give her the right to force egg whites and steel-cut oatmeal on your breakfast table.

Second, paternalistic interference often backfires—it frequently doesn't produce the good consequences it's meant to produce. Typically, defenses of paternalism focus on how badly people advance their own ends. However, showing that people are poor guardians of their self-interest isn't enough to vindicate paternalism; to do that, paternalists need to show that state actors will advance people's ends less badly than they do. By analogy, showing that Steph Curry misses a lot of three-point shots isn't enough to justify sending him to the bench. To do that, you'd need to show that Curry's replacement will miss fewer shots (he won't). We shouldn't simply assume that paternalistic regulators will be better informed or less biased than those they are regulating. After all, they're only human themselves and so they're just as flawed as the rest of us.

In fact, you'll typically be in a better position to look after yourself than a paternalistic regulator for two reasons. First, as John Stuart Mill argued, most people are the experts about their own well-being. This isn't to say that most people are good at predicting which course of action would be best for them, just that they're likely to know better than anyone else. Suppose your grandmother is having some hip pain. Should she get a hip replacement or should she try physical therapy first? Your grandmother is in a better position to know the answer than you are, even if you happen to be an orthopedic surgeon. You might be an expert on orthopedic surgery, but not on how that surgery will fit into your grandmother's life plans. Your grandmother is the expert on the time she can spare for recovery, her health insurance and financial situation more generally, her work and family commitments, and so on.

Second, even if a paternalistic regulator somehow does know what's good for you better than you do, they don't have strong incentives to actually do it. Maybe you're a smoker and a switch to vaping would be an improvement. Suppose you don't know that, but a legislator does. Even so, that legislator may have stronger incentives to oppose vaping in an effort to placate their supporters in the tobacco industry. Who's more likely to care about your long-term health, you, or your state senator?

DEATH

People's rights to decide what happens to their own bodies extend to even the most serious kinds of choices, including deadly ones. Some paternalists argue that people should be prevented from making deadly choices because the stakes are so high. Others argue that people don't have the right to die because it's an irrational choice. On this view, suicide is irrational because it is contradictory to say that someone has a right to destroy their autonomous capacities in virtue of the value of autonomy. Another argument alleges that permitting a legal right to die would cause people to feel pressured by their family members to end their lives. And some religious people oppose the right to die because they think it's immoral for a person to kill themselves or to assist in a killing, even if it is voluntary.

Yet many states and countries permit people to end their lives when they judge that living for longer would make their lives as a whole worse. Consider a recent example of a euthanasia patient in Switzerland:

MEDICAL AID IN DYING

At the age of 71, Peter Smedley's health was beginning to seriously decline due to an incurable, terminal, degenerative disease. Peter traveled to the Swiss Dignitas Clinic, where he was able to purchase and use deadly drugs. He died peacefully in his wife's arms.

Peter believed that, in his circumstances, a shorter life would be a better one. If public officials prevented him from ending his life at the Dignitas Clinic, they would have forced him to endure months of continued suffering and decline and a potentially painful death.

Those who deny that all people should have a legal right to die might reply that medical aid in dying should be allowed for people like Peter, but not for people who would otherwise live long and healthy lives. Yet this reply is inconsistent with longstanding prohibitions on medical paternalism in other clinical contexts. Even young and healthy patients have the right to refuse lifesaving antibiotics, blood transfusions, and surgery. Here's another influential case:

BURN VICTIM

Dax Cowart was severely burned in a propane explosion, which also caused him to become blind and to experience some mobility impairments. Throughout his recovery, he begged hospital workers to discontinue lifesaving treatment and to allow him to die. Hospital workers forced him to receive treatment. Later, Dax got married and became a successful attorney.

Even though Dax presumably had a life that was worth living after the accident, the hospital workers violated his right to refuse lifesaving medical care. So too, even if some people who seek out deadly drugs and medical aid in dying would go on to have happy lives, it is nevertheless wrong for public officials to force them to stay alive against their wishes.

PHARMACEUTICALS

Most would agree that the state should permit people to decline to take a prescription pill that could prevent a heart attack, even when the benefit of taking the pill is high and the cost is low. Is the decision not to take the drug unwise? Probably. But it's not unlawful. And yet, if a patient wants to use a prescription drug in the first place, public officials require her to first get a permission slip from her doctor:

PRESCRIPTIONS

Sally wants to try a new drug that could potentially limit the frequency and duration of her migraine headaches. The drug costs $50, but she cannot legally purchase the drug from her pharmacist unless she also spends $100 to meet with a neurologist first.

As long as Sally is informed about the potential risks and benefits of the drug, she should not need to convince her physician to allow her to take it. Here again, Sally's doctor might be an expert about headaches, but Sally is the expert about her own values, risk tolerance, and budget.

Of course, it would probably be a good idea for Sally to see a neurologist about her headaches. But it would be wrong for public officials to compel her to see a doctor on the grounds that she should get a checkup. Insofar as prescription requirements are justified as a way of encouraging patients to get checkups and to undergo screening, public officials are implicitly appealing to the premise that they have the moral authority to limit people's bodily rights in order to compel people to go to the doctor. Gynecologists have long justified prescription requirements for contraceptives on the grounds that prescription requirements encourage women to comply with recommended HPV and STI screening. Yet all women have rights to control their own fertility. So even if prescription requirements are intended to promote women's overall health, they still violate women's rights.

The libertarian argument for bodily rights is sometimes made in terms of self-ownership. We can say that people in effect own themselves, and this gives them the right to harm themselves and their bodies. But we can also put this point in terms of medical self-defense. Consider another circumstance where patients have an interest in accessing prohibited pharmaceuticals:

RIGHT TO TRY

Abigail Burroughs was diagnosed with head and neck cancer as a teenager. She sought access to an investigational colon cancer drug that she and her care team believed would extend her life. Public officials prohibited her from accessing the drug.

Patients like Abigail have the right to defend their own lives. Policies that prohibit patients from accessing unapproved drugs that have the potential to extend their lives violate patient's rights to save their lives. Though it may look like these patients die from cancer, or Parkinson's, or cystic fibrosis, or whatever other deadly diseases they have, they really die from pharmaceutical regulations that delay their access to care.

Economists sometimes refer to the patients who die prematurely due to excessive pharmaceutical regulations as the invisible graveyard. Not only does this graveyard include the patients who died of treatable conditions while they waited for a drug to gain approval, it also includes all the patients who currently suffer and die of diseases that lack a feasible cure because the regulatory process for drugs deters innovation:

DRUG LOSS

Georgette suffers from a gastrointestinal condition that currently has no cure. There is some theoretical reason to think that stem cell therapy could cure her illness. Yet stem cell therapeutics are heavily regulated and the high costs of regulation prevent researchers from investing in stem cell therapy for patients like Georgette.

Deregulation promotes pharmaceutical innovation. When regulators provide expedited approval for a class of drugs, more new drugs are introduced into that sector of the drug market. No one can know for sure how many promising treatments and cures we haven't seen yet because of pharmaceutical regulators' interference in the drug market, although we do know that pharmaceutical innovation has been one of the leading causes of increased life expectancy over the last century. Yet public officials are too often blind to the risk that their seemingly safety-oriented regulations are more dangerous than a more risk-acceptant regulatory structure would be.

As an alternative to the existing regulatory structure, libertarians have proposed various solutions that could balance a patient's interest in having safe drugs and safe regulations. A moderate solution is regulatory reciprocity, where regulators agree to automatically approve drugs that have been approved in other jurisdictions.

A more radical approach is a safety-only standard, where patients can purchase and use drugs that have passed a preliminary testing phase and drug makers could seek additional certification after the drug is on the market.

The most radical solution is a system where public officials don't stop any adults from using any drugs. In the absence of regulation, private certification can ensure the safety and quality of products. Under this model, non-governmental agencies could test drugs, food, and so on to determine whether or not they're safe to consume. And unlike the FDA, if a certifier proves unreliable, it'll go out of business, which provides it with a strong incentive to be reliable. Private agencies already certify whether food is organic or kosher, whether makeup is cruelty-free, and whether appliances and cars are likely to be reliable. Even if such a proposal is not politically feasible, it is morally ideal from a libertarian perspective.

And just as patients should be free to make their own medical choices when it comes to pharmaceuticals and medical devices, they should be free to make their own choices about medical providers. Libertarians since Milton Friedman have been sharply critical of medical licensing policies, which can constrain the supply and raise the cost of medical care providers:

MEDICAL LICENSING

In order to practice family medicine, psychiatry, or any other medical specialty, public officials legally require that physicians attend an accredited school, pass a series of tests, and complete a series of internships. This process is expensive and time consuming. Public officials authorize physicians' trade associations to oversee their own certification process. This enables existing physicians to artificially limit the supply of people who can become doctors, which contributes to health worker scarcity and high costs.

Medical licensing laws also apply to nurses, dentists, midwives, sonogram technicians, phlebotomists, and dental hygienists. Furthermore, public officials uphold scope of practice regulations that prohibit most kinds of health workers from providing routine care or prescriptions without being supervised by a doctor. Everyone working in these industries must spend months or years completing expensive training, while patients and taxpayers bear the costs of this investment. In many cases, patients might value the opportunity to see a trained healthcare worker, but some patients might prefer to see a lower-cost, unlicensed provider instead. Yet medical licensing policies prevent people from making cost-conscious decisions about their own healthcare.

Certification limits access to healthcare and contributes to rising costs in other corners of the industry too. Many jurisdictions require hospital and birthing center developers to acquire a certificate of need before building a new facility. Like medical licensing, the certificate of need process often requires gaining approval from industry professionals who have an interest in limiting competition—keeping prices high and restricting supply.

In sum, policies that require patients and providers to obtain a permission slip from public officials in order to make or provide health services are inefficient and harmful. These policies massively benefit existing stakeholders while preventing patients from accessing more innovative or customized care. These policies also prevent people from deciding for themselves how to trade off health against other priorities they might have. And medical regulations often violate patients' rights to make their own medical decisions while driving up the cost of healthcare. A libertarian approach to medicine rejects the paternalism of the current system in favor of a market in medical services that gives patients the authority to make important healthcare decisions.

PREGNANCY

Libertarians disagree about the ethics of abortion, but they are generally opposed to policies that enable public officials to restrict abortion rights. Consider this case, which illustrates the distinction between abortion ethics and abortion policy:

ABORTION

Diane learns that she is pregnant, and she wants to end her pregnancy. Her sister believes that Diane should continue the pregnancy, on the grounds that her fetus has moral status. Public officials tell Diane and her doctor that if she doesn't carry the pregnancy to term, they could go to jail.

Even though Diane's sister believes that abortion is unethical, she doesn't stop Diane from terminating her pregnancy. In contrast, the public officials who prohibit abortion not only believe that abortion is unethical but also believe that they are entitled to compel Diane to continue the pregnancy. In general, libertarians support Diane's right to choose even if they also agree with Diane's sister that she ought to remain pregnant.

Some libertarians support abortion rights because they deny that a fetus has moral status. If a fetus doesn't have moral status, then abortion is morally similar to contraception, in that it is a medical decision that enables women to choose whether and when to have a child. Since the libertarians who hold this view also think that women have the right to use contraception, they support abortion rights.

Other libertarians argue that even if a fetus does have the same kind of moral status that people have, meaning that it has legally enforceable bodily rights, those rights should not entail a right to live inside a woman's body. After all, mothers have legally enforceable bodily rights too. Presumably, you are a person who has a legal right to not be killed. Now imagine that you wanted to use another person's body as a human shield during a hailstorm. Or imagine that you got sick and you wanted to forcibly remove another person's kidney in order to save your own life. Even if your human shield or kidney donor would survive the attack, and even if you needed to attack them in order to save your own life, it would still be wrong for public officials to legally require that people who are well-placed to serve as human shields or kidney donors do so. Similarly, even if a fetus has a legal right to life and needs to use his mother's body to survive, public officials still should not require that women remain pregnant by prohibiting abortion.

On the other hand, there are libertarians who hold that a restrictive abortion policy is in principle justified because each fetus has moral status, which includes enforceable bodily rights. In this view, public officials can legitimately prohibit women from ending their pregnancies for the same reason that they can legitimately prohibit people from killing infants and children. So if an unborn child is a person who has the same moral status as other people, then the prohibition of abortion is justified. That said, even some libertarians who do not think that women have an enforceable right to end their pregnancies may nevertheless hold that public officials should not legally prohibit abortion because prohibition would backfire. For example, if people can travel to access abortion elsewhere and if some people illegally provide abortions, then prohibiting abortion might not reduce rates of abortion enough to justify the negative consequences associated with black markets in abortion care.

Libertarians are therefore divided on abortion policy because they disagree about the nature of people's enforceable rights and whether a fetus is a person who has enforceable rights. For other reproductive health questions, libertarians generally affirm the moral importance of reproductive freedom in light of the myriad ways that state intervention violates pregnant women's reproductive autonomy by limiting their options during childbirth:

BIRTH

Gretta is pregnant with her second child. Her first child was delivered via Cesarean. She would like to attempt a vaginal birth after a Cesarean (VBAC) for her second delivery. However, she cannot find a hospital-based provider who will support this birth plan. Physicians are reluctant to support VBACs because they can be held legally liable for complications that arise during delivery. Frustrated by her limited options, Gretta chooses to attempt a home birth instead.

Patients like Gretta are not legally permitted to waive their right to hold a physician liable for birth-related injuries. Medical licensing regulations and other legal restrictions on obstetric care also discourage physicians from opening birthing centers that offer alternatives to a hospital birth. Even in places where women have a right to choose to terminate a pregnancy, public officials still routinely limit women's reproductive freedom if they choose to give birth.

Or, consider a case that is based loosely on the details of the *Griswold v. Connecticut* Supreme Court decision:

BIRTH CONTROL

Public officials prohibit people from accessing birth control on the grounds that it would encourage them to have immoral sexual relationships. Estelle opens a clinic to provide birth control to married women. Public officials arrest Estelle and she must pay a fine for violating the law.

For one, Estelle Griswold was not doing anything wrong by providing birth control to *married* women, even if public officials were right that sex between unmarried people is immoral. But also, sex between unmarried people is not immoral. And even if premarital sex *were* immoral, public officials still would not have the authority to limit people's access to birth control as a way of deterring it.

Though libertarians support a right to access contraception, they do not support policies that subsidize it or mandate that insurance providers pay for birth control. Rather, libertarians hold that birth control should be neither prohibited nor encouraged by the state. When public officials mandate that private insurance providers pay for contraceptives, they force religious people to privately subsidize conduct that they view as immoral.

Some people support subsidies and mandates for contraception because they worry that too many people are having children. But as the economist Julian Simon has argued, a rising population is something to celebrate, not something to fear, as long as states do not interfere with the price system:

FERTILITY

As the population of a society increases, so does demand for food, energy, and other life-sustaining products. In a society with a free price system, increased demand creates an incentive for suppliers to find ways to deliver food, energy, and other products more efficiently. New workers sort into occupations according to their comparative advantage, further contributing to economic growth and innovation.

Many libertarians are natalists, meaning that they think that it is a good thing to have more children. In part, the argument for natalism parallels libertarian arguments for open borders, which we will discuss later. In a free society, where people are empowered to trade with each other in ways that make both sides better off, creating more people not only benefits the children who would not otherwise have existed, the rest of us also benefit from eventually having the opportunity to trade with them and enjoy all the innovative new stuff the next generation will create.

In contrast, anti-natalists who worry about rising populations often implicitly assume that societies will not effectively allocate resources in a way that enables everyone to have a decent life. Yet these anti-natalists assume this because they tend to support anti-market policies!

DRUGS

Another argument in favor of restrictions on the right to make risky choices proceeds from the premise that some people don't understand the risks of what they are doing. Consider a famous case from John Stuart Mill's *On Liberty*:

BRIDGE CROSSING

"If either a public officer or anyone else saw a person attempting to cross a bridge which had been ascertained to be unsafe, and there were no time to warn him of his danger, they might seize him and turn him back, without any real infringement of his liberty; for liberty consists in doing what one desires, and he does not desire to fall into the river."

Mill himself was generally opposed to paternalism, but even he believed paternalistic interference could be justified in cases like these—that is, cases where the interference stops someone from doing something that would ultimately frustrate their desires. Here the pedestrian only *thinks* that he wants to cross the bridge. If he had accurate beliefs about the danger, he'd turn away on his own. But unfortunately, he mistakenly believes the bridge is safe and presses on. So the paternalistic bystander who stops the pedestrian is merely helping him get what he really wants, which is to stay safe and not fall into the river. Consequently, the pedestrian can't complain about the interference. If anything, a "thank you" is probably in order.

One might think that addictive drugs are like this. For example, sometimes people who use addictive drugs later say that if they knew how hard it would be to stop, or how dangerous the drug is, they wouldn't have started:

HEROIN USER

Kyler decides to start using heroin, knowing that it is very addictive and dangerous. He enjoys using heroin, but he also regrets starting to use the drug. Because of his drug use, Kyler is homeless and unemployed.

Yet there are several reasons why stories like Kyler's do not justify paternalistic drug laws, even if drug users claim that they regret taking drugs. First, it is more socially desirable for drug users who struggle due to their addiction to say that they disavow their drug use than to say that they are making a rational tradeoff between the welfare they experience from using drugs and the welfare they forego due to using. Second, the science of addiction shows that drug addicts are capable of refusing their drug of choice, even if it is very difficult for them to refuse. Even addictive choices are voluntary. Third, drug users are typically aware of the risks of addiction, contrary to some media portrayals of opioid addiction. And fourth, most importantly, drug prohibition makes substance use more dangerous because manufacturers cannot be held legally liable for adulterated products. Prohibition also makes drug use more dangerous insofar as public officials also prohibit people from accessing therapy that could treat addiction or prevent overdoses.

Suppose, though, that drug users cannot make a voluntary choice to use drugs, at least after their initial decision to use them, because addiction undermines a person's capacity to make voluntary choices. Even so, drug criminalization would be inappropriate. Consider a dilemma raised by Michael Huemer. On one horn of the dilemma, if the initial choice to use drugs is voluntary, then it would be wrong to criminalize drug use because people have the right to autonomously choose to act in ways that risk their future autonomy. For instance, one may play professional football and risk chronic traumatic encephalopathy. You may also decline to take a drug that's necessary to prevent you from suffering an autonomy-destroying neurological condition Alternatively, if addicts really do not voluntarily consent to limit their long-term autonomy, then, assuming that the criminal law primarily punishes choices that people are morally responsible for, it would be wrong to criminalize drug use because drug users would not be responsible for their addictive behavior.

Some paternalists may reply that even if drug use is a free, informed, and voluntary choice that addicts believe is the best way of promoting their overall interests, public officials may still reasonably prohibit it if prohibition would reduce premature deaths from drug use on balance. In this way maybe prohibiting drug use is like mandating seatbelt use:

SEATBELTS

Tim doesn't like to wear a seatbelt. He knows that it puts him at a greater risk of dying in a car accident, but he also knows that he is a safer driver than many other people and he's willing to take the risk for the freedom of riding unbelted. One day Tim is pulled over by a police officer and given a ticket for riding unbelted. If he doesn't pay it, he could face criminal penalties.

Libertarians reject paternalism in these cases as well. Even if public officials can prevent people from dying in car accidents by enforcing a seatbelt mandate, these mandates are nevertheless a violation of people's entitlement to ride unbelted and free from the threat of police interference.

Here again, the principle that people may take risks with their own health for reasons that observers regard as trivial is supported by our commonsense judgment in a range of cases. A thrill-seeker has the right to swim in shark-infested waters just for the rush. A patient is at liberty to refuse to take their heart medication simply to avoid the chalky aftertaste.

A different kind of justification for paternalism relates to the idea that people should be prevented from making dangerous decisions since these decisions can impose burdens on their loved ones. Consider the case of drinking as an illustration of this kind of argument:

DRINKING

Bob got a big bonus at work. He could use the money to pay off some credit card debt or to help his family pay for a vacation, but instead he chooses to spend it on alcohol. Later, he regrets his choice.

People often feel that they have special obligations to their family members, so one might think that public officials are entitled to ban risky decision-making as a way of preventing people from letting their loved ones down.

But even if people do have special duties to consider their loved ones' well-being, here again, these duties are not enforceable. When elderly people choose euthanasia, their adult children may be distressed by that choice, but the children have no entitlement to prevent their parents from choosing how to die. Similarly, Bob's decision to drink away his bonus rather than spend it on a family vacation must have been awful for his family, but it shouldn't be unlawful. Drinking and being a bad partner or father makes you a jerk, but not a criminal.

The crux of this argument for paternalism is whether Bob's family had an entitlement to the money. If Bob would have been within his rights to simply hand over the bonus money to his drinking buddies as a gift, then he also would have been within his rights to spend the bonus at the bar. On the other hand, if Bob's family did have an entitlement to Bob's financial support, then even this entitlement would not justify a prohibition on drinking per se. Rather, it would justify a law that requires parents and spouses to provide for their loved ones.

To sum up, one must always ask whether the cost affiliated with some sort of risky behavior is criminal or just bad. Sometimes, people who make dangerous, self-harming choices are bad friends, students, employees, and citizens. But so are conscientious and prudent people! And in any case, it is perfectly legal to be lazy, inconsiderate, rude, and self-absorbed. So, as Huemer has argued, public officials cannot prohibit dangerous and self-harming behavior such as drug use on the grounds that it makes people more likely to do something that is not itself criminal. To appreciate the absurdity of the contrary view, consider:

HARRY POTTER

Public officials acquire solid evidence indicating that citizens who read Harry Potter and the Philosopher's Stone *are more likely to read* Harry Potter and the Chamber of Secrets. *They proceed to ban the sale of* Harry Potter and the Philosopher's Stone *to reduce the chances that citizens will read* Harry Potter and the Chamber of Secrets.

There are several reasons why the public officials' behavior is absurd—the one relevant to our argument here is that reading *Harry Potter and the Chamber of Secrets* isn't a crime! So it would be bizarre to criminalize the sale of *Harry Potter and the Philosopher's Stone* to prevent people from doing something which is perfectly legal. Similarly, banning drugs on the grounds that they may make users unproductive or disengaged is bizarre given that it's perfectly legal to be unproductive and disengaged.

One might respond that some kinds of dangerous decision-making increase people's chances of committing crimes that violate other people's rights. For example, suppose that drug users and drinkers are also more likely to be violent or to steal. If so, should doing drugs and drinking be prohibited? The answer is going to be complicated. The mere fact that doing X makes you more likely to commit a crime doesn't imply that X should be criminalized. For instance, suppose that being in poverty makes you more likely to commit a crime. Even if this is true, it should still be legal for people to impoverish themselves by giving away all of their money and quitting their jobs, because people have property rights and the right of occupational choice. So too, even if drug users and drinkers are more likely to commit crimes, if people have bodily and property rights that entail the rights to do drugs and drink alcohol then the heightened risk of crime is not a sufficient reason to limit those rights.

On the other hand, there are unresolved questions of just how high the risk of crime has to be before public officials have a good case to prohibit the activity. People who drive drunk are so much more likely to commit vehicular homicide that public officials may conclude that drunk drivers are liable to be stopped and punished, but not that alcohol should be banned. All political philosophies struggle to resolve controversies about how much risk public officials should tolerate though; this issue is not distinctive to libertarianism.

Libertarians give a similar response to some paternalist arguments that propose broad restrictions on liberty to protect a subset of the population. For example, paternalists sometimes oppose heroin legalization because it would make it easier for children to access heroin. This is a fair worry, but it can be addressed with a more targeted solution than across-the-board prohibition—for instance, harsher penalties for selling heroin to children. By analogy, if people were worried about underage driving, the solution wouldn't be to criminalize *all* driving but rather ratchet up prevention efforts and penalties for underage driving.

A final argument against these kinds of prohibitions on risky decision-making is that all laws create more power for the state. At first glance, a paternalistic intervention like a seatbelt mandate might not seem like a big deal. But the mandate gives the police another reason to pull drivers over. When agents of the state have discretionary power, they tend to exercise it as the expense of marginalized groups. For instance, a Black driver is more likely to be stopped than a white driver and more likely to be searched during a stop. And when police officers pull people over, terrible things can happen, including civil rights violations, brutality, and even murder (victims of police abuse are also more likely to be Black). In brief, the consequentialist anti-paternalist argues that if our failings make us unfit to be in charge of our own lives, they make us even less fit to be in charge of the lives of others.

ENHANCEMENT

Libertarians believe that everyone owns their own body, and public officials violate this right when they prohibit people from modifying their bodies. For example, consider people who want to take drugs that will make them stronger or faster:

PERFORMANCE ENHANCING DRUGS

Tobin is a bodybuilder who uses steroids and other performance enhancing drugs to increase his strength and endurance. He knows that there are long-term risks, but he doesn't care about his future wellbeing as much as he values impressing his friends at the gym and winning competitions.

In many jurisdictions, public officials prohibit people like Tobin from using some kinds of performance enhancing drugs. Yet it's hard to reconcile these prohibitive policies with people's freedom to choose other medical interventions:

FACE TATTOOS

Erik "the Lizardman" Sprague, a former philosophy graduate student, tattooed his face and body to look like it was covered in lizard scales. He also modified his tongue to make it look more like a lizard tongue. He is a professional performance artist and an active member of the body modification community.

In both cases, people like Tobin and Erik have a compelling interest in making potentially risky choices for the sake of other values, even if they have idiosyncratic values that most people would not share (to be clear, we're referring to Erik's decision to modify his body to look like a lizard, not his decision to enter graduate school in philosophy—although the point might also apply there!).

A classic libertarian argumentative strategy is to point out that the law fails to treat cases alike. Why should public officials allow the Lizardman to modify his body so that he is more entertaining to watch, while prohibiting athletes from doing the same? This inconsistency reveals that public officials should either prohibit the Lizardman's modification or permit PEDs in sports. Yet to prohibit the Lizardman from modifying his body in the service of his professional ambitions as an entertainer would be a form of government overreach. Therefore, given that the Lizardman has a right to modify his body in the service of his occupational freedom and self-expression, so too do professional athletes.

A body modification choice doesn't even need to be in someone's professional or artistic interest in order for it to be a protected choice that they are entitled to make. Sometimes, public officials ought to allow people to make harmful body-modifying choices. For example, public officials should permit people to gain or lose a lot of weight, even if their weight gain or loss causes health problems and functional impairments. Public officials should also permit imprudent cosmetic surgery:

COSMETIC SURGERY

Kylie is an aspiring influencer who has had ten cosmetic surgery procedures that made her appear more photogenic and stylish. She knows that each surgery has short-term and long-term risks, but she doesn't care about her future wellbeing as much as she values getting more followers. Unfortunately, the surgery doesn't cause her to gain more followers and she regrets the pain and expense.

In this case, Kylie's decision to permanently modify her body backfired, just as body modifications for the Lizardman could have backfired as well. But just as entrepreneurs are entitled to risk their savings or their reputations in the pursuit of an untested idea or a grand new venture, so too are people like Kylie entitled to risk their bodies for the sake of their professional ambitions.

One line of argument against Tobin, Erik, and Kylie's rights to modify their bodies in order to achieve their long-term goals is that permitting this kind of behavior is unfair to other people who want to compete in athletic competitions, the entertainment industry, or on social media but don't want to modify their bodies. For this reason, some philosophers have argued that public officials should restrict access to at least some forms of bodily enhancement and modification, not for the sake of people like Tobin, Erik, and Kylie but for the sake of everyone else in their industries. These arguments are motivated by a concern that no one benefits from ever-increasing athletic, entertainment, or beauty standards, and that without regulation, people will feel competitive pressure to modify their bodies in increasingly risky ways in order to succeed.

The libertarian rejoinder to this line of argument is to question the claim that cultural norms surrounding athletic performance, entertainment, and appearance arise primarily due to competitive social pressure. To see why this is a questionable claim, consider why people would feel that bodily modification gave them a competitive advantage. Chess players and bankers, for example, do not feel pressure to dramatically modify their bodies, even though they are also in competitive fields. These examples reveal that people choose to modify their bodies in order to gain an advantage in a competitive context where having certain physical traits really is an advantage. Ability and appearance norms in athletics, entertainment, and social media contexts are an expression of those community's values. Even if some people feel excluded, shamed, or judged by their inability or unwillingness to comply with normative standards of appearance, this fact alone is not a sufficient ground for government regulation or censorship. Consider an analogy to other cultural contexts:

MODESTY

Martha is a member of a conservative religious community. In her community, women are encouraged to dress modestly. Some women cover their arms and legs, while other women cover their hair. A few women cover their whole bodies. Martha would prefer to wear short skirts and tank tops, but she feels social pressure to cover her arms and legs.

In this case, it would be wrong for public officials to restrict or censor religious dress on the grounds that some religious norms make many people feel judged, excluded, or pressured to comply. Similarly, it would also be wrong for officials to cite these kinds of reasons as a justification for regulations that restrict what people can do with their own bodies.

The idea that people own their bodies—and are therefore entitled to modify their bodies however they want—is at the foundation of many libertarian theories. It is also a foundational justification for permitting trans people to access gender-affirming care:

GENDER-AFFIRMING CARE

Belle seeks gender-affirming surgery and hormones, even though she does not expect the surgery to improve her mental health in the long-run.

Some justifications for permitting trans people to access gender-affirming care emphasize the mental health benefits of transitioning. Yet from a libertarian perspective, these benefits are not necessary to justify the practice. All that is required is that each person is entitled to modify their bodies however they see fit, as long as the modifications are essentially self-regarding.

Difficult cases arise when a person's desire for bodily modification is seemingly indicative of a broader inability to make rational decisions. People with anorexia are sometimes compelled to receive treatment on these grounds. Yet libertarians are very skeptical of any kind of compulsory treatment or prohibition on bodily modification because even people who seem to have very idiosyncratic preferences (like Erik the Lizardman) may be making the choice that is best for them. Consider another case like this:

ELECTIVE AMPUTATION

Hank is a patient with Body Identity Integrity Disorder (BIID). He pays an orthopedic surgeon to amputate his leg. After the surgery, Hank feels much more at home in his new body.

Even if Hank's desire to amputate his leg is the result of a neurological impairment or a mental illness, he is entitled to change his body however he likes. The more difficult question is whether public officials or healthcare providers ought to be required to subsidize Hank's amputation. We address this question in Chapters 4 and 5.

Before moving on, we'd like to spotlight a curious feature of a lot of paternalist thought and practice. People are perfectly willing to criminalize some practice because it's risky while at the same time permitting an even riskier practice. Refusing to wear a seatbelt is less risky than refusing to take a life-saving medication, yet we tend to allow the latter but not the former. This is a bit like allowing people to gamble $100,000 but not $100. If you're permitted to perform the more harmful action, why aren't you permitted to perform the less harmful action? Of course, you could resolve this problem by prohibiting both, but we suspect most readers would not want to take up this option.

FOOD

Sometimes we have information that would help us make better decisions but we don't use it to form true beliefs because of our vulnerability to weakness of will and cognitive biases. For instance, you might read statistics indicating your likelihood of suffering a serious car accident but dismiss them because you assume, wrongly, that you're better than the average driver. This sort of optimism bias may cause you to buckle your seatbelt less frequently than you would if you had accurate beliefs about your risk of crashing your car.

We're also susceptible to a short-term bias, where we are unwilling to pay small short-term costs for substantial long-term gains. Cognitive biases could explain why we pile up too much debt and eat too much sugar. To counteract these biases, regulators could tax, or even ban, unhealthy food (for example).

One problem with public health policies that aim to encourage citizens to make better decisions is that public officials have their own biases, which may blind them to the risks of their policies. Consider the case of soda taxes:

SODA TAXES

In an effort to reduce obesity, city officials implemented a soda tax, which charged consumers a small fee per ounce of sugary drink purchased.

For an obesity-minded public health official on a budget, this kind of policy looks like a promising solution to the obesity epidemic. The tax was designed to encourage people to quit their unhealthy soda habits without requiring a costly public investment in behavioral change.

Yet the public officials who have passed these kinds of taxes often fail to account for the unintended consequences of their policies. In some cases, people can avoid these taxes by purchasing sugary drinks just outside of the city limits. Or, people might trade soda for juice, even though juice is also a sugary drink, in order to avoid the tax. Or, people might consume additional calories elsewhere in their diets. For these reasons, soda taxes do not seem to reduce calorie consumption or weight in the places where they are enforced.

Even worse, these taxes are regressive. Taxes are passed onto consumers (deliberately, since the taxes aim to deter people from purchasing soda) and the lowest-income consumers take on most of the tax burden because they are less likely to drive to purchase soda outside the city lines. So a well-intentioned public health policy backfires because it does not achieve its public health goals but it did disproportionately burden the city's lowest-income residents.

This case represents a more general pattern of misguided paternalism among public health officials when it comes to food. Too often, public health officials and politicians pass policies that impose their vision of what healthy eating, healthy weight, and healthy lifestyle entail without considering that the people they serve might have different values and different ideas about health and diet.

SEX

A second problem with appealing to cognitive biases to justify paternalism is that people have the right to make biased decisions, even when those decisions end badly. Take the right to marry the partner(s) of your choice. Here are some eminently sensible principles to follow when assessing prospective spouses. Your partner should share your religious beliefs and your preferences for having children. They should live nearby because long-distance relationships are expensive, emotionally draining, and often unsuccessful. It's usually a mistake to date a co-worker. It's good to date someone who has similar taste in movies, recreation, and vacations. A lounge-at-the-pool person might not want to marry a hike-up-the-mountain person. These are all important boxes to check.

But of course, none of this matters when you meet someone with an adorable smile who strikes you as the person you didn't know you were missing all along. Each of the sensible principles for choosing a partner scatters like so much dust in the wind. You say, "We'll make the long-distance thing work." "He'll want kids once he gets older." "She'll convert before we get married." People in love assume that they will be exceptions to the rule even if that assumption isn't supported by the broader population-level evidence. This idea is encapsulated in a conversation from the sitcom *Arrested Development*:

> Tobias: "You know, Lindsay, as a therapist, I have advised a number of couples to explore an open relationship where the couple remains emotionally committed but free to explore extramarital encounters."
> Lindsay: "Well, did it work for those people?"
> Tobias: "No, it never does. I mean, these people somehow delude themselves into thinking it might, but . . . but it might work for us."

Irrational desires and feelings often motivate romantic choices, taking sober reasoning along for the ride. And given how important romantic partnerships can be to people's overall well-being, if ever there were a sphere of human activity that was ripe for paternalistic intervention, it would be romantic choices.

But now imagine if a group of technocrats in Washington started regulating people's dating decisions. Maybe they start filtering Tinder results and fine people for going out on unapproved dates. Or maybe they try to make people consider partners in a non-discriminatory way, or they try to make sure that the worst off have the best possible romantic prospects. Even if these technocrats were good at their jobs, people would surely resent the interference because public officials don't have the moral authority to dictate dating. And here it's also important to recall the earlier point that public officials are people too. So just as newlyweds have optimism bias about their own marriages and struggling couples may delude themselves into thinking that an open relationship can solve their underlying incompatibility, public officials are likely to be overly optimistic about their own capacities to promote people's long-term well-being in romantic relationships.

If this whole thought experiment sounds absurd, it's worth remembering that public officials have taken an interest in people's romantic lives for most of human history. Historically, states prohibited premarital sex, adultery, and divorce, in addition to gay relationships. Not long ago, two men were arrested for having consensual sex:

LAWRENCE V. TEXAS

John and Tyron are having sex when the police enter John's apartment and arrest them both.

In the United States, the Libertarian Party was, for a long time, the only party that publicly supported gay people's legal right to sexual autonomy. In contrast to the two major political parties, libertarians supported gay marriage since the 1970s.

Today, libertarians advocate for the privacy and sexual autonomy of people who choose to sell sex. People should be free to choose a sexual partner based on their ability to pay just as they are free to choose a partner based on other facts, such as looks, sense of humor, or shared values. When it comes to people's sex lives, different people value different things and markets can enable people to meet enthusiastic and willing intimate partners when otherwise they may not be able to find anyone. Here's an example:

SEX WORK

Don has money but he struggles to find attractive women who are interested in an intimate relationship with him. Melania is attractive, and she is willing to have sex with Don if he pays her. Public officials prohibit Don from paying Melania for sex. If Don is caught paying Melania for sex, they could both go to jail.

Though technocrats and scientists may be experts about the risks of sex work in general, this expertise doesn't make them experts in deciding whether that risk is worth taking for Melania.

Paternalists might defend the prohibition on sex work on the grounds that it is a dangerous industry. The problems with this argument are the same as the problems with many of the foregoing arguments. First, prohibition may just make a risky industry even riskier by making it more difficult for sex workers to report abuse to the police. And second, public officials are especially unreliable judges of whether a particular risky industry is worth it because their intuitions are often clouded by normatively extraneous factors that go beyond mere considerations of risk. For example, some voters have very strong moral intuitions about sex, purity, and bodily integrity which cause them to react negatively to choices that violate sexual taboos or which involve someone's bodily integrity. If enough people think this way, then officials have electoral incentives to affirm these views. This may explain why public officials support prohibitions on risky sex work, but they do not similarly advocate for a prohibition on commercial fishing, logging, military service, or professional football.

BODILY MARKETS

All labor markets are bodily service markets although some might not look like it at first glance (for instance, even if you work as a professor, you're using your fingers to type and vocal chords to lecture). But some bodily service markets, such as sex work or kidney sales, are more dangerous than others.

People also have strong anti-commodification intuitions about things they view as sacred, such as sex and body parts. Squeamishness and anti-commodification attitudes may in part explain why public officials prohibit blood and kidney sales but permit blood and kidney donation, even though this position seems somewhat strange. After all, the reason why you get to decide whether or not to donate your own blood is because it's *your* blood—but if it's your blood, it seems as though you should get to decide whether or not to sell it. By analogy, if it's your car, you may give it away for free, but you may also sell it.

The following case illustrates why policies prohibiting markets in body parts can also be harmful:

KIDNEY MARKETS

Diane needs a kidney. Her sister takes a week off work and donates a kidney to her, saving Diane's life. Dane needs a kidney but no one in his family is a match. Dane's neighbor Dylan is willing to give his kidney to Dane, but only if Dane pays him $10,000 so that Dylan can pay off a loan. Public officials prohibit Dane from paying Dylan. Dane dies of kidney failure and Dylan declares bankruptcy.

As a first pass, it looks like public officials permit people to donate their kidney out of altruism but not for money. The prohibition on kidney markets is even stranger, though, if we imagine that Diane's sister donated her kidney not out of altruism, but because Diane provides free childcare to her children. Still, Diane's sister would have been legally permitted to donate her kidney. Yet if it's permissible to donate something for a financial reason, then it should also be permissible to sell it in the market. The same argument applies to sex work. Some people choose their sexual partners at least partly for financial reasons. Yet when a couple makes the arrangement explicit, public officials threaten them with criminal penalties.

These examples also illustrate how prohibitions on sex work and kidney markets are counterproductive insofar as officials' goal is to protect people's safety and well-being. By prohibiting sex work, officials force people like Melania to work in an "underground" labor market where she has less access to legal and police protection. By prohibiting kidney markets officials prevent people like Dane from saving their own lives. In these cases, the risks of prohibition exceed the risks of permitting a bodily service market.

An intuitive objection to kidney sales is that sellers shouldn't be permitted to take the risk associated with selling their kidney. But this objection fails for a familiar reason: we allow people to take far greater risks—for example, climbing dangerous mountains and even agreeing to euthanasia. So to permit dangerous mountain climbing but not the sale of kidneys is strange—especially considering that mountain climbing is recreational while kidney sales could save thousands of lives by incentivizing people to supply kidneys to those who would otherwise not receive one. Plus, the risk objection speaks against not only kidney sales but also unpaid kidney donations, given that they carry the same risk. Yet few are willing to criminalize kidney donations to spare the donor the risk.

One might reply that the problem with kidney sales is not simply that they are risky but rather that provide people with an incentive to take a serious risk with their health that they otherwise wouldn't take. Yet we allow people to accept payment to do other risky things like drive a truck, mine coal, and more.

Of course, you could find it objectionable that people are forced to take the risks associated with a dangerous surgery or job out of necessity. Maybe you think the fix for this is a social safety net that ensures that people don't sell a kidney or drive a truck out of economic desperation. That's fair enough—and we'll return to questions of redistribution later—but notice that this argument only speaks in favor of a social safety net; it does not speak in favor of banning payment for doing something risky such as giving someone a kidney or mining coal.

What's more, by paternalistically banning bodily service markets like sex work or kidney sales, the state merely removes an option without adding any better ones; indeed, it removes the option that the citizen actually thinks is their best one, as evidenced by their decision to take that option over all of the alternatives. On its own, a ban harms those it purports to help by taking away their "best bad" option.

To illustrate the point, consider an analogous argument that is clearly absurd. Suppose someone argues in favor of banning temporary warming shelters on the grounds that no one should have to use them to escape the cold rather than, say, high-quality permanent housing. Just as they aren't likely to sell their kidneys, millionaires don't use warming shelters—only the economically vulnerable are likely to do so. But we suspect that few people would find the argument for banning warming shelters compelling. Simply banning them wouldn't place people in high-quality permanent housing and would in fact worsen the condition of those in need of shelter. Just like selling a kidney is a bad option, staying at a warming shelter is a bad option. But both are sometimes the *best* bad option. Of course, none of this speaks against the goal of creating conditions that enrich everyone to the point where they are no longer forced to accept a bad option due to economic necessity. But in the meantime, public officials shouldn't take away an option from people who already lack good options.

Other bodily service markets are more controversial than sex work and kidney markets. Specifically, markets that involve surrogacy, vital organs, or the full alienation of one's bodily autonomy are more morally complex than markets that merely involve risky bodily work:

SURROGATE MOTHERHOOD

Scott and Amy are unable to have children without medical assistance. Scott and Amy pay Shelly to gestate twins for them. Shelly gestates the twins but changes her mind about giving the twins to Scott and Amy. Public officials do not require Shelly to give the twins to Scott and Amy.

In these cases, public officials must decide whether parental rights should originate with the parent who gestates and gives birth to a child or the parent who initiates the conception and gestation of a child. States vary in how they answer this question. One reason that some people advocate for a law that grants parental rights to the gestating parent is that the alternative strikes them as a form of baby selling. But libertarians may reply to this objection by asking whether baby selling is really as bad as it sounds:

BABY MARKETS

Dave and Eric would love to start a family but they cannot conceive on their own. Marlene recently had a baby and she does not want to raise the child— she wants to travel the world. Marlene offers to sell her parental rights to Dave and Eric for $400,000. Public officials hear about this plan and announce that they will not uphold a transfer of parental rights if Marlene was motivated by a pecuniary incentive. Marlene raises a child she did not want to raise and Dave and Eric remain involuntarily childless.

This example shows that markets in parental rights can facilitate mutually beneficial agreements between consenting people, and a prohibition on these markets can result in an inefficient allocation of parental rights.

One might defend a prohibition on markets in parental rights on the grounds that children will fare better under a system where people cannot buy their way into parenthood. Yet this reply assumes that people who would be interested in selling their parental rights would be better parents than people who are willing to pay a lot of money for the chance to become parents. If nothing else, the argument against markets in parental rights requires further empirical investigation in order to justify anti-market limits on parental rights.

Consider also that even libertarians should endorse regulations on markets in parental rights. Parents have duties to care for their children and promote their interests. So the state may institutionalize regulations to ensure that buyers of parental rights will be competent parents. This point should help assuage worries about a parental rights market. Think of this way: take whatever regulations you believe should be in place to screen prospective adoptive parents and imagine they're in place to screen prospective buyers of parental rights. For instance, you'd probably want prospective parents to pass a background check, secure character recommendations, allow in-home visits, and more. Buyers of parental rights could be subject to all of these regulations—the only difference is that cash will change hands.

Another controversial bodily service market involves markets in vital organs, such as hearts and lungs. Here again, though these markets often arise when people are facing very difficult circumstances, prohibiting these markets does more harm than good:

HEART MARKETS

Nick is very ill and he needs a heart transplant. Jonas is thinking about ending his life. He decides that he would like to end his life in a way that benefits others, so he offers to sell his heart to Nick for $1,000,000, specifying that the money will go to Jonas's family. Public officials prohibit Nick and Jonas from making the exchange. Nick dies of his illness and Jonas kills himself in a violent way.

As above, if Jonas really owns his body, then he can decide to sell his heart to Nick. If people have the right to access medical aid in dying, then they should also have the legal right to choose the way that they die. And if people have the right to end their lives for any reason, then they should be permitted to choose to end their lives in order to financially benefit their families.

The most morally controversial bodily service market for libertarians isn't baby selling or heart markets, it's the case of voluntary slavery:

VOLUNTARY SLAVERY

Toby signs up to work on a commercial fishing boat for six months. If he chooses to leave earlier than his contract, he will be required to pay a steep financial penalty. Ana signs up for the military. If she decides to leave early, she will experience significant financial penalties. Kristine signs up for a one-year term where she will alienate her occupational freedom in exchange for a very high wage. Public officials will enforce Toby's and Ana's contracts, but they refuse to uphold Kristine's contract with her employer and Kristine's employer faces criminal penalties if public officials learn about the arrangement.

These kinds of cases are tricky for libertarians because they reveal a tension in libertarian thought. On the one hand, libertarians hold that no one should ever be forced to labor. Historically, libertarians were abolitionists. Many libertarians oppose taxes because they view it as a kind of forced labor. On the other hand, libertarians hold that people should be allowed to make almost any kind of contract that they want, including contracts that authorize other people to force them to labor. And libertarians also hold that, insofar as people make these contracts voluntarily, public officials should uphold and enforce them.

One way of honoring both of these libertarian commitments involves an appeal to the idea that people can change over time in ways that invalidate their previous voluntary commitments. So while a person may be entitled to consent to a voluntary labor agreement for six months, they will not uphold that contract permanently. This kind of argument is not without costs. It seems that insofar as it justifies limits on labor agreements, it also requires that public officials enable people to opt out of other contracts such as mortgages or student loans. For this reason, the ethics of voluntary slavery remains an unresolved subject in libertarian thought.

To the extent that the foregoing case for bodily service markets strikes some readers as objectionable on the grounds that poor people may be disproportionately compelled to sell their bodies in these ways, libertarians have three responses to this line of response. First, poor people are more likely than millionaires to sell their labor on a dangerous commercial fishing vessel, but few take this to be a reason to ban commercial fishing. Second, though some people participate in bodily service markets like kidney selling, sex work, and surrogacy because these are the only jobs that will enable them to meet their basic needs, typically the people who participate in these markets are also motivated by flexible hours, a high wage, or the fulfillment they get from doing the work. And third, insofar as one is concerned that people who participate in bodily service markets are motivated only by material considerations, this concern would not justify a prohibition on bodily service markets. Rather, as noted, this concern supports libertarian proposals for a universal basic income, which would ensure that no workers take a job solely because they need it to survive.

PUBLIC HEALTH

Public health policy aims to promote the health-span of an entire population. Throughout history, public officials addressed public health concerns by providing sanitation services, educating people about personal hygiene, and enforcing quarantines. Mass vaccination programs became a key component of public health policy in the twentieth century, following the development of vaccines for smallpox and polio. These diseases have largely been eradicated today, and life expectancy has markedly improved as a result of other vaccination campaigns against diseases like measles and pertussis. As state capacity expanded in developed countries over the course of the twentieth century, so did the welfare state, the administrative state, and armies of public health busybodies who supported many of the paternalistic regulations that we've already discussed in this chapter. At the same time, some old public health policies remain, as officials continue to enforce policies that aim to protect people from contagious diseases and reduce their exposure to environmental toxins.

Today's public health officials continue to promote vaccination campaigns as a way of preventing disease-related mortality and also as a way to limit the costs of disease management. People who get vaccinated not only protect themselves from diseases or disease symptoms but also protect unvaccinated people by reducing the chances that a disease will spread in a population. This is called herd immunity, and it is a public good that presumptively benefits everyone. Yet a population can only benefit from herd immunity to the extent that people get vaccinated, which is why most public health officials support vaccine mandates:

VACCINE MANDATES

Public officials require vaccination for all children who attend public school and for all public employees.

Some libertarians support vaccine mandates on the grounds that people are not entitled to use public schools or to keep their jobs as public employees as a general matter, so a vaccine mandate of this sort would not violate anyone's rights. Others think of contagious transmission as a kind of violence, because diseases cause bodily injuries. According to this view, just as public officials are entitled to uphold laws that protect people from reckless gunfire or drunk drivers, mandatory vaccination policies don't violate anyone's rights because no one has a right to put other people's health at risk. Also, to the extent that public officials are sometimes entitled to coerce citizens in order to solve collective action problems and provide public goods, mass vaccination campaigns could be justified in this way.

Other libertarians are skeptical of vaccine mandates because they oppose government policies that empower state actors to conscript people into projects that they would not otherwise contribute to. According to this view, vaccine mandates violate people's bodily rights because they punish people for refusing vaccination.

The crux of this disagreement between libertarians is that pro-mandate libertarians think vaccine mandates can sometimes be a way of protecting people's bodily rights whereas anti-mandate libertarians view mandates as a violation of people's bodily rights. Partly, they might disagree because they disagree about the extent that people's bodily rights include rights against the risk of contagious transmission. Or, people might disagree about the extent that state actors have a right to violate people's rights for the sake of overall well-being or to provide public goods. These disagreements do not arise solely within libertarian thought. People with other political ideologies also disagree with each other about vaccine mandates due to more foundational disagreements about the nature and limits of individual rights.

In contrast, libertarians are more univocal in their views about public policy when it comes to regulations that limit people's conduct in private contexts for the sake of public health:

SMOKING REGULATIONS

Public officials prohibit people from smoking in public places. They also prohibit private businesses from allowing people to smoke indoors. They censor some kinds of tobacco advertising and require that cigarette manufacturers include graphic warning labels on their packaging.

Though public officials may reasonably ban smoking in courthouses and public schools, libertarians argue that they do not have the authority to tell private business owners what they can do with their own property. Indeed, most people would agree that public officials lack the authority to tell homeowners and their guests that they may not smoke in the homeowner's kitchen. Public health restrictions on tobacco advertising also censor truthful speech about the benefits people can get from smoking and compel speech by private actors when they require manufacturers to put graphic warning labels on their products. Though smoking is hazardous and secondhand smoke can cause health problems too, business owners are entitled to decide for themselves whether the benefits outweigh the costs of allowing employees and patrons to smoke. People who want to avoid secondhand smoke can avoid businesses that allow it.

Public health scholars and officials are often critical of libertarianism on the grounds that people frequently use their liberty to make unhealthy choices, and then pass the costs onto others. This line of argument provides further justification for paternalistic laws like seatbelt mandates since taxpayers are required to pay for people's healthcare, including the costs of surgery and physical therapy for people who are injured in car accidents due to riding unbelted.

Yet this argument drifts away from a purely paternalistic justification because it aims to protect third parties from being harmed due to a seemingly self-destructive choice.

Consider how a public health official might appeal to an argument like this to justify paternalistic drug laws:

SOCIAL COSTS

Mavis sees Keith at the local hospital after an overdose. She knows that her tax dollars pay for medical care for people like Keith. Mavis resents that she has to pay for Keith's bad choices.

Of course, many libertarians will claim that public officials should not require people like Mavis to subsidize health care for risky decision makers like Keith. But libertarians also question the premise that people who make risky choices do impose greater costs on the health system. After all, the grim truth is that people who die prematurely typically die more quickly and in lower-cost ways than healthy people who experience a slow and costly decline in their eighties and nineties.

The social cost justification for public health regulations also seemingly holds that people, including Keith, have enforceable rights to receive medical care, which they cannot waive in exchange for the right to make risky choices. (Otherwise, Keith could waive his right to medical care in exchange for the right to use drugs.) But if Keith did have enforceable and inalienable rights to access medical care then presumably people like Mavis would be morally obligated to satisfy that right to health care. And if so, then taxpayers like Mavis would have no complaint against Keith's exercising his right to access health care.

To make this point clearer, consider an analogy to free speech. Imagine that public officials censored speech on the grounds that people who say controversial things might cause civil unrest. Say, for example, that a civil rights leader was legally prohibited from speaking in public on the grounds that his speech could draw a crowd, which would then require that the police attend the event to protect people's property and to prevent violence. In this example, the fact that providing police protection is costly is not grounds for censoring the leader's speech. Speakers are not preemptively liable to be censored for the sake of sparing public officials the cost of doing their jobs. On the other hand, if health care is not a right, as most libertarians believe, then people like Mavis may not be compelled to help people like Keith, and public officials should not force Mavis to pay the price of Keith's choices.

A similar justification for public health regulations is one that reframes the cost of seemingly self-harming behavior as harmful to others in virtue of the non-pecuniary social costs, such as the psychological harms that people experience by witnessing their fellow citizens suffer:

PSYCHOLOGICAL HARMS

Elsa sees the wreckage of a terrible motorcycle accident on the side of the road. She is traumatized by the experience, and she avoids driving for months after the incident.

It's very plausible that watching people make bad choices or suffer from their risky decision-making can be distressing. It's not plausible that public officials are entitled to limit citizens' freedom to shield their tender-hearted compatriots from distress. If a swimmer drowns in rough waters, he has not wronged the horrified onlookers by dying in public. This justification for paternalistic laws also has unacceptable implications in cases where people are unreasonably squeamish or too-easily distressed. There are people who find it distressing to see gay couples kissing, immodestly dressed teenagers waiting in line for a dance club, cancer patients at the gym, or burn victims eating at a diner. But gay couples, club kids, cancer patients, and burn victims aren't doing anything wrong, even if their presence is distressing to the people around them. So too for people who make self-harming decisions.

SUMMARY

The political slogan "my body, my choice" has far-reaching public policy implications beyond current debates about reproductive healthcare. Libertarians often affirm a principle of self-ownership, which means that people are entitled to decide what to do with their own bodies. This principle is at odds with policies that restrict people's bodily autonomy, including restrictions on medical freedom, recreational drug use, and intimate partnerships. Even if a person exercises their bodily autonomy in ways that are bad for their well-being in the long run, no one else has a right to decide what happens to their body. Plus, an appeal to people's unreliability as decision makers doesn't support paternalism because we should expect public officials to be at least as unreliable when they make choices for an entire population. For these reasons, libertarians oppose paternalistic and moralistic restrictions on bodily choices.

FURTHER READING

- Abigail Alliance for Better Access v. Von Eschenbach. 2007, 495 F. 3d 695. Court of Appeals, Dist. of Columbia Circuit.
- Andreyeva, Tatiana, Keith Marple, Samantha Marinello, Timothy E. Moore, and Lisa M. Powell. 2022. "Outcomes Following Taxation of Sugar-Sweetened Beverages: A Systematic Review and Meta-Analysis." *JAMA Network Open* 5 (6): e2215276. https://doi.org/10.1001/jamanetworkopen.2022.15276.
- Brennan, Jason, and Peter Jaworski. 2022. *Markets without Limits: Moral Virtues and Commercial Interests.* Routledge.
- Cowart, Dax, and Robert Burt. 1998. "Confronting Death Who Chooses, Who Controls?" *The Hastings Center Report* 28 (1): 14–24.
- Feinberg, Joel. 1989. *Harm to Self.* Oxford University Press.
- Flanigan, Jessica. 2014. "A Defense of Compulsory Vaccination." *HEC Forum* 26 (1): 5–25. https://doi.org/10.1007/s10730-013-9221-5.
- Flanigan, Jessica. 2016. "Double Standards and Arguments for Tobacco Regulation." *Journal of Medical Ethics* 42 (5): 305–311.
- Flanigan, Jessica. 2017. *Pharmaceutical Freedom: Why Patients Have a Right to Self Medicate.* Oxford University Press.
- Flanigan, Jessica, and Lori Watson. 2019. *Debating Sex Work.* Oxford University Press.
- Friedman, Milton, Rose D. Friedman, and Grover Gardner. 1962. *Capitalism and Freedom.* Vol. 133. Chicago: University of Chicago Press.
- Fry-Revere, Sigrid. 2014. *The Kidney Sellers: A Journey of Discovery in Iran.* Carolina Academic Press.
- Griswold v. Connecticut. 496AD, 381 US 479. Supreme Court.

- Hall, Lauren K. 2019. *The Medicalization of Birth and Death*. Johns Hopkins University Press.
- Hart, Carl. 2014. *High Price: A Neuroscientist's Journey of Self-Discovery That Challenges Everything You Know about Drugs and Society*. Harper Perennial.
- Huemer, Michael. 2009. "America's Unjust Drug War." In *The Right Thing to Do: Basic Readings in Moral Philosophy*, 223–236. Rowman & Littlefield Publishers.
- Lawrence v. Texas. 2003, 539 US 558. Supreme Court.
- Mill, John Stuart. 1966. *On Liberty*. Edited by John M. Robson. London, UK: Macmillan Education.
- Posner, Richard A. 1987. "The Regulation of the Market in Adoptions." *Boston University Law Review* 67 (1): 59–72.
- Russell, Charlie, dir. 2011. *Choosing to Die*. KEO North.
- Saul, Stephanie. 2009. "Building a Baby, with Few Ground Rules." *The New York Times*, December 12, sec. U.S. www.nytimes.com/2009/12/13/us/13surrogacy.html.
- Savulescu, Julian, and Nick Bostrom, eds. 2009. *Human Enhancement*. 1st edition. Oxford: Oxford University Press.
- Shallat-Chemel, Lee, dir. 2004. "The One Where Michael Leaves." *Arrested Development*. Fox.
- Sprauge, Erik. 2025. "The Lizardman." https://sites.google.com/view/the-lizardman/home.
- Thrasher, John. 2019. "Self Ownership as Personal Sovereignty." *Social Philosophy and Policy* 36 (2): 116–133. https://doi.org/10.1017/S026505 2519000396.

3

CONSCIENCE, EXPRESSION, AND ASSOCIATION

Libertarians defend an expansive conception of freedom of conscience, expression, and association. Public officials are not entitled to dictate what people believe or say, nor are they entitled to tell people whom they may associate with, or not. Some libertarians are committed to these values because they believe that a society that tolerates even false and immoral speech and unpopular ways of living is more likely to ultimately arrive at true beliefs and flourishing communities than more restrictive societies. Libertarians also emphasize the dangers of empowering censors to regulate ideas and speech, given that censors are subject to the same biases and prejudices as those they would censor. Similar considerations also weigh in favor of an expansive right to free association, which permits nearly any form of economic, religious, or fraternal association entered with the consent of its members. Critics of libertarianism argue that this approach permits too much hate speech and discrimination. In this chapter, we'll describe the case for freedom of expression and association and address objections to the libertarian view.

RELIGION

The relationship between religious authority and political authority is complicated. Religion can undermine and destabilize state

DOI: 10.4324/9781003270720-3

power because religious people recognize a source of authority that can override governmental authority. This is why political leaders have historically tried to restrict religious speech and expression. At the same time, when states adopt a national religion, political leaders can strengthen and reinforce their claims to authority, which is why some of the most politically repressive government officials today limit their citizens' freedom in the name of religion.

Consider how, throughout history, some of the most striking challenges to political authority were motivated by religious convictions. For example, here's a story that is thousands of years old:

ANTIGONE

Antigone must choose whether to obey the law or fulfill a sacred religious obligation to bury her deceased brother, who has been labeled as a traitor. Antigone chooses to follow her religious duty, in defiance of political authorities.

Or, in the 1600s, as the European Wars of Religion unfolded in the wake of the Reformation, public officials in England and Scotland demanded that citizens pledge allegiance to the King and affirm his status as the leader of the Church. Religious citizens who refused were punished and killed for challenging the King's authority:

LOYALTY OATHS

Margaret Wilson was a religious teenager who denied King James II's authority as the head of the Church. After Wilson refused to swear an oath to the King, she was executed by the King's official representatives.

Here again, public officials viewed people's religious beliefs as a threat to political authority. Wilson wasn't a libertarian—the concept of libertarianism (or even liberalism) was not a prominent part of most people's political consciousness at the time. But Wilson's refusal to swear an oath of loyalty to a political official is just one of many examples of how religious conviction was one of the earliest factors that led people to challenge state power.

Though the earliest arguments for freedom of conscience, expression, and association appealed to the importance of religious liberty, they ultimately demonstrated the value of these freedoms for everyone. After all, if it makes sense for public officials to tolerate a religious practice, they should also tolerate that practice for everyone else too. This is why, even today, many people's commitments to libertarianism are motivated in part by a strong commitment to religious liberty.

The example of religious exemptions for helmet laws illustrates how a person who values religious liberty may ultimately conclude that these values entail a broader commitment to liberty for everyone else:

SIKH DELIVERYMAN

Aseem is a Sikh whose religion requires that he wear a Turban. Aseem's job requires that he ride a motorcycle to deliver packages in the city. Public officials allow Aseem to ride a motorcycle without a helmet, but if Aseem's Christian coworker Jacob rides without a helmet he will receive a ticket and he must pay a fine.

Other religious exemption policies include exemptions to drug and alcohol prohibitions that permit people to use drugs or alcohol for religious purposes, and exemptions to compulsory schooling requirements for religious families. In each case, religious exemption policies may initially strike people as a way of respecting religious freedom. Yet any argument for religious exemption policies actually reveals that public officials have been unnecessarily limiting everyone else's freedom all along because any reason for granting a religious exemption to a law is also a reason against the law itself. Public officials who grant religious exemptions concede that they are not in a better position than Sikh cyclists to decide whether it's worth it for a Sikh deliveryman to wear a helmet. But that same logic applies to other deliverymen too, so no one should be required to wear a helmet.

In this way, granting the importance of religious liberty reveals the value of liberty for everyone else too. As the philosopher Brian Barry once argued, if a law is justified, then public officials should enforce it uniformly. If uniform enforcement strikes us as wrong, that is a reliable indicator that public officials lack the authority to enforce the law for anyone.

ASSOCIATION

If public officials should respect people's freedom of religion, they must also respect people's freedom to do the kinds of things that religion requires. Namely, officials should respect people's freedom to choose whom they associate with and what they think or say. And as in the case of the Sikh deliveryman, the reasons for respecting these freedoms for religious people are also reasons to respect everyone else's freedom to associate, think, or speak without interference from public officials.

Consider, for example:

COMMUNE

A group of religious people decide to buy some land and share all their property in common. Though some people trade with the broader community, they do not recognize property rights within their community.

The early Christians arranged their affairs in this way, as have religious communities throughout American history and Israelis who choose to live on a kibbutz. In these cases, people fulfill their religious commitments through communal living, but the reasons for respecting intentional religious communities are also reasons to respect any group of consenting adults who choose to share their property with like-minded people.

Other important freedoms also require freedom of association. For example, the rights to choose where to work or whom to marry require the rights of free association. People also exercise their rights to freely associate with others when they join sports teams, go to college, or sign up for a book club. Freedom of association includes the freedom to create a new club, team, family, or business. And it also includes the right to refuse to associate with people. Public officials aren't entitled to tell people whom they can befriend, or to mandate that they treat all potential friends and partners equally, or to require people to show up for each other. At the same time, members of private associations are entitled to tell other members whom they can associate with and what they must do for others to remain in good standing within the organization. So while it would be wrong for the mayor of your town to tell you that if you didn't check in on your elderly neighbor she'd kick you out of town, the pastor at your church would be within his rights to threaten to excommunicate you for failing to attend church meetings. The key difference between these cases is that one consents to the authority of a private association when one voluntarily agrees to join it.

CONSCIENCE

Just as public officials are not entitled to mandate how people practice their religion, or how they express other community-oriented values, officials more generally lack the authority to tell people what they should think or stand for. Consider, for example, conscientious objection to military service:

QUAKERS

Daniel is a Quaker who interprets the Bible as requiring pacifism, even during wartime. Public officials draft young men for a war, but Daniel refuses to fight because it would violate his pacifist convictions.

Most libertarians are opposed to conscription for anyone. Here again, the case for a religious exemption to a policy illustrates why the policy is misguided in the first place. In this example, the case for conscientious objection to military service is compelling because many people have the intuition that it would be wrong to force someone to make a life-and-death decision that violated his most deeply held convictions. But people also have deeply held convictions that are not religious, and even a secular pacifist should have the right to refuse military service.

Similar arguments apply to policies that might initially seem less significant. For example, even health insurance regulations can implicate matters of conscience for some people:

CONTRACEPTION COVERAGE

Mary Elizabeth is the principal at a large religious school. Her religion prohibits people from using contraception. Public officials mandate that all large employers must pay for insurance plans that subsidize contraception. Mary Elizabeth objects to contraception, so she refuses to pay for an insurance plan that covers it.

In this case, public officials should not threaten Mary Elizabeth with legal penalties if she refuses to pay for a health plan that subsidizes contraception. And this example illustrates the broader problem with a policy that requires non-governmental employers to purchase private insurance plans without giving them the freedom to choose employee benefits that reflect their values.

In order to respect people's freedom of conscience, public officials should minimize the extent that public policy requires people to violate their values and religious commitments. At the same time, freedom of conscience and association also require that public officials allow people to form groups with like-minded people who share their beliefs and values. This is why people should not have rights of conscientious refusal in private associations, since private groups may have a legitimate interest in defining their membership based on matters of conscience.

Even when respecting people's freedom of conscience makes it harder for public officials to govern, libertarians still argue that people are entitled to express their values and beliefs without censorship or punishment. Here's an extreme example:

SEDITION

An activist writes a series of op eds arguing that people should organize to overthrow the government. After reading his work, a few people try, and there is a riot at the capitol.

Historically, public officials have incarcerated political activists for sedition in cases like these. Or, consider US policies that punished people who supported communism during the Cold War. Even if public officials were authorized to regulate matters of conscience for the sake of the public interest, permitting officials to restrict conscientious expression could backfire because officials would have incentives to regulate these matters for their own personal interests at the expense of the public.

SPEECH

Freedom of speech encompasses the more specific rights that people have to express their religious beliefs and other values. It also includes artistic freedom, academic freedom, the freedom to campaign for a political candidate, the freedom to advocate for immoral behavior, the freedom to gossip, the freedom to insult people, the freedom to create profane and obscene content, and even the freedom to make false claims. In general, libertarians hold that all these kinds of speech should be legally protected from censorship or punishment.

There are two sides of the libertarian case for freedom of speech—speaker-based justifications and listener-based justifications. Speaker-based justifications for freedom of speech appeal to the foregoing arguments for freedom of religion, conscience, and association. Most people have ideas and projects that are important to them, and they have a very strong interest in expressing these ideas and pursuing these projects without interference. Additionally, a person's speech and expression do not usually violate anyone else's rights against interference. Consequently, public officials who use legal threats and punishment to coercively repress speech or expression interfere with people who are not liable to be interfered with.

Speaker-based justifications for freedom of speech oppose censorship on the grounds that it violates the rights of speakers, even when speakers are expressing themselves in ways that other people find obscene or socially destructive. Consider this case:

STRIPPERS

Candy is an artist who choreographs interesting dance routines for patrons of the arts. Unlike some dancers, Candy takes off her clothes during her dance routine. Sometimes she spins around a pole or interacts with audience members.

Candy's interest in expressing herself through dance is just as legitimate as any other choreographer's or dancer's interest in doing the same. The fact that some people disapprove of her artistic expression is irrelevant to the question of whether Candy has a legal right to dance, just as the fact that some people disapprove of rap music would in no way justify a policy that prevented radio stations from playing it. People who don't like Candy's dancing can simply decline to pay for her show, in the same way that people who disapprove of rap music can just change the channel.

Though limits on speech and artistic expression are especially burdensome to people like Candy, censorship is immoral even when it doesn't violate a speaker's rights. Consider the example of a book ban for a deceased author:

BANNED BOOK

George wrote a political novel that was widely considered subversive and dangerous. He gave it to his publisher right before he died. After the publisher printed and sold a few thousand copies, public officials prohibited the publisher from printing any more copies of George's novel. Retailers were prohibited from selling existing copies, and public officials confiscated and destroyed all the remaining copies they could find.

In this case, George is dead, so he doesn't have an interest or right to express himself anymore. Nevertheless, it would be wrong for public officials to ban and destroy George's novel because their censorship would prevent the rest of us from reading and learning from his work.

Listener-based justifications for freedom of speech also explain why the libertarian commitment to freedom of speech extends to protections for speech that includes clear falsehoods. At first glance, it might be unclear why officials must respect people's rights to say that the sun revolves around the Earth or that aliens built the Eiffel Tower. In this case, it's not that false speech is valuable for listeners in its own right (although it can be if it is interesting or entertaining). Rather, libertarians argue that public officials should not censor speech on the grounds that it is false because a legal system that permits false speech is more likely to ultimately promote true ideas than a legal system that censors false speech. There are two reasons for this claim. First, people are often overconfident in their ability to pick out which claims are true and which are false. Second, people can learn about the truth by encountering falsehoods.

The first listener-based reason that public officials should permit false speech goes like this. False speech occurs because speakers are fallible, immoral, misinformed, and wrong. People who promulgate falsehoods usually don't know that they're saying something that isn't true, they're just overly confident in their own judgment. Yet the very same human failings that give rise to false speech explain why public officials are in no position to censor it. Like the rest of us, public officials can also be fallible, immoral, misinformed, and wrong. But it's always easier to see other people's flaws than one's own, which is why public officials are very likely to be overly confident in their own judgments about which views merit censorship.

Relatedly, remembering that public officials are as fallible as the rest of us should make anyone wary of authorizing the state to regulate speech. Political actors are not wise and benevolent guardians of the public interest; they're institutionally constrained and have incentives to appeal to their voters and to advance their own political careers. In virtue of their institutional roles, public officials are limited both in their impartiality and in their information. As an example, a politician may say that it is good for everyone if the state restricts trade to benefit domestic producers, not because this is a true statement about economics, but because it gives them an electoral advantage in their district. Everyone recognizes that public officials have incentives to lie and mislead people, at least when they're talking about the other side. This alone is a reason to doubt any policy that gives public officials even more power to influence which information citizens can access.

Of course, there are still cases where someone can say definitively that a given belief is false. Libertarians needn't be skeptics or relativists to support freedom of speech. Here we encounter the second listener-based reason for free speech: people should be permitted to speak freely because the truth is important, but we are unlikely to discover it if public officials do not permit a free exchange of ideas. Each of us can only be confident in our beliefs if we can see why our beliefs are true, and this means that we must be allowed to hear and consider competing viewpoints. Suppose our earlier arguments were mistaken and the state should, in fact, force you to buckle your seatbelt. Even so—and at the risk of being immodest—we'd expect you to have at least gained a deeper understanding of the correct view by grappling with our defense of the (let us stipulate) incorrect view and seeing where it goes wrong.

The case for censorship also has a bit of a Goldilocks problem in specifying which kinds of false claims public officials need to prevent people from seeing. After all, if a claim is obviously false, then public officials shouldn't need to censor it because they can just explain why it is an obvious falsehood and listeners will realize that it's wrong. On the other hand, if it's not obvious that a claim is false, then public officials cannot be confident that they are censoring a falsehood. Here the best way to establish that the claim is wrong is to permit people to discuss it out in the open air.

ADVERTISING

With the general libertarian case for freedom of speech and association in hand, we can now turn to a few specific cases where libertarian views of speech and expression stand in contrast with other approaches. Consider first the issue of commercial speech and advertising. Libertarians hold that governmental censorship of speech is just as wrong when it targets a corporation as it is when it targets an individual. The fact that some people use speech to make money doesn't mean that their interest in speaking is less legitimate, and listeners benefit from freedom of speech whether speakers are working or not.

To see why public officials should treat commercial and non-commercial speech similarly, consider whether press freedom is a form of commercial speech:

NEWS COMPANY

A large news company makes billions of dollars each year by producing interesting content and selling advertisements. The journalists and editors at the news company are highly motivated to make the company more profitable.

How is the news company different from a company that advertises its own product, where the people who make the product are highly motivated to make their company more profitable? In both cases, journalists and advertisers are motivated to convince people to consume their product, but they also have creative motivations and a professional obligation to tell the truth. Commercial speech is so morally similar to journalism that anyone who supports freedom of the press as a basic requirement for a free and open democracy should support freedom of commercial speech for similar reasons.

The fact that commercial speech should be protected with the same force as individual speech and freedom of the press reveals that some existing restrictions on commercial speech are clearly unjust. For example, public officials are not entitled to censor truthful advertising that advocates for lawful conduct solely on the grounds that they disagree with the advertisers' message. Today, officials enforce regulations involving censorship of this sort:

OFF-LABEL DRUG MARKETING

Physicians often prescribe drugs off-label, meaning that the drugs are prescribed to treat conditions that they were not initially approved to treat. Off-label prescribing can be safe, effective, and evidence-based. Yet public officials prohibit drug manufacturers from advertising truthful information about off-label uses.

In this case, public officials censor pharmaceutical companies' truthful speech about their products, even though off-label prescribing and treatment is legal and often beneficial. Both the speaker-based and listener-based justifications for freedom of expression support manufacturers' right to communicate information about whether their products can treat conditions off-label. Manufacturers have an interest in expanding the market for their product and patients and physicians have an interest in learning about promising new evidence-based treatment options. Manufacturers could even disclose that they were advertising a drug for an off-label use if regulators would allow drugmakers to tell the full truth about their products.

In contrast, other cases of commercial speech regulation are clearly justified on libertarian grounds. Though libertarians argue that public officials should never censor speech solely on the grounds that it is false, they also argue that people cannot consent to a transaction or contract if they were misled about the terms and conditions of the exchange. The difference between these two cases is that prohibitions on fraud do not censor of speech on the grounds that it is false; rather, fraud standards regulate speech to ensure that sales and contracts are fully consensual.

For example, imagine a health food company falsely claims that they do not use any artificial flavorings, antibiotics, or genetically modified ingredients in their products. Their customers cannot consent to purchase and eat their product because they don't actually know what they're buying. In cases like these, regulations that prohibit fraud and misbranding are not speech restrictions; they're protections for people's property and bodily rights. The consumers who purchase the mislabeled health food cannot give meaningful consent to the exchange with the health food company because they have been deceived about the product they're buying. So just as a patient whose physician withheld information about the risks and lied to him about the benefits of surgery cannot give informed consent to the procedure, so too, a customer who was misled about the product cannot meaningfully participate in the transaction.

Now, a libertarian would likely prefer a system where public officials punished fraudulent marketing, adulteration, and mislabeling through the court system. If consumers could hold manufacturers legally liable for misleading them and the threat of legal penalties were sufficient to deter misleading marketing, then public officials would not have reason to preemptively punish or censor commercial speech that they deemed false. However, unlike other people who say things that are false, fraudulent, and misleading, marketers are liable to be preemptively interfered with because they violate their customer's rights when they sell products or services under false pretenses. For this reason, libertarians are not in principle opposed to preemptive censorship of false commercial speech. Rather, the question of whether fraudulent speech should be prevented through regulation or punished through the courts depends on which institutional arrangement would most effectively protect consumers' rights against deception.

In some cases, it can be tricky to determine whether commercial speech is deceptive because people disagree about how much information consumers are entitled to know. Here's a recent case that illustrates this point:

COMPELLED SPEECH

Local officials passed a law requiring cell phone retailers to tell their customers that there is a chance that they could be exposed to more than a federally permitted level of radiation if they carry phones in their pockets.

Whether this policy is justified depends on whether consumers are entitled to know about the chances of radiation exposure. This ambiguity isn't unique to commercial speech. In medical contexts, health workers must discern how much information a reasonable patient has an interest in knowing about the risks and benefits of a procedure. When people are dating, they must discern how much their potential partners are entitled to know about their sexual history, credit score, cosmetic surgery, and career prospects.

Libel law is another case where ethical questions about the permissibility of commercial speech regulations ultimately amount to questions about people's more general rights:

LIBEL

A national newspaper reported that a prominent celebrity, who claims to be an ally for women, behaved in a misogynistic way. The celebrity disputes the newspaper's claims and sues the newspaper on the grounds that they disparaged him in a way that will diminish his earning potential going forward.

In this case, if people have enforceable rights to the earning power associated with their reputations, then public officials could legitimately punish libelous commercial speech, or even libelous non-commercial speech, such as gossip. But if people do not have enforceable reputational rights, then public officials would not be entitled to censor or punish even false information about people.

Libertarians are likely to disagree about the extent that people have enforceable rights to know about the risks of consumer products or to maintain their reputations. Yet libertarians generally oppose policies that compel or prohibit these kinds of commercial speech preemptively. Rather, libertarians argue that public officials are more likely to reliably track consumers' interests in information or people's interests in avoiding reputational harm if they gain information about these interests through the market. For this reason, when the scope of people's entitlements to information and the strength of their reputational rights are unclear, civil courts are a better institutional option for addressing the harmful effects of false information in commercial contexts.

CAMPAIGN FINANCE

Some proponents of speech restrictions argue that public officials are entitled to limit political speech in order to safeguard the fairness of elections. These arguments are motivated by cases where a candidate or party can gain a competitive advantage by spending more money on campaigning and publicity. Though many libertarians dislike political speech as much as the next guy, they nevertheless argue that public officials should not enforce legal limits on political speech and spending because these kinds of limits would violate people's speech and property rights.

Consider an influential court case that people cite to motivate arguments for limits on political speech:

CITIZENS UNITED

A nonprofit organization made a documentary about a political candidate. Public officials ordered that the organization refrain from publicizing the documentary until after the election.

In the United States, organizations like Citizens United are allowed to make unflattering documentaries about political candidates. Critics of this policy argue that it gives rich people and rich interest groups more of a voice when it comes to politics, just because they can buy a bigger microphone. If everyone in a political community is entitled to an equal say, the argument goes, then unfettered political speech could violate that entitlement.

Proponents of legal limits on political speech sometimes say slogans like "money isn't speech," but the line between speech and the use of property is actually pretty blurry. Suppose the state banned you from buying and wearing a Che Guevara shirt or from posting a sign with the name of your favorite candidate in your front yard. These bans violate your freedom of speech, even though in some technical sense, they merely restrict how you use your property. Or consider that you have the right to buy a dozen copies of this book and distribute them to friends, family members, and neighbors to persuade them to become libertarians. We strongly urge you to exercise this right; this book makes a wonderful birthday gift!

Free speech often involves spending money, and people have the right to use their money to promote whatever they care about—their religion, their artistic vision, their personal brand, or their preferred particular political outcome. This is why people have the right to spend their money on political campaigns.

Of course, a yard sign's impact on political outcomes is small. However, people may exercise their rights in ways that can have a significant impact on political outcomes. Take freedom of speech. A celebrity endorsement of a candidate has far more power to influence the outcome than, say, our endorsements. Nevertheless, anyone, libertarian or otherwise, who is committed to respecting people's speech rights may not restrict endorsements or charismatic speech in the name of securing equal political influence. So, it's unclear why they may restrict people's property rights in the name of securing equal political influence.

Public officials also cannot distinguish between grassroots political expression and political speech that is likely to make a substantial difference, such as large campaign donations. Imagine, for example, that a billionaire decides to purchase a million yard signs for his preferred candidate. Or that a million people all donate $10 to a filmmaker so that he will make a political documentary. In both cases, political speech has grassroots components while also making election spending less equal.

Even setting aside rights-based concerns about campaign finance regulations, these restrictions on speech and property rights come with other tradeoffs too. In some countries, public officials cap donations or limit candidates' campaign spending during elections. Donation caps may reduce corruption and incumbency advantages, but they can also force candidates to spend more time raising money from small donors and less time connecting to constituents and passing legislation. Spending limits may appear to level the playing field, but limits can also distort the fairness of campaigns by preventing more popular candidates from effectively mobilizing and organizing their supporters. It's also important to recognize that social scientific research on campaign finance has not even definitively established that money *does* buy elections.

People should not interpret the principle of equal political influence in a way that requires that everyone has an equal chance to affect the outcome of an election. Rather, the principle only prohibits laws that formally restrict people's entitlement to vote or run for office. Some policies, such as the disenfranchisement of felons, may violate this principle, but legal protections for freedom of speech and property rights do not.

Lastly, we'll note that the rich are motivated to "buy elections" because they want to bend the redistributive and regulatory powers of the state to their own benefit. Maybe they'd like subsidies from the government or restrictions that put their competitors at a disadvantage. However, the libertarian state has far less redistributive and regulatory power than others, making it a far less valuable prize to buy. As a result, we should expect campaign spending to be a less pressing issue for a libertarian society than for the alternatives. After all, billionaires aren't spending tens of millions of dollars to acquire as much marshmallow fluff as possible because there's not much to be gained from stockpiling marshmallow fluff.

DISCRIMINATION

Libertarians generally oppose anti-discrimination laws. Proponents of anti-discrimination laws argue that these laws are necessary to repair for historical legacies of state-sponsored discrimination and ongoing prejudice. Libertarians reply that these policies are unnecessary, counterproductive, or that they violate people's rights. In this section, we'll talk about anti-discrimination laws in a general way.

In the next sections, we'll address more specific issues related to libertarianism and discrimination.

To begin, notice that many kinds of rights permit people to indulge in behavior that's morally wrong in general and discriminatory in particular—the distinction between behavior that's awful and behavior that should be unlawful is especially important here. And this is true of rights that almost all non-libertarians recognize. For instance, the right of free association entitles people to make racist choices of dates, friends, and spouses. A racist's decision to only invite white people to his poker game is awful, but it isn't unlawful. Or consider the following case:

RACIST FAMILY

Jeff falls in love with Beth and they agree to get married. Beth is a different race than Jeff; Jeff's family is racist and shuns him and writes him out of their wills.

The behavior of Jeff's family is deplorable and could in many ways ruin his life. Yet their right of association entitles them to make this deplorable choice.

We can go on. The right to vote entitles people to cast sexist votes, such as only voting for male candidates. The right of occupational choice entitles people to only apply for jobs offered by female employers. Abortion rights permit a woman to have an abortion because she wants a child of a different sex. Speech rights allow people to make bigoted comments. Property rights entitle people to boycott sellers of a certain race or sex. Here's the key point: critics of the standard libertarian view of the legality of discrimination also believe that citizens are within their rights to engage in many forms of discrimination. The main difference is simply that libertarians believe that there aren't principled grounds for treating employment decisions as unique.

Libertarians support free markets. Policies that prohibit discrimination limit the kinds of market exchanges people can make. These policies prevent people from gaining reliable information about supply and demand and they can make markets less efficient. Consider a simple case of employment discrimination to see why:

EMPLOYMENT DISCRIMINATION

Based on decades of experience, the owner of a women's clothing boutique believes that women are likely to sell more dresses, denim, swimsuits, and accessories than men, so she does not consider men for sales positions.

In this case, the owner's hiring decisions are based on her interest in quickly finding someone who will sell as much product as possible. Of course, the owner's discriminatory search process means that she may overlook highly effective salesmen, some of whom could be even better than the person she hires. But the process could still be efficient if the cost of a more fine-grained search process that required her to give equal consideration to all applicants exceeded the potential benefit of finding a more productive employee. And if she's wrong about male applicants, then she places herself at a competitive disadvantage because rival boutiques will learn that they can hire male sales associates and draw business from her store.

In this case, we can ask two ethical questions about the discriminatory owner. First, did she treat male applicants unfairly? Second, was she entitled to discriminate?

Whether the discriminatory owner treated men unfairly depends on whether she discriminated on the basis of an aspect of applicant's identity that shouldn't matter for the job. In this case, the owner may argue that the sex of a sales associate is relevant to their productivity since women seem to sell more product. She doesn't even have anything against men, she's just trying to sell dresses. On this interpretation of the case, women are presumptively more qualified for the job for the same reason that advertisers tend to choose female models for clothing and jewelry campaigns.

Here we'll also note that this concern about discrimination doesn't apply exclusively to commercial transactions. Suppose a political party's data suggests that a woman is more likely to win the local election than a man. Party leaders might throw their support behind the female candidate simply on the grounds that she's more likely to win. Although this decision may be morally objectionable, few would make it illegal.

Another way of viewing the case holds that she did treat male applicants unfairly because being a man shouldn't be the kind of thing that matters for a retail sales job. It only matters because her customers have prejudicial attitudes toward men, and by favoring women in the hiring practice, the owner is only re-enforcing those attitudes.

For the sake of argument, let's assume that the owner treated male applicants unfairly. Should she have a legal right to do so, or should public officials require that she give equal consideration to all applicants and hire some men? If the owner's customers prefer female sales associates, a policy that required the owner to hire male applicants may benefit some men, but it would make a female applicant worse off by preventing her from getting a job at the boutique, it would make the owner worse off by diminishing her sales, and it could make her customers worse off too.

The case for a policy that required the owner to consider and hire some men is that, eventually, her female customers might abandon their prejudicial view of salesmen. But if the objection to the discriminatory owner's hiring practice is that she is depriving men of the opportunity to work in a field where they are less productive, albeit in virtue of customers' attitudes, then without changing underlying consumer attitudes a policy that requires the owner to hire men could backfire by entrenching the negative stereotypes it sought to correct. So while it might seem like a bit of inefficiency is a price worth paying for the sake of equal treatment and equal opportunity, it's not clear that a prohibition on discrimination would secure those values.

Moreover, a policy that prohibited the discriminatory owner from choosing her employees would also violate the owner's freedom of association rights. As the philosopher Matt Zwolinski has argued, people have morally significant interests in choosing who they work with in the same way they have morally significant interests in choosing their friends and romantic partners. Consider a modified version of the case:

SEXIST EMPLOYMENT

The owner of a women's clothing boutique believes that men are untrustworthy and obnoxious, so she does not consider men for sales positions even though, if hired, they would sell as much product as her female employees, if not more.

Even in this case, it would be wrong for public officials to force the owner to hire men, even though they are as, or more, qualified. If she wants to take an economic hit for the sake of her sexist ideology, it is her business.

This point is actually less controversial than it seems at first glance. Because an employer is just a buyer of labor, to say that an employer is within her rights to not hire men is just another way of saying that she is within her rights not to buy labor from men. Here again, even non-libertarians believe that people are within their rights to make sexist buying decisions, meaning that it would be wrong to coercively interfere with a consumer's choice to only buy apples from female farmers at the market, even if a man is selling apples of a similar quality for a lower price. And even if non-libertarians disapprove of religious congregations that exclude women from the clergy, they also generally agree that the congregations are entitled to do so.

Consider also that most people agree that employees are entitled to choose where they work and who they work for. Imagine a man who refuses to take orders from a woman, and so only applies to male-owned businesses. He places himself at a disadvantage in the labor market by limiting his options, and he should consider changing his sexist attitude. But it would be wrong for public officials to legally require that he consider female bosses and apply to jobs at woman-owned firms. Likewise for prejudicial employers. They shouldn't discriminate, but public officials shouldn't intervene when they do.

This is not to say that libertarianism offers no remedies for employment discrimination. For one, the market offers remedies for discrimination without getting legal sanctions involved. If the prejudicial owner is treating male applicants unfairly, she may pay a price for her discriminatory practices by overlooking highly productive applicants or if people find out about her policy and decide to boycott her store. Turning away qualified employees and paying customers is bad for business. Over time, non-discriminatory businesses will tend to outcompete discriminatory businesses in the marketplace. Maybe upholding discrimination is worth it to some employers who are so prejudiced that they are willing to pay an economic price to avoid people from a disfavored group. But in cases where market incentives do not deter discrimination, legal remedies are unlikely to effectively deter discrimination either because most anti-discrimination laws are enforced via financial penalties. If market-based incentives cannot overcome someone's commitment to discrimination, legal deterrents probably won't either, especially because it's easier to evade legal detection than it is to evade competition for high-quality workers and feedback from customers.

Similar arguments apply in other domains. Consider a recent case of discrimination against potential customers:

CONSUMER DISCRIMINATION

A baker refuses to bake a cake for a gay wedding, believing that gay marriage is immoral.

Should public officials threaten the cake baker with legal penalties for refusing to sell wedding cakes to gay people? Any argument for punishing the baker would seemingly assume that people have an enforceable entitlement to cake-decorating services or that public officials have the authority to compel bakers to endorse relationships that they privately disapproved of. When someone becomes a baker, he doesn't make himself liable to compulsory cake-decorating mandates from public officials. So even if the baker should have made the cake for the gay wedding, he acted within his rights when he refused. And for similar reasons, customers should have a legal right to refuse to buy cakes from religious bakers, for example, on the grounds that the customers disapprove of religious views about marriage.

Consider another recent case where a business owner refused to serve a customer:

KNIFE SHOP

A neo-Nazi asks the owner of a knife shop to inscribe Nazi symbols on his knife. The owner refuses.

The owner of this knife shop should be applauded for refusing the neo-Nazi's request. But notice that the right that protects his laudable choice to refuse service is the very same right that protects deplorable choices to refuse service, just as the rights that protect someone's laudable choices to speak or associate are the very same rights that protect their deplorable choices to speak or associate.

In a sense, any legal system that compels people to hire or serve people against their will is effectively conscripting people to labor under conditions that they did not choose. Here again, this is not a uniquely libertarian position—any liberal who endorses freedom of occupational choice should agree. When we view people as consumers or employees, it's clear that any policy that compelled people to refrain from discrimination when choosing where to shop or work would be excessively intrusive and ineffective at the goal of promoting social equality. So proponents of anti-discrimination laws should ask themselves why they think these laws are a good idea when it comes to employers and vendors.

Intuitively, people might support anti-discrimination laws out of a concern that, if prejudicial attitudes are widespread enough, some people will be unable to meet their basic needs:

HOUSING DISCRIMINATION

Many landlords refuse to consider tenants who are immigrants because they are opposed to immigration.

Imagine in this case that anti-immigrant attitudes are so strong that it's difficult for immigrants to find housing. A proponent of anti-discrimination law will say that landlords should be legally required to consider immigrants. In contrast, a libertarian will notice that there is a lot of demand for housing and limited supply, due to the landlords' prejudicial attitudes. In circumstances like these, people can make money by contributing to the supply of housing in the area. Assuming that zoning isn't an issue, developers can build new housing for immigrant families and people can convert their basements and garages into rental units. Even if developers and residents also have anti-immigrant attitudes, they also value opportunities to make extra income. The landlords who discriminate against immigrant families pay a price for their prejudice as they compete to attract reliable tenants. Each of these policy responses to anti-immigrant landlords might not succeed, but an advantage of the libertarian solution is that it can solve the housing problem in a way that doesn't limit anyone's freedom of association or property rights.

RACISM

In any society, some people will probably say racist things and choose to associate with people on the basis of race. Some people argue that public officials should prohibit racist speech and ban racist behavior. As the previous sections about freedom of speech, freedom of association, and anti-discrimination law suggest, libertarians disagree. Libertarians maintain that public officials should be very reluctant to interfere with people's freedom, even when they use that freedom in ways that are morally criticizable, including racist speech and association. Additionally, policies that aim to reduce racial disparities are generally ineffective and they can even backfire.

In our experience, a lot of people have reservations about libertarianism primarily because it seems to permit too much racist conduct. People think this in part because racist separatist groups and neo-Confederates sometimes appeal to libertarian values like free speech and freedom of association when they defend their entitlement to organize and advocate for their racist political projects. Some members of these groups even call themselves libertarians. Other people who identify as libertarians maintain that these groups do not accurately represent libertarianism, but they acknowledge that libertarians do oppose policies that would censor members of these groups.

To get a better sense of why people suspect that libertarianism cannot adequately repudiate racism, think about how a libertarian society would treat a deeply racist person:

RACIST

Sal is a white supremacist. He dislikes Black people and he thinks that they are inferior to white people. Sal discriminates against Black people and avoids them whenever he can. He writes essays defending his racist views, and he forms a racist club where he and other racists can complain about Black people. Sal doesn't talk much about his racist views at his church or in his broader friend group anymore, because most people think that racism is a sign of poor character.

In a libertarian society, Sal would have a legal right to discriminate, publish his racist essays, and meet with his fellow racists. Other people would have a legal right to criticize Sal, refuse to employ him, and exclude him from their businesses and private associations. Sal would have a right to refuse to date or befriend anyone who is Black. If he owned a business, he would have a legal right to refuse to hire Black people as employees. He could choose to boycott Black businesses. And in a libertarian society, Sal would also have a right to move to a predominantly white neighborhood.

Critics of libertarianism argue that Sal's example is a *reductio* of the view. If the libertarianism protects people like Sal's right to discriminate, write hate speech, and form racist associations, then so much the worse for libertarianism. But the first thing to notice about the libertarian society is that most of the racist things that Sal has a right to do in a libertarian society, he would also have a right to do in *any* liberal society. The only difference is that libertarians treat economic liberties in the same way that other liberals treat civil liberties. Most people agree that racists should be legally permitted to only date within their own race or to choose to live near other white people, even though people's choices about partnership and housing can, in the aggregate, widen social and economic divides between racial groups. Again, choices that are awful aren't automatically unlawful.

The similarity between economic liberties and civil liberties also extends to strategies for fighting racism. Free speech liberals argue that citizens should counter racist speech with anti-racist speech rather than censorship. They should respond to racist marches with anti-racist countermarches. Similarly, libertarians argue that citizens should counter racist economic behavior with anti-racist economic behavior—say, by boycotting Sal's racist business.

Also, it's not clear whether legally censoring Sal and prohibiting him from forming a racist association would deter Sal more than social sanctioning and criticism would. One might reply that this is a false dichotomy because people could use both legal and social sanctions to stop Sal. But legal responses to racism make social responses to racism less effective. Here's why. Public officials in some countries do prohibit people from joining hate groups or distributing hate speech. These laws might prevent some people from adopting racist beliefs, but they also drive racist behavior, speech, and organizing underground. Policies that prompt people to illicitly access racist speech and to form secret racist associations make it harder for law enforcement agencies to monitor hate groups for violent activity. These policies also prevent anti-racists from publicly responding to racist speech and showing racists—and everyone else—where it goes wrong:

DARYL DAVIS

Daryl is a Black musician who actively seeks to engage with members of the Ku Klux Klan to challenge their racist beliefs. Davis has persuaded dozens of people to leave the Klan.

If racist speech and association happen covertly, then anti-racists have less opportunity to sanction and criticize it.

Lastly, critics of libertarianism who argue that Sal's freedom of speech and association should be restricted encounter a series of dilemmas, regardless of how they make their case. Either they support viewpoint-based restrictions that prohibit anti-Black speech and association for the sake of racial justice or they support universal restrictions that prohibit whole categories of speech and association on neutral grounds.

Say that someone supports viewpoint-based restrictions on speech and association, meaning that public officials are empowered to censor and prohibit anti-Black speech and association for the sake of racial justice. If a society were deeply racist, then public officials are unlikely to use the power to enforce viewpoint-based restrictions in ways that advanced racial justice. Instead, they would likely use the power to censor and prohibit specific viewpoints in ways that punished anti-racist groups and Black people. In contrast, if a society is anti-racist, meaning that most people are committed to racial justice, then public officials would be more likely to censor and prohibit Sal's viewpoint, but censorship and prohibition would be less necessary for at least a couple of reasons. First, there would be far fewer instances of racist speech and conduct in this society. And second, an anti-racist public could effectively fight Sal's racism by ostracism and boycotting him.

Another issue with empowering public officials to impose viewpoint-based restrictions on speech and association is that insofar as public officials restrict Sal's conduct on the grounds that they disapprove of his viewpoint, they could justify restricting other politically subversive or unpopular viewpoints on the same grounds. Even if one doesn't value Sal's right to promote his racist viewpoint, one might be more sympathetic to other unpopular communities, such as vegans, furries, communists, Mormons, atheists, or nudists.

Alternatively, say that someone supports universal restrictions that prohibit whole categories of speech and association on neutral grounds. For example, someone might say that public officials should restrict Sal's speech and association because no one should have the right to publish anything that disparages racial groups or discriminate on the basis of race. But a policy like this could make it more difficult for people to exercise their freedom of speech and association in ways that advance racial justice:

AFFIRMATIVE ACTION

Susan is a committed anti-racist who works in the HR department of a large company that makes frozen food products. Most people in management or leadership roles are white. A few employees are planning to retire in the next year, and Susan argues that the company should only consider Black applicants to fill those positions. The CEO of the company agrees, and the company rejects all white applicants for the open positions.

Though Susan is an anti-racist, she is also a proponent of racial discrimination in hiring. Other anti-racists may similarly discriminate by prioritizing Black vendors and suppliers for their businesses. Black people may have an interest in forming clubs and professional associations that only they can join, either as a way of building social capital, resisting racism, or just because they want to. If public officials issued a universal ban on any racial discrimination, these kinds of associations would be illegal too.

Many people who support affirmative action also think that public officials should prohibit racial discrimination. Pointing out that private companies that practice affirmative action engage in racial discrimination reveals that many people agree that, at least in some cases, people are entitled to make associative decisions on the basis of racial preferences. This doesn't mean that affirmative action should be illegal. It shows that many people aren't opposed to racial discrimination per se.

The main moral objection to Sal's behavior isn't that it's discriminatory, it's that his behavior is racist. Sal expresses a negative view of Black people, entrenches historical injustices in the culture, compounds race-based socioeconomic inequalities, and exhibits poor character. But if officials were justified in prohibiting racist speech and association on the grounds that it's needed to prevent people from expressing racist views, widening disparities, and exhibiting poor character, then that justification would also weigh in favor of an enormous range of restrictions on other kinds of conduct that have similarly negative effects. For example, people's romantic partnerships, purchasing decisions, real estate investments, and educational choices can also express derogatory and racist views, display poor character, or widen racial disparities. That few people would support anti-racist regulations in these other domains suggests that racism alone is not a sufficient justification for prohibition or regulation.

Critics of libertarianism might reply that restrictions on racist speech and associations are necessary because racists like Sal used to control the government, so now public officials must enforce anti-racist civil rights policies that counteract longstanding injustices. During the civil rights era, public officials in the United States passed legislation that prohibited discrimination and aimed to promote equal opportunity for everyone, regardless of race, as a way of correcting for centuries of racist policies, including slavery, Jim Crow, and segregation.

As a first pass, libertarians would respond to this line of criticism by pointing out that these racist policies were clear violations of libertarian principles. The legal institution of slavery is the opposite of everything libertarians stand for. Jim Crow laws placed restrictions on private businesses and violated people's freedom of association. And public officials actively promoted segregation by segregating public schools and buildings and by subsidizing the development of racially segregated communities. These historical injustices did not arise due to too much libertarianism.

Second, if the public officials who work for the government have an obligation to repair for previous officials' racist policymaking, they should consider less government intervention—not more. For example, racial disparities in exposure to policing, which we address in a later chapter, still contribute to social and economic disparities between groups. Public officials still enforce zoning regulations and public school funding models that uphold racial inequalities across geographic lines. Before turning the coercive power of the law to private companies and individuals, officials should consider their own ongoing role in maintaining historical inequalities. And to the extent that state-based solutions are preferable, libertarians favor direct reparations for victims of historical injustice (more on this later).

Third, it's hard to know whether many of the policies that aimed to narrow socio-economic gaps between racial groups have actually been effective. One issue is that anti-discrimination law is very difficult to effectively enforce at scale, while existing wage regulations can make things even harder for people who already face discrimination in the labor market:

DISADVANTAGED TEENAGERS

Black and Hispanic teenagers have a hard time finding work because employers discriminate in favor of white and older workers and minimum wage requirements prevent them from competing with white and older workers by offering to work for less. This policy prevents Black and Hispanic teenagers from gaining valuable work experience and building credentials for the labor market going forward.

To this kind of an argument, one might reply that the minimum wage is good because it ensures that employers hire Black and

Hispanic teenagers at the same wage they'd pay anyone else. But that reply doesn't really address the problem, which is that some employers are reluctant to hire Black and Hispanic teenagers who lack work experience. Public officials make this problem worse when they prohibit Black and Hispanic workers from working for less, thus preventing them from gaining work experience. In this way, a seemingly egalitarian economic policy actually protects privileged groups from economic competition.

Fourth, if market-based responses to racial injustice are unlikely to work because so many employers, vendors, and consumers are racist, then political solutions are unlikely to work for the same reason. If someone said, "The market will enforce anti-racist policies," critics of libertarianism would be skeptical. They'd say look, there's no such thing as the market—only individual economic actors with certain incentives. But if someone says, "The state will enforce anti-racist policies," people think that sounds perfectly normal. Yet here it's important to recognize there's no such thing as the state—only individual political actors with certain incentives. If anything, it's more costly to indulge bigotry in the market than at the ballot box. Consider two cases:

MARKET RACISTS

The owners of the local sandwich shop are openly racist. As more people learn about their racism, it becomes taboo to purchase sandwiches from them. Even people who were secretly racist don't want to be seen there. A rival sandwich store opens in the same strip mall. Soon, the racist shop closes.

and

VOTING RACISTS

A few people in the neighborhood are openly racist. As more neighbors learn about their racism, it becomes taboo to go to their parties. Some neighbors are secretly racist. They don't go to the racist neighbors parties, but when the city council election comes up, they vote in the same way as the openly racist neighbors. Others in the neighborhood are shocked by the results.

These two cases illustrate that people are more likely to act in a bigoted way when they act in their capacity as voters because voting enables people to advocate for their racist agenda privately, without fear of social sanction and without placing themselves at an economic disadvantage.

For these reasons, it's not clear whether a libertarian legal system or some other kind of liberal democratic legal system would have more racist consequences. In any democratic society, racists are allowed to cast racist votes for racist public officials. So insofar as racism is widespread within a society, anti-racists have strong presumptive reasons to be wary of any legal system that expands the scope of public officials' authority to interfere with people's personal and economic choices. And if racism is not widespread within a society, then anti-racists have little reason to worry about a legal system that fails to sanction a small number of bigoted citizens because they are unlikely to influence public policy and they are likely to experience significant social sanctions too.

ACCOMMODATIONS

Libertarians oppose policies that prohibit discrimination, even when discrimination is unfair and immoral. Again, the fact that something is awful is not a sufficient ground for making it unlawful, and public policy is usually a bad way to change people's minds anyhow. For similar reasons, libertarians are also generally opposed to policies that require employers and private associations to make accommodations or to provide specific goods and services to people for the sake of equal treatment. These kinds of accommodation requirements include policies that require employers to pay workers during periods of medical or childbirth leave, policies that require private schools to provide equal support for men's and women's sports, and policies that require that private businesses be accessible to people with disabilities.

Here again, libertarians aren't saying that employers shouldn't pay workers to take leave. And libertarians aren't saying that private businesses shouldn't accommodate people with disabilities. Rather, libertarians are saying that public officials shouldn't *force* businesses to do these things because policies that require employers and property owners to make accommodations in these cases violate people's rights and are likely to backfire in any event.

To see how accommodation policies can backfire, consider the example of employer-subsidized maternity leave:

MATERNITY LEAVE

Kelly is a payroll specialist for a large factory. She reviews and approves everyone's paycheck each week. When Kelly has a baby, she takes three months of maternity leave. During this time, she does not review or approve anyone's paychecks. Instead, her employer hires a temporary worker, Jane, to do manage payroll while Kelly is on leave. Jane loses her job when Kelly returns to work.

In these sorts of cases, public officials may require large employers to provide employees with at least some paid maternity leave as a way of supporting women who give birth. But policies like these disproportionately burden employers with the responsibility of supporting new mothers and babies. If public officials are justified in ensuring that all new mothers can take off work, then *all* women should have access to this benefit, not just women who work for large firms. And correspondingly, all taxpayers should subsidize the benefit, not just large employers. In short, if there is a *general* enforceable obligation to provide maternity leave, then large employers in particular should not be solely responsible for providing it. A policy that places the burden of supporting new mothers on large employers means that those who hire young women risk paying for a costly disruption to operations if their employee gets pregnant. This dynamic may make employers reluctant to hire young women, which would be counterproductive insofar as the goal of maternity leave requirements is to support women in the workforce.

Regulations that mandate equal resources for men's and women's sports are another case where public officials disproportionately burden private groups with the costs associated with providing equal opportunities to everyone:

SPORTS EQUALITY

A small private university has several sports teams. Many of the men at the university wrestled in high school, and they want to wrestle at the college level too. The university can afford to create a men's wrestling team, but they are legally required to add a women's sports team as well. Due to low interest, recruiting and sustaining another women's sports team is infeasible, so the university is legally prohibited from adding a men's wrestling team to their official athletic programming.

In these cases, the mandate that private actors provide equal resources to both men and women effectively means that they cannot respond to unequal demand for resources from men and women. This is another example of the way that regulations can backfire by preventing people from responding to information about different people's preferences.

Disability accommodation requirements also disproportionately burden private actors with the costs of giving people equal opportunities. They also violate private actors' property rights:

WHEELCHAIR RAMPS

Uma owns a small coffee shop. The building has a bathroom in the back, but it is small and there is a step between the bathroom and the dining area. Curtis is a wheelchair user who notices that the bathroom is inaccessible. Curtis reports Uma's shop to public officials. Uma must pay a fine and build a ramp to the bathroom, which will require her to remove a table from the dining area. To pay for this, Uma raises prices on coffee, fires an employee, and works overtime.

A wheelchair ramp requirement would make it more expensive for Uma to run her business and increase the fixed costs of opening a new storefront. These requirements therefore benefit large companies at the expense of smaller entrepreneurs, and limit competition in storefront industries. In theory, accommodation requirements would also drive up the costs of goods and services or diminish wages. After all, the money to build a ramp for Curtis has to come from somewhere.

Libertarians would deny that a private business in particular has an enforceable obligation to pay the cost of making their space accessible to Curtis. Consider the following argument:

> If someone may sell no coffee, they may sell coffee without universal access.
> Someone may sell no coffee.
> So, they may sell coffee without universal access.

Let's break this down, starting with the first premise. If you don't sell coffee at all, then you aren't providing anyone with coffee. By contrast, if you sell coffee in a shop that not everyone can access, then you're at least providing *some* people with coffee. And it seems better (or at least not worse) to provide *some* people with coffee than *no* people with coffee.

What about the second premise, that it's permissible to sell no coffee? We doubt many would argue that anyone who is able to sell coffee has an obligation—indeed, an obligation that the state may enforce with coercion—to sell coffee. After all, we assume many people who could afford to start a coffee shop nevertheless haven't. It doesn't look like they've done anything wrong. And it certainly doesn't look like the state may *force* people to open coffee shops. This argument supports the conclusion that Uma is entitled to open a coffee shop that doesn't have a ramp because Curtis doesn't have an enforceable right to have full access to coffee shops.

The libertarian conclusion is also supported by the claim that less burdensome disability accommodation requirements apply to registered historic buildings when officials determine that modifying the building to make it more accessible would threaten the historic significance of the building. People usually are not entitled to violate other people's enforceable rights in order to preserve historically significant architecture, so historical exemptions to accommodation policies amount to an implicit acknowledgment that Curtis does not have an enforceable right to have full access to buildings that are open to the public.

In each of the cases above, public officials intervene in private associations in order to compel people to provide equal opportunities for all citizens. But it is not the responsibility of a private business owner in particular to bear the full cost of providing people with equal opportunities. The mere fact that Uma provides the community with coffee doesn't mean that she has a special obligation—that is, an obligation that no other community member has—to ensure that everyone who visits her shop can access every part of it. Even if Curtis had an enforceable right that all public spaces be accessible to him as a wheelchair user, it would be wrong for public officials to force Uma in particular rather than the general public to pay the full cost of providing Curtis with a ramp. More generally, reforms to support women in the workplace, girls in sports, or people with disabilities in public spaces ought to be funded by *all* taxpayers. Or, as we discuss in Chapter 4, states could provide such support indirectly by providing all citizens with a basic income to ensure their access to goods like maternity leave and gourmet coffee.

CAMPUS SPEECH

The case of speech on college campuses synthesizes a lot of the foregoing discussions of freedom of speech and association because some colleges enforce speech codes that prohibit students, faculty, and staff from using uninclusive or insensitive language. In these cases, libertarians are generally of two minds. On the one hand, they typically defend free speech on campus for all the standard reasons that they defend freedom of speech in general. On the other hand, libertarians also defend freedom of association, and some schools that enforce speech codes are private associations. Here again, it's important to keep in mind the distinction between things that people have moral reasons to do and things that people should be legally required to do. Institutions that claim to care about academic freedom and the pursuit of truth have especially strong moral reasons to refrain from private censorship of unpopular viewpoints. At the same time, private, voluntary associations are entitled to enforce speech codes for their members, even if those codes are harmful.

Libertarian positions on campus speech therefore vary depending on whether the campus is a private or public school. To see why, consider two cases where a college's interest in freedom of speech may conflict with their interest in maintaining a distinctive religious or cultural identity:

PUBLIC VS. PRIVATE COLLEGES

Kris teaches at a religious college that does not receive any government fund-ing. If he is critical of the school's religion, he could lose his job. Katy teaches at a public university. If she is critical of the school's affirmative action policy, she could lose her job.

In these cases, the administrators at the religious school are entitled to require that Kris refrain from criticizing the school's religion, but the administrators at Katy's school are not entitled to punish Katy for expressing a different viewpoint.

Consider Kris's case first. Public officials are not entitled to censor the religious administrators at his private college because the members of Kris's religious school are entitled to freely associate with (or disassociate from) whomever they like, including Kris. If the admin-istrators agree that they do not want to associate with people who oppose their religion, they are under no obligation to continue to employ faculty who criticize the religion.

In contrast, the administrators at Katy's school are public employ-ees. As public employees, they are not entitled to censor Katy's speech by threatening to fire her because this would consist in a public official enforcing a punitive sanction against someone on the grounds they disagreed with the content of her speech.

One may reply to this claim by saying that Katy is just like Kris in that she should be subject to an at-will employment standard, that is, her employer may fire her for whatever reason they'd like. But because Katy's employer is the government, terminating her employment is not a mere expression of private opinion. Rather, if a university administrator fired Katy, he would be using his author-ity as a public official to sanction someone's speech on the grounds that he disagreed with the content. Public employers should be more constrained in their capacity to censor employees compared to private employers because they are not working on behalf of an entirely free association. Public employers derive their funding through coercive taxation and they claim an entitlement to author-ity and funding on the grounds that they are advancing a common interest. In most cases, libertarians deny that they are entitled to authority and funding. But if ever there were a chance for these institutions to be morally justified, libertarians would agree with other taxpayers that public employers should use their power to advance a common interest rather than their partisan or sectarian ideological projects.

When taxpayers invest in a public university, they may reasonably expect that the university prioritize fulfilling its role in providing public goods. This requires upholding protections for free expression because one of the best justifications for subsidizing higher education is that universities promote scientific innovation and new ideas. For this reason, universities have especially strong reasons to foster communities of free and open inquiry so that employees and students can better test scientific theories and produce daring and innovative cultural products. Another justification for subsidizing higher education is that universities educate and certify workers. Here again, the taxpayers have an interest in subsidizing institutions that uphold principles of open inquiry. Students who are leaving their families for the first time benefit from encountering new ideas that may make them uncomfortable in a safe and supportive environment before entering the workforce. College is also a time for self-discovery, and insofar as this is part of the reason that higher education is worth the investment, students have an interest in encountering a range of ideas and perspectives to see what resonates with them.

Private universities that accept government funding occupy a middle-ground position between these two kinds of schools because they receive taxpayer support but their administrators and faculty are not public employees. In these cases, the reasons in favor of tolerating censorship for the sake of freedom of association are weaker than they are for religious schools and the reasons in favor of protecting free speech on campuses are weaker than they are for public universities.

In defense of the public school administrators who threatened to fire Katy, one might reply that they were advancing a public interest in diversity, equity, and inclusivity (DEI). This line of argument raises an interesting question about the kinds of policies that many public and publicly funded universities have encountered in recent years:

DEI AND SPEECH

Mariana is very committed to social justice and campus inclusivity. One day she overhears a facilities worker call the new recycling program "retarded" as they are emptying a series of classroom wastebaskets. Mariana reports the facilities worker for using insensitive language, and the worker loses his job.

This is a stylized example but there are many cases that take a similar form. Universities sometimes enforce punitive sanctions against students and employees who say or do things that undermine DEI initiatives on campus, such as using slurs, supporting disfavored political causes, making disparaging remarks about disadvantaged groups, committing microaggressions, and using insensitive language. Proponents of these censorious policies argue that censorship is necessary in order to ensure that every student has an opportunity to succeed. They also argue that campus administrators are capable of effectively and equitably applying censorious policies in ways that will narrow opportunity gaps.

Yet this case for campus censorship is committed to two conflicting assumptions. First, proponents of DEI censorship assume that universities are so non-inclusive that administrators must be empowered to punish and sanction people. Second, they assume that the administrators at these profoundly non-inclusive institutions will reliably use their power to promote inclusivity. Both of these assumptions are unlikely to be true at the same time.

If the first assumption is correct, then people should have little confidence that administrators will use their power to make their community more inclusive. The example of Mariana illustrates how seemingly inclusivity-minded or egalitarian censorship is likely to backfire because the people who have the least power on a campus are sometimes the most likely to encounter administrative sanctions for their speech.

Yet if the second assumption is correct and administrators are reliably on the side of people from disadvantaged identity groups, then censorship is unnecessary because people on campus can still be broadly assured that the administration disapproves of that disparaging speech. Either way, public school administrators cannot claim that restrictions on campus speech are a necessary and effective way to promote diversity, equity, and inclusion.

SUMMARY

The earliest defenses of libertarian ideas appealed to people's interests in acting on the basis of their conscience and religious convictions. Freedom of expression and association are the foundations of any libertarian philosophy. Because libertarians take these freedoms very seriously, they oppose policies that censor even the most abhorrent speech. Libertarians also argue that the reasons in favor of respecting freedom of association in private relationships are also reasons for public officials to permit freedom of association in economic contexts, even if people choose to associate in ways that are discriminatory. The fact that someone's speech or association is morally criticizable is rarely a reason for public officials to interfere with them.

FURTHER READING

- Bagenstos, Samuel R. 2006. "The Perversity of Limited Civil Rights Remedies: The Case of Abusive ADA Litigation." *UCLA Law Review* 54 (1): 1–36.
- Barry, Brian. 2002. *Culture and Equality: An Egalitarian Critique of Multiculturalism.* Harvard University Press.
- Bedi, Sonu. 2015. "Sexual Racism: Intimacy as a Matter of Justice." *The Journal of Politics* 77 (4): 998–1011. https://doi.org/10.1086/682749.
- Brock, Peter. 2002. *Liberty and Conscience: A Documentary History of the Experiences of Conscientious Objectors in America through the Civil War.* Oxford University Press.
- Citizens United v. Federal Election Com'n. 2009, 558 US 310. Supreme Court.
- Flanigan, Jessica, and Alec Greven. 2021. "Speech and Campus Inclusivity." *Public Affairs Quarterly* 35 (3): 178–203.
- Graber, Mark A. 2023. *Transforming Free Speech: The Ambiguous Legacy of Civil Libertarianism.* University of California Press.
- Klinker, David. 2003. "Why Conforming with Title IX Hurts Men's Collegiate Sports Comment." *Seton Hall Journal of Sport Law* 13 (1): 73–96.
- MacRobert, A. E. 2010. "Were the Wigtown Martyrs Drowned? A Reappraisal." *Dumfriesshire and Galloway Natural History*, 121.
- Neumark, David, and Jyotsana Kala. 2024. "Do Minimum Wages Reduce Job Opportunities for Blacks?" Working Paper. Working Paper Series. National Bureau of Economic Research. https://doi.org/10.3386/w33167.

- Neumark, David, and William L. Wascher. 2008. *Minimum Wages*. MIT Press.
- Sophocles. 1989. *Antigone*. Pioneer Drama Service, Inc.
- Vallier, Kevin. 2014. *Liberal Politics and Public Faith: Beyond Separation*. New York: Routledge. https://doi.org/10.4324/9781315818122.
- Volokh, Eugene. 2010. "Speech Restrictions That Don't Much Affect the Autonomy of Speakers." *Constitutional Commentary* 27: 347.
- Zwolinski, Matt. 2006. "Why Not Regulate Private Discrimination Editors' Symposium: The Rights and Wrongs of Discrimination." *San Diego Law Review* 43 (4): 1043–1062.

4

PROPERTY RIGHTS AND TAXATION

Libertarians disagree about matters of distributive justice, but they are generally unpersuaded by arguments for a welfare state. We begin by explaining why libertarians disagree about distributive justice. Many libertarians are skeptical of enforceable duties of aid. On the other hand, they recognize that existing property systems are difficult to justify on libertarian grounds. We then argue that, to the extent that the state should enforce duties of assistance, it should do so by directly transferring income or providing vouchers rather than providing goods like education in kind. Just as food is privately produced and distributed in a free market and the income of the poor is supplemented with food stamps, so too can education and other goods be privatized and paired with vouchers or income for the poor. We argue that such a system will expand the effective freedom of the poor and better meet their needs than a traditional welfare state.

PRIVATE PROPERTY

Property rights give people the legal right to, among other things, exclude others from using something. If someone owns a house, he may prevent others from entering without his permission. He can also decide

DOI: 10.4324/9781003270720-4

how his house is used without needing authorization from anyone else. For instance, he wouldn't need to ask his neighbors if they agree whenever he redecorates or invites a guest over.

All libertarians endorse strong rights of private property, that is, property rights held by individuals, but they do so for different reasons. According to one account, affiliated with the philosopher Robert Nozick, your ownership of a piece of property is justified if it was transferred to you voluntarily. If you used the income your employer voluntarily paid you to buy the couch from Steve that he voluntarily sold to you, it's rightfully yours. If you burglarized Steve's house and stole the couch, it isn't.

In brief, a transfer of property is just as long as all parties consent to it. The argument for this view appeals to an intuitive similarity between property rights and body rights. When it comes to questions about medicine, sex, or drug use, the question we need to ask is whether everyone involved in an interaction consented to the terms. Similarly, when it comes to questions about houses, money, and contracts, the only question we need to ask is whether all parties to a transaction consented to the terms. Indeed, some libertarians argue that property rights are closely connected to bodily rights because economic choices are often choices about people's bodily labor or the products of their bodily labor.

This view of property rights may seem counterintuitive to some people because it doesn't consider whether people deserve their property. Roughly speaking, deserving something amounts to having worked hard to earn it or having done something morally meritorious to warrant it. According to the view of property rights sketched above, whether someone deserves to own a piece of property is irrelevant to whether they have a right to it. What matters is whether they got their property in a way that didn't violate anyone else's rights. To motivate this intuition, imagine that you received some undeserved property:

LUCKY GIFT

Your office does a holiday gift exchange and you end up with a scratch-off lottery ticket. As chance you have it, you've got a winning ticket that pays out $1,000,000!

Even if you are the laziest and meanest person in your office, if the scratch-off was freely given to you as part of the gift exchange, the winnings are yours. As Nozick would argue, the ticket is yours because your co-worker freely gave you the ticket and the lottery freely agreed to pay that amount to the winner. If you care about desert, you could decide to give the prize to a person who works harder than you, or someone who is more saintly. But it would be wrong for someone else to snatch the winning ticket from your hands on the grounds that it could have gone to someone better.

Indeed, as a general rule, people own lots of things that they do not deserve. For example, some people are born with healthy bodies or natural talents that they did not work hard or do good deeds to get. But they are still entitled to decide what happens to their bodies, despite this fact.

Thinking about how some people are born lucky does raise a related moral complication about how people get the property they have. Namely, if everyone is entitled to property as long as they justly acquired it, how does someone acquire property rights in the first place? If we trace the history of some property back far enough, we'll reach a point where no one owned it (or it was unjustly seized from someone—more on that later). So how could someone justly acquire property out of untouched nature if it wasn't voluntarily transferred to them by a previous owner? To put the point differently, how can parts of the world be privatized in the first place?

Nozick, following John Locke, argued that someone can acquire land (and other natural resources) for themselves as long as they leave "enough and as good" for others to own. This might seem impossible. If someone fences off some land and claims it as her own, then no one else can use it. So doesn't that mean that she's made others worse off? After all, everyone was previously able to use that land and now they can't.

But not only does privatization not make others worse off, it actually makes them *better off*. To understand why privatization can make people better off, consider the incentives people have to produce in a world without private property rights:

A WORLD WITHOUT PROPERTY

No one recognizes or enforces property rights, meaning that no one recognizes anyone's entitlement to exclude anyone from using any part of the Earth. Frank is thinking about planting a garden to grow vegetables, but he decides against it because he realizes that any passerby could then grab the carrots and lettuce that he put his time and effort into growing. Why work to make the land more productive when none of the food he grows will end up on his family's table? So Frank's diet consists of only whatever he can manage to hunt and gather.

This case actually understates the difficulties that arise in a world without property rights. Indeed, the philosopher David Schmidtz argues that satisfying Locke's demand to leave "enough and as good" for others *requires* privatization. If Frank is unable to fence off any property as his own, he has a strong incentive to, say, chop down whatever trees happen to be growing for firewood without planting any new ones to replace them. After all, any passerby could chop down the trees he worked to plant, so why bother? Consequently, the propertyless world incentivizes people to leave *less* for others. By contrast, privatization enables people to exclude other people from using the things they produce, giving everyone an incentive to produce, not only for themselves, but for other people in the community too:

THE FIRST FARM

Members of the political community announce that if Frank fences off some land and prevents others from harvesting the fruits of his labor, they will uphold his right to exclude people from that land. This policy gives Frank a reason to invest the time and effort it takes to grow vegetables. But there's only so much lettuce one family can eat, and Frank's garden produces more than he needs. Frank's neighbors, who planted some apple trees, find themselves with a surplus of apples but a shortage of lettuce. So Frank agrees to trade his surplus lettuce for his neighbors' surplus apples. Both families now have lettuce and apples whereas they'd have neither if they weren't able to fence off some land.

In short, both families can eat better thanks to privatization. One might still object to this system on the grounds that it only benefits landowners, but even people who don't own any property benefit from institutions that incentivize production:

LABOR MARKET

Imagine that Frank and his neighbors can produce more lettuce and apples than both families can eat, but they don't have enough family members to do all the productive work that could be done on their farms. Each family can hire other people, exchanging lettuce and apples for labor.

Here again, private property rights facilitate win-win transactions where food goes to people who otherwise wouldn't have enough to eat and a helping hand goes to people who otherwise wouldn't have enough labor to produce at their full capacity.

The example of the first farm also illustrates a consequentialist justification for private property rights; namely, that private property rights give people incentives to produce goods and services that other people value. When you go to work, you are providing a service that someone else values—that's why they're paying you. But you wouldn't work very hard, or at all, if your co-workers could take as much out of your paycheck for themselves as they like. So if you weren't able to enforce a property right to your paycheck, you would lack the incentive to show up and provide a service that your employer values. Similarly, if your employer couldn't ensure that they could profit from their business, they wouldn't have an incentive to set up shop and hire people like you. Private property rights enable strangers to help each other out when they otherwise wouldn't have incentives to do so.

A further justification for private property rights follows from an analogy to other kinds of rights. Liberals and libertarians agree that the state ought to prioritize the protection of civil liberties such as freedom of association, freedom of religious practice, freedom of speech, and so on. Public officials should enforce protections for these freedoms so that everyone in a political community can choose and pursue their own way of life. Some libertarians argue that the justification for property rights is the same as the justification for all these other liberal rights. Private property rights enable people to take up long-term projects such as building and maintaining a home, running a business, starting a church, or publishing a newsletter. In order to choose and pursue your own way of life you need the freedom to, for instance, make your own decisions about buying and selling books, electronics, appliances, transportation, food, housing, clothing, entertainment, and so on. In this way, property rights are often preconditions for other liberal rights and they are also important in their own right.

Critics of libertarianism may reply that these arguments do not justify giving people property rights in whatever they acquire through a free exchange; it only supports markets. Market socialists, for example, support economic policies that enable companies to use prices to determine the price of goods on the basis of supply and demand, but which redistribute each company's profits so that they are shared by everyone else in the political community. A problem with market socialism is that it doesn't incentivize production as well as a system that gives people property rights in the things they create. To see why, consider this case:

COFFEE MEMBERSHIP

You are thinking about opening an innovative new coffee shop that charges a monthly membership fee instead of asking patrons to pay for each individual drink. You live in a capitalist economic system, so you do a lot of research to see if enough coffee drinkers would value this service enough to pay the $130 monthly membership fee, which would make the shop profitable. If your research is sound and the café is a success, you'll get rich. But if you miscalculate and choose the wrong location, coffee menu, or staff, you will lose all your savings.

In a market socialist economy, consumers could still decide whether to spend $130 per month on a coffee shop membership. But in a market socialist system, launching a new business is still a lot of work and producers would have fewer incentives to research and invest in this new idea if socialist redistributive tax policies would prevent them from getting rich selling coffee shop memberships.

This line of argument shows why it's more likely that an economic system that gives people property rights in the things they create will promote innovation and encourage people to use natural resources as efficiently and productively as they can. This justification for property rights is instrumental. Even if people don't have natural rights to property, public officials could still be justified in enforcing property rights in virtue of the enormous social benefits of the property system.

This broadly instrumental line of argument also supports intellectual property rights, which are controversial among libertarians. To see why, consider a stylized example of how patents work:

PATENTS

In January, Chris had a great idea. In February, he asked the mayor to promise that if anyone else had that idea, the mayor would order the police to violently prevent them from making any money off of it. The mayor agreed. In March, Jess had the same great idea, and set out to make some money. The mayor notified her that she would face serious penalties if she made any money from her idea, because unbeknownst to her, Chris had the idea first and he called dibs.

To some libertarians, the patent system looks like an unjustified government monopoly. If the state is not special, then what gives the mayor the authority to tell Jess that she can't profit from her idea just because Chris came up with the idea slightly earlier?

But to other libertarians, the patent system looks like another case where enforcing private property rights has enormous benefits for everyone. The libertarian case for patents appeals to the idea that patents are a way of using markets to incentivize innovation and discovery. Pharmaceutical innovation, for example, is one of main reasons that life expectancy has increased over the past century:

PATENTS FOR DRUGS

Patients benefit from pharmaceutical innovation, but it's very expensive to develop and test a new drug. Once someone has invented a new drug, however, it is not very expensive to produce more of it. In order to convince drugmakers to invest in new drug development, public officials tell drugmakers that they will have the exclusive rights to sell and produce their new drugs for several years. This exclusive right to produce and sell drugs is so valuable, it incentivizes lifesaving drug development.

Without patents, there would be fewer incentives to invest in drug development, which is hugely expensive, because once a drug exists other people can manufacture it at a low cost without having paid for all the research it took to create the first pill. Patents give drug companies the assurance that they can eventually profit from drug development by promising them a temporary exclusive right to sell new drugs.

Both libertarians are right about intellectual property rights. When public officials enforce intellectual property rights, they uphold a government monopoly that constrains people's economic freedom and they uphold a policy that has enormous social benefits. Whether any particular intellectual property conventions are justified on libertarian grounds depends not only on which version of libertarianism is correct but also on the magnitude of the benefits. The most socially beneficial intellectual property protections are patents in pharmaceuticals because innovation in this sector has prolonged and improved countless lives. Other kinds of intellectual property rights, such as copyright protections for authors, are more difficult to justify on these grounds.

THE COMMONS

Not all libertarians are 100% on board with the foregoing case for private property rights. Some libertarians are Georgists, following the ideas of the economist Henry George. Georgists believe that everyone is equally entitled to benefit from the use of natural resources, and that a system that gives some people exclusive rights to use and control natural resources cannot be justified on the grounds that they leave enough and as good for others. Rather, Georgists claim that no one has a right to exclude others from using land or to keep the full profits that come from using the land. Enforcing property rights can also violate people's natural rights to move about the Earth without encountering violence or threats:

RAMBLER

Lloyd doesn't want to buy or sell anything, including his labor. He wants to wander the Earth unencumbered, hunting, gathering, and scavenging for food. One day, Lloyd walked onto someone's farm, and the farmer legally threatened Lloyd with force for trespassing on their property.

Any system that enforces property rights to land and natural resources threatens people like Lloyd. Though the farmer may be using the land more productively than Lloyd is, and though Lloyd may have plenty of other good options for walking, Lloyd might claim that he is just as entitled to use the land as the farmer is, so the farmer shouldn't have a legal right to threaten Lloyd just for crossing an invisible, man-made boundary.

As a way of addressing the potential rights violation that enforcing private property rights to land would entail, Georgists often support a land value tax, which would require landowners to pay a tax based on the value of their land, excluding any improvements made to it. Several scholars in the libertarian tradition, including Adam Smith and David Ricardo, supported land value taxes alongside more general support for free trade. A land value tax is attractive because it would still incentivize landowners to use their land as productively as possible, unlike property taxes that punish landowners who increase the value of their property by improving it. A land value tax would also encourage landowners to sell under-developed land and it would discourage people from holding vacant lots in high-demand areas.

As for where the land value tax revenue would go, Thomas Paine proposed that each citizen receive a portion of the total land value tax, which would somewhat address their entitlement to the value of the land that they are excluded from using. On this view, people like Lloyd may still be coercively prevented from walking onto other people's farms, but they would receive payments from landowners. This kind of redistribution could satisfy any entitlement Lloyd has to a share of the value of the Earth's resources, without requiring landowners to permit Lloyd to trespass on their property.

Alternatively, if everyone owns the Earth in common, then public officials could also respect these entitlements by enforcing property rules that give everyone an equal entitlement to the full value of all natural resources. Some states manage natural resources in this way, for example, by sending citizens regular dividends from the sale of state resources. The problem with this approach is that, unlike a land value tax, which would incentivize people to use land and resources as productively as possible, a property system that gave every citizen an equal entitlement to the value of all natural resources risks disincentivizing production or encouraging depletion.

To see how a common property system could disincentivize production, imagine a case where all resources are held in common, including resources in space:

ASTEROID MINING

The year Is 2050 and valuable minerals are spotted on an asteroid. An entrepreneur invests billions of dollars in a company that will mine those minerals. Critics object to the privatization of the asteroid by the mining company on the grounds that the asteroid belongs to everyone.

It's expensive and risky to try to extract minerals from an asteroid. If the minerals could benefit humanity, then public officials should want to incentivize people to discover and acquire them by enabling them to profit from their efforts if they succeed. But if asteroid mining companies were compelled to share these minerals equally with everyone, including those who didn't contribute to their extraction, it wouldn't be worth their while to take the risk. This is why a property system in natural resources should permit people to profit from owning land or resources, because when natural resource owners profit, they do so by using the resources to benefit the rest of us too.

In other cases, a property system where all natural resources are held in common can also encourage the depletion and degradation of those resources. Private property rights give property owners the authority and incentive to use resources efficiently and to prevent other people from degrading or depleting land or other resources. Private property owners who are short-sighted, destructive, and inefficient harm themselves when they diminish the value of their property. In contrast, public officials in communist societies did not have personal incentives to maintain the value of natural resources.

Rather, they often rewarded administrators for meeting centrally planned production targets, which gave them incentives to use natural resources in short-sighted and inefficient ways.

More generally, when public officials view land as a commonly owned resource, their investments in infrastructure and other regulations of the built environment often encourage people to live in ways that are inefficient and wasteful. For example, public officials enforce zoning laws that limit landowners' property rights by constraining their legal rights to modify their property as they see fit. Zoning laws constrain the supply of housing in ways that make housing more expensive for everyone and discourage people from living in more efficient multi-family dwellings:

ZONING

Alan would like to build an apartment building in a neighborhood that primarily has single-family homes, but public officials prohibit him from building on the grounds that it would change the character of the neighborhood.

Libertarians are nearly unanimous that officials should let developers build new apartment buildings. The main reason to support zoning reform is that building apartments would simply be an exercise of Alan's property rights. And single family zoning laws for housing not only prevent people like Alan from providing affordable housing, they prevent low-income people from moving to a neighborhood where they would like to live. These policies then affect the price of housing all the way up the income distribution because prices all rise as a result of limited supply.

We'd bet that nearly every libertarian has been asked, "who will build the roads?" in response to arguments for private property rights and free market institutions. The short answer to this question is that private property owners can build roads too. In some countries, private companies manage roads and collect revenue from drivers, rather than all taxpayers, to fund road maintenance and expansions. Housing and commercial real estate developers build the roads that their future residents and customers will use. In developing countries, industrial manufacturers often build or improve the roads they will use to transport their products.

The longer answer to questions about road building is that the public management of roads is actually a great case study of why privatization and markets can outperform public management of the commons:

ROADS

Public officials claim the authority to build roads, but they don't reliably maintain them. Many roads are plagued by dangerous potholes, which contribute to traffic delays, damage cars, and cause accidents. Domino's Pizza delivery drivers often encounter pot holes on their delivery routes, so they started the Paving for Pizza campaign, which consisted in the pizza company paying townships to fill their potholes.

Public roads are low quality because it's difficult for citizens to hold public officials accountable for road maintenance. Voters might value better roads, but they also punish elected officials who raise their taxes. At the same time, when public officials are reluctant to limit citizens' use of the roads, they become congested and fall into disrepair more quickly.

Whether roads are publicly or privately owned, the solution to low-quality roads is road pricing, such as electronic tolling, restrictions on who can use a road, or dynamic pricing for high-traffic areas:

CONGESTION PRICING

Cars are equipped with meters that charge drivers to use roads. The price of using the road increases at times when there is more demand, such as during rush hour. This system avoids congestion-related traffic jams.

Regardless of whether it's used by state actors or private owners, congestion pricing is an example of how enforcing markets in goods and services can improve the quality of a good or service for everyone. No one likes sitting in traffic, but traffic jams happen because drivers do not personally bear the cost of their contributions to congestion. In contrast, congestion pricing directly improves the quality of roads in two ways. First, requiring that drivers pay to use the roads during busy times reduces traffic. And second, congestion pricing generates revenue and incentives for improving the roads, since drivers would be less willing to pay to drive on low-quality roads.

A critic of this line of argument might argue that public officials should not privatize common spaces and resources because private actors are more likely to exploit and abuse citizens than public officials would. For example, consider the case of parking meter privatization:

PARKING

Strapped for cash, the city of Chicago sold their parking meters to a private equity firm. The firm immediately raised prices.

Critics argued that the private equity firm was exploiting citizens, but the firm actually just recognized that street parking in the city was massively underpriced. After all, privately owned parking garages charged much higher fees. Though people appreciated below-market prices for street parking when they found a parking spot, they did not appreciate the traffic that drivers caused in their search for an open spot. Cheap parking spaces subsidize drivers. Because people can consume high-value land at a below-market rate they are more likely to drive instead of walking or taking public transportation, even though driving is more dangerous to pedestrians and harmful to the environment. In this way, yet again, a policy that seemingly gives everyone equal access to a common resource ends up diminishing the quality of the resource and distributing it in an inefficient way.

These arguments in favor of privatization also explain why public officials should not appropriate private property, even to achieve a public-spirited project that would (theoretically) benefit everyone:

EMINENT DOMAIN

Public officials want to build a road from the city to a growing suburb. To make room for the road, they seize several people's property, including some people's homes, which they destroy to make way for the road.

The worst problem with eminent domain is that public officials sometimes seize and destroy people's homes and land and then fail to complete the project that justified the seizure. But even when public officials do use people's property for some public purpose, they rarely pay the full market price.

Officials justify eminent domain on the grounds that some property owners might hold out on selling their land to the government unless officials pay them an exorbitant price that far exceeds the market rate. But libertarian critics of eminent domain would reply that private companies face similar issues all the time.

KELO V. CITY OF NEW LONDON

Public officials in New London Connecticut granted a private developer the power to use eminent domain to make way for a potential pharmaceutical plant. The developer seized a residential neighborhood, including Suzette Kelo's home. The neighborhood was bulldozed, and it has been a vacant lot for decades.

Though the US Supreme Court upheld this use of eminent domain, few would defend a law that permitted private businesses to seize other people's property in this way. The *Kelo* decision was so egregious that dozens of states strengthened their eminent domain laws to prevent the injustice that Suzette and her neighbors experienced from ever happening again. But the moral reasons that weigh against the private appropriation of people's property also weigh against government officials' appropriation of people's property. Even when the public benefits from economic development and public investments in infrastructure, if the benefits are so insignificant that business owners and officials are unwilling to adequately pay property owners, then these benefits cannot justify confiscating people's property.

INCOME TAX

In the previous section, we reviewed libertarian arguments for some kinds of property taxes. Specifically, we noted that some libertarians defend land value taxes. In contrast, libertarians are generally much more critical of income taxes because the income tax involves the appropriation of the fruits of a person's bodily labor:

THE WORKWEEK

Sally works 40 hours a week, five days a week, Monday to Friday. Twenty percent of her income is taxed. This means that every Monday, Sally works for the government, while from Tuesday to Friday, she works for her own benefit.

Or, recall the tale of the slave, where a person was forced to work for one master, then many. We initially presented the tale as a way of illustrating the limits of public officials' authority in democracies. But the tale of the slave also illustrates moral objections to the income tax. When public officials tax Sally (or the slave's) income, they are taking the money that someone pays Sally for her labor. In this way, income taxes force Sally to labor without compensation. Thinking of the income tax in this way shows why libertarians like Nozick believe that income taxes violate people's rights. When the state taxes 20% of your labor income, it means, in effect, that 20% of your time on the clock is spent working for the state's purposes rather than your own.

Someone might respond to the claim that taxes violate people's rights by disputing whether people really have rights to all of their income in the first place. After all, maybe the rich have a moral duty to transfer some of their property to the poor, so that they can at least meet their basic needs. Even if the rich do have a duty to assist the poor though, libertarians claim that such a duty would not be enforceable. They contend that if there were an enforceable duty to assist people who are in dire need such a duty would have unacceptable implications across a range of other cases.

To begin to make the case for this claim, it's worth emphasizing that just because someone has very strong moral reasons to do something (such as help those in need) doesn't mean that they are liable to be forced into doing it:

DEATHBED WISH

Wendy's mother's dying wish is to spend her final hours reminiscing with Wendy. Instead, Wendy decides to spend that time watching Dumb and Dumber.

Assuming that Wendy and her mother have a good relationship, Wendy has done something wrong. She should have visited her mother. But it would also have been wrong for Wendy's sister to show up at her house, kidnap her, drive to the hospital, and force Wendy to reminisce with her mom. And it would be even more wrong for a police officer to barge into Wendy's house and threaten her with jail time if she doesn't relive the good old days for a few hours. Though Wendy's behavior was awful, it isn't—and shouldn't be—unlawful.

Similarly, the mere fact that someone is obligated to assist people in need doesn't imply that public officials may force them into doing it even in cases where the stakes are literally life or death. Consider that the right of bodily autonomy prohibits the state from institutionalizing compulsory blood draws even if a blood tax were necessary to prevent a severe blood shortage. The right of occupational choice prohibits the state from coercing a heart surgeon into delaying her retirement even though doing so could save the lives of dozens of patients. And for similar reasons, libertarians oppose conscription even when there are significant threats to national security. In each of these cases, potential donors, doctors, and soldiers have strong moral reasons to volunteer their bodies and time to save other people's lives. But they do not forfeit their rights to decide what happens to their bodies and time just because other people stand to benefit.

On this point, consider also Judith Thomson's famous defense of abortion rights:

VIOLINIST

You've been kidnapped and wake up to find that a famous violinist has been plugged into your kidneys. He needs to stay plugged in for nine months to survive. If you unplug yourself, you can go about your life, but the violinist will die.

Thomson concludes that even if your body is the only thing keeping the violinist alive, you cannot be forced to remain connected to him. She acknowledges that it "would be very nice of you" to stay plugged in, but he has no right to the use of your body to stay alive.

This argument is presented in defense of a legal right to abortion, since, in her view, public officials are not entitled to force women to use their bodies to provide life-saving assistance to those in need.

Thomson maintains her claim that duties to provide life-saving assistance are not enforceable even in cases when the cost of helping him is rather low. She writes that even if a person, say Henry Fonda, could save her life only by walking across the room and laying a hand on her fevered brow, "I have no right to be given the touch of Henry Fonda's cool hand on my fevered brow." This example is not as far-fetched as it may initially seem. People have actually sued their family members for the right to use another person's body in order to save their own lives:

MCFALL V. SHIMP

McFall was suffering from a rare disease and needed a bone marrow transplant to dramatically increase his chance of survival. Shimp, McFall's cousin, was the only match, but he refused to donate. McFall sued Shimp in an attempt to force the donation. The judge determined that Shimp could not be forced to donate, but also criticized Shimp's refusal to help voluntarily.

Here again, even if Shimp had a duty to help in the sense of having compelling moral reasons to be a bone marrow donor, he did not have an *enforceable* duty to help. It would have been wrong for public officials to show up at his doorstep and threaten him with jail time if he didn't give McFall his bone marrow.

These cases simply show that the right of bodily autonomy may not be compromised for the sake of easy aid. But one might object that property rights are different since taking someone's money doesn't involve trespassing the boundaries of their bodily autonomy. This is an intuitive objection. Perhaps we should grant stronger protection to body rights than property rights because the cost of violating body rights is greater than the cost of violating property rights. We suspect this is true in many cases, but not all. Ask yourself this: If the state offered to exempt you from taxation for the rest of your life in exchange for your participation in a yearly blood draw to address blood shortages, would you take the deal? Our hunch is that most people would, and this suggests that bodily property is more similar to other kinds of property than it may seem at first.

Consider another case, which we adapt from Ryan Davis, that casts doubt on an enforceable duty to use one's property to provide aid:

HERMIT

Hermione lives alone on a small plot of land. She's entirely self-sufficient, subsisting only on what she can hunt and gather on her property. She receives no assistance from others, but also provides no assistance to others.

Even if you think Hermione does something wrong by not using her property to assist others, it's doubtful that she should be *compelled* to do so.

Lastly, general opposition to Bad Samaritan laws which impose an enforceable duty of easy rescue on bystanders to crimes and injuries also supports the libertarian claim that people do not have enforceable duties to use their property to provide help to people in need. If, in virtue of people's property rights, they should not be legally compelled to use their phones to call 911, to let people use their cars or boats to rescue people in need, or to permit the homeless to camp on their property, then these same rights more generally support the claim that people should not be legally compelled to transfer their property to other strangers in need.

This is not to say that public officials should *never* violate property rights in order to save lives. Even Nozick suggests in *Anarchy State and Utopia* that rights may be violated to avert moral catastrophes. To motivate this idea, consider a bad mashup of Bruce Willis movies:

DETECTIVE SPACE HERO

Willis is a grizzled New York detective who plays by his own rules. As it happens, he needs to get to NASA immediately to prevent an asteroid from destroying the planet. The problem is, he doesn't have a car. So he hotwires a BMW and speeds away to save the world.

Plausibly the detective space hero did the right thing, even though he didn't respect the car owner's property rights. Property rights, then, may be overridden to prevent sufficiently bad outcomes. But the violation of the rights still merits some kind of a remedy, even if it was the right thing to do at the time. After he saves the world, Willis should apologize to the BMW owner, repair any damages, and compensate the BMW owner for the violation.

Cases like these do not show that property rights are somehow weaker, or less stringent than bodily rights though. After all, in some cases, people may have compelling moral reasons to violate other people's bodily rights. Consider a scenario inspired by Peter Singer's influential essay, *Famine, Affluence, and Morality*:

DROWNING CHILD

A child is drowning in a shallow pond. The only way to save her is to push a champion swimmer into the pond.

Plausibly, you should push the swimmer into the pond, but it doesn't follow that the swimmer was liable to be pushed. After she saves the child, she may rightly demand compensation for the hardship she experienced when you assaulted her. As in Thomson's examples, which established the right to abortion, the swimmer may claim that she was not liable to be pushed simply because she was well-placed to rescue a child.

In each of these cases, a bystander's rights can be overridden in emergencies. But neither of these cases invalidates the moral force of property or bodily rights in ordinary contexts. And virtually none of the state-compelled redistribution of property that takes place in the real world is analogous to the confiscation involved in the BMW case. For one thing, most redistributive taxation doesn't provide life-saving assistance to people in imminent danger. Maybe the analogy could work if Americans were taxed to provide funds for, say, the Against Malaria Foundation; but that's not the sort of redistribution that the US government undertakes.

BASIC INCOME

Not all libertarian thinkers (or perhaps libertarian-adjacent thinkers) oppose redistribution. Some consequentialists defend a universal basic income (whereby all citizens receive a certain amount of money at regular intervals) or a negative income tax (whereby poor citizens receive payments that steadily decline as they become richer). Even those libertarians that oppose redistribution in principle sometimes defend a UBI as an improvement over the status quo. To see one reason why, consider the following case:

VACATION OFFER

Your boss wants to reward your stellar work performance, so she offers you a choice. You can either receive a vacation package worth $10,000 or $10,000 in cash.

You should choose the cash. Why? Because if you want the vacation, you can use the cash to buy it. If you want something other than the vacation, you can buy that instead. So the cash makes you no worse off and potentially better off.

In the same vein, citizens are better off receiving cash payments than the specific bundle of goods and services provided by the welfare state. If they want that specific bundle, they can buy it; if they'd rather have something else, they can buy that instead. So a UBI gives people the freedom to acquire the specific quality and quantity of goods and services they prefer rather than the specific quality and quantity of goods the government wants them to have. If you're still unconvinced:

SOCIAL SECURITY SWAP

A public official proposes to replace Social Security—a cash transfer—with government-run retirement facilities that provide on site food and entertainment.

Now even if, like us, you're skeptical of the merits of Social Security, you should see that this proposal is a downgrade. The reason is simple: moving to a government-run facility isn't in the best interests of every retiree. Many would rather have the resources to travel, advance their education, or train for a triathlon. And those retirees would *do* want to live in a retirement facility are no worse off for having cash that they can use to pay for it.

A further benefit of the UBI is that it doesn't create "benefit cliffs":

FEEDING THE SMITHS

The Smiths bring in $29,000 per year, which makes them eligible for $2,000 in food assistance. Jane Smith gets a promotion and a small raise at work, bringing the household income to $30,000 per year. Consequently, they now earn too much to qualify for the benefit. The $1,000 salary increase results in a loss of $2,000 in food assistance.

Clearly, this system creates poor incentives, as it effectively punishes people for being more productive and earning more income. A UBI doesn't have this problem, as the payments don't decrease when income increases.

GOVERNMENT SPENDING

In the previous section, we presented libertarian arguments against the income tax that appealed to the idea that people do not have enforceable duties of assistance. Granting that there are enforceable duties of assistance would have intuitively implausible implications in a range of cases, so public officials should not threaten or compel people to part with their time, bodily labor, or property in order to help people in need.

To this line of argument, some readers may reply that they are comfortable accepting that there are enforceable duties of assistance in all the foregoing cases, assuming that the assistance is effective and beneficial on balance. This consequentialist line of response denies that any rights are so sacrosanct that public officials must respect them instead of saving an innocent life. But consequentialists also have reasons to oppose the income tax because redistributive taxation is not effective and beneficial on balance. Consequentialist libertarians oppose income taxes on the grounds that these taxes discourage people from making an income, slow economic growth, and distribute resources in an inefficient way.

The consequentialist case against redistributive taxation can be counterintuitive because, at first glance, it might seem like taxes are good because the rich don't benefit much from marginal increases in their income and wealth, compared to the benefits that transferring that money to the poor would bring. So even if taxes deter productive labor to an extent, the benefits to the poor could make up for these losses. Think of burritos. If you're hungry, the first burrito you eat is transcendent. The second burrito might still be satisfying, but not as good as that first burrito. And you're very unlikely to enjoy a third burrito. On this view, redistributive taxation isn't a big deal because it's mostly taking people's third burritos, which they don't even enjoy that much anyhow.

This argument appeals to the idea of diminishing marginal utility, which means that the more someone has of something, the less happiness it brings. If people value money the way they value burritos, then this argument would support redistributing from the rich to the poor. For example:

BILL AND PENNY

Bill is a multibillionaire who finds a roll of quarters on the sidewalk. That $10 will bring him little, if any, satisfaction. What could Bill buy with that $10 that he doesn't already have? He's got a mansion, a garage full of vintage cars, and a private jet. Bill could use that money to buy lunch at McDonald's, but he could've afforded a million Big Macs anyway. Penny, on the other hand, is penniless. She can't afford food, so that $10 means a lot to her—it can prevent her from starving. In this case, taking $10 from Bill and handing it to Penny would have good consequences, even if Bill would rather keep the money he found, because the transfer helps Penny more than it harms Bill.

However, this argument does not do much to justify existing redistributive tax policies because existing redistributive taxation is ineffective. For one, a lot of the money that people pay in taxes doesn't even make it to the poorest members of their political community. Government transfers don't directly move money from the pockets of the rich to the pockets of the poor because the groups that can most effectively advocate for benefits are unlikely to be the most disadvantaged people.

Of course, showing that real-world redistribution could be more efficient and progressive than it is doesn't show that it isn't an improvement over no redistribution. Penny might still take the flawed system that gives her a little over a system where she gets nothing at all.

But tax policies aren't just an inefficient way of helping poor people like Penny, they can be harmful to the poor when they slow economic growth. Taxes on labor income and capital reduce the supply of labor and capital, just taxes on carbon emissions reduce the supply of carbon emissions and taxes on cigarettes reduce smoking. This reduction in the supply of labor and capital will, in turn, reduce the rate of economic growth and thus make people poorer over the long run.

Economic growth is important because everyone who works for a wage is providing a service that (presumably) someone else finds beneficial enough to pay for. Companies and workers make money by becoming more efficient, improving their skills, finding new services to offer and finding new ways to provide more for less. Think of the ways that large retailers have improved the material living conditions of America's poorest households by finding ways to efficiently deliver a range of products that were previously prohibitively expensive. These retailers also expanded the labor market for low-skilled workers. While it's true that the owners of large retailers profit from this system, so do their workers and consumers. Taxing wealth and income to fund a welfare state can be harmful to the poor because it deters production, which benefits everyone.

To be fair to the pro-tax side, though taxes deter economic growth in some ways, they can also promote economic development in other ways. For example, policies that tax citizens to pay for universal education, healthcare, and childcare might enable people to participate in the workforce when they become adults. Taxpayer-funded investments in infrastructure and basic science may provide the foundation for private-sector innovation. But taxation-defenders must show not only that there are some benefits to taxation and government spending, but that these policies are beneficial on balance.

A closer look at the ways that public officials spend tax revenue challenges the case for redistribution as a policy that is beneficial *on balance,* because the benefits of redistributive taxes are unlikely to outweigh the costs of a system that discourages productive, mutually beneficial exchange and innovation. Today, existing redistributive tax policies don't even seem to aspire to benefit people on balance; they mostly take money from the rich and redistribute it to groups that are politically powerful. As noted, most of the resources that are redistributed to people in a political community don't benefit the poorest of the poor in that community. And redistributive taxes certainly don't go to the poorest people on Earth.

The biggest item in the United States federal budget is Social Security, a retirement-benefit policy that transfers income from younger workers to provide a basic income to older people:

SOCIAL SECURITY

Young workers typically enter the workforce with debt and without wealth. They then pay taxes, which are transferred to older people who had their entire lives to save for retirement and who are often capable of working. Though some elderly people are disabled, poor, and unable to work, public officials provide Social Security retirement benefits to people who are capable of working, to people who earn a high income, and to people who are wealthy.

Some people think that Social Security is like a savings account because public officials misleadingly refer to it as a trust fund. This is not true. Social Security is funded through general taxation. The revenue goes to the US treasury and recipients of Social Security retirement benefits do not have a right to the benefits even if they previously paid taxes.

To understand why libertarians are skeptical of the merits of Social Security, let's revisit an earlier case:

ELDERLY TRANSFERS

Sarah seizes Tim's property to pay poor elderly people. She also wants to pay some rich elderly people so that they like her more and will support her plan to pay poor elderly people. So Sarah decides to just transfer Tim's money to anyone who is old, rather than targeting the poorest elderly people in her political community. Sarah actually pays the rich elderly people more money on a monthly basis, and since poorer elderly people don't live as long as richer elderly people Sarah ends up transferring a lot of what she took from Tim to wealthy old people who live nearby. Sarah lies to everyone and tells them that she's actually just paying the old people money that they previously contributed. But Sarah's actually giving them money she took from Tim.

It seems clear that Sarah acts wrongly when she seizes Tim's property. As suggested earlier, Sarah's violation of Tim's property rights might be justified if it were needed to, for instance, save a life; here, however, the violation merely helps Sarah top off the retirement income of the elderly.

Healthcare for elderly people and low-income people is another large spending category in the United States federal budget. Yet here again, the benefits are unclear. A lot of health spending at the end of people's lives provides little benefit because those patients have a limited life expectancy anyhow. Low-income people receive government-provided health insurance, but the long-term health benefits of having access to this insurance are very limited because other factors, such as behavior, environment, and genetics, have a much bigger effect on people's long-term health. And when government involvement in healthcare is paired with pharmaceutical price controls in an attempt to keep down costs, it diminishes long-term pharmaceutical innovation.

Defense and veteran's services are another big budget item in the United States. We will address the ethics of war and global justice later in this book, but for now, we'll just register our skepticism that funding the US military is an efficient way to help poor Americans. Taxes also fund subsidies for student loans, a policy that primarily benefits people who already have a comparatively high earning potential and a strong incentive to invest in their education. We could go on.

The point is that even if someone could, in principle, justify redistributive taxation as a way of benefiting the poorest members of a political community, in practice, that's not how taxes work. Instead, sympathetic and politically powerful groups benefit from redistributive policies, even if they are comparatively wealthy or capable.

Proponents of redistribution sometimes argue that public officials should redistribute resources as a way of protecting people from hardships that are primarily due to bad luck. They sometimes use the term "social insurance" to describe these policies. The problem with thinking about redistribution as a form of social insurance is that there are some kinds of choices that people should not receive insurance for. Policies that provide people with insurance in these cases create a moral hazard, meaning that the policies encourage people to make risky choices because risk takers do not bear the full costs of the risk when it goes wrong:

PUBLIC FLOOD INSURANCE

Barney bought a home in an area that is prone to flooding. No one will sell him flood insurance. When his home floods, he asks public officials to pay for him to relocate and resettle. He then purchases a home in the same uninsured, flood-prone area.

In this case, public officials redistributed resources from taxpayers who bought homes in safer areas to Barney, who knowingly bought a home in an area that was prone to flooding. Why should public officials subsidize Barney's choice? Similarly, public bailouts for failing companies are not a form of insurance against the risk that the economy might change; they are a form of redistribution from workers in profitable industries to workers in unprofitable industries. These subsidies incentivize homeowners and investors to make riskier choices, knowing that their fellow taxpayers will pay the price if it doesn't work out.

For other kinds of redistribution, such as healthcare policies for elderly people, it makes even less sense to think of these programs as a form of insurance because the risk that people are supposedly insuring against is almost sure to occur. The reason that there are not private markets in health insurance for elderly people is that their medical services are so expensive that too few young people would voluntarily purchase a policy that also paid for the care of the elderly.

Redistributive policies that tax people to pay for social services like healthcare and retirement benefits are not insurance policies, but public officials use the language of insurance to describe these

policies because it gives taxpayers the impression that they are paying for a benefit that is comparable to something that they would
otherwise purchase in the marketplace. Yet the rhetoric of "social
insurance" misrepresents the true nature of government spending,
which is often a straightforward transfer of resources from young
working people to wealthier elderly people.

The case for redistributive taxation in the United States looks
even worse if we consider that even the poorest Americans are some
of the richest people to have ever existed, and many people in other
countries are far worse off today. An American at the domestic poverty line is among the top 15% or so of earners worldwide. Very few
American tax dollars go to help the global poor. Even worse, the US
government spends a lot of taxpayer money enforcing immigration
restrictions which trap people in developing countries where they
have much more limited economic prospects. Immigration restrictions not only harm the global poor by preventing them from moving to the US and improving their real living standards but also harm
US citizens who would benefit from selling goods and services to
them and hiring them as workers.

Considering the well-being of future generations also undermines
the case for redistributive taxation because future people are likely
to benefit from today's gains in overall productivity far more than
redistributive taxation. To see why, think of all the ways that we
are the beneficiaries of the technological advances and improved
living standards that our grandparents and parents created for us.
We enjoy technology, lifesaving drugs, and cultural products that
are better than our ancestors could ever have imagined. The typical
American's material standard of living is, in most ways, better than
that of the richest people on Earth a century ago. (John Rockefeller
didn't have an iPhone, ChatGPT, NBA League Pass, Netflix, or
Ozempic.) We live longer, more comfortable lives than any previous generation, and it is, for the most part, still getting better for
humanity year after year. Taxes on labor income and capital investments are likely to discourage these kinds of advances. And even
a small decline in this growth can compound over time in ways
that massively disadvantage future generations. If the economy had
grown at an even slightly slower rate in the past century, then people
today would be far poorer.

Relatedly, if future generations' well-being matters at all, the case for debt-financed government spending is weaker as well. When governments issue treasury securities to fund spending projects, they borrow from people's pension funds, state, local, and foreign governments, and foreign investors. This practice means that governments compete with industry for funding, which can make it harder for businesses to take on debt so that they can invest in their own growth. When governments take on increasing levels of debt, they need to offer higher interest rates to attract new buyers for the debt. When this happens, other borrowers must also offer higher rates so that they can compete for funding, which also makes it harder for people in the industry to borrow. In this way, national borrowing, like taxes, can harm future generations by slowing growth. A high national debt can also harm people when the costs of borrowing increase to the point that debt policy contributes to inflation and causes political instability.

INCOME INEQUALITY

Another justification for redistributive taxation is that it can reduce income inequality within a political community. The egalitarian case for redistribution is different from the consequentialist case for redistribution because egalitarians hold that public officials should aim to reduce income disparities between the rich and the poor even if reducing these disparities does not improve the material conditions of the poor. Libertarians generally disagree with the claim that public officials should enforce policies that reduce economic inequality as such. After all, there are inequalities between the rich and those seem completely benign—we hear few calls for reducing the gap between Warren Buffett and Elon Musk.

Consider also the absurdity that follows from claiming that people should reduce material inequality as such:

LEVELING DOWN

Alice is in pain, poor health, and has a reduced life expectancy. Bob is even in worse pain, in worse health, and has an even shorter life expectancy. An egalitarian medical researcher offers to inject Alice with a virus that will increase

*her pain and reduce her health and life expectancy even further in order to
eliminate the health gap between her and Bob.*

It's clear that Alice shouldn't accept the virus. It is morally gro-
tesque for the researcher to suggest that she should. But if there
were moral reasons to reduce inequalities as such, then Alice would
have reason to accept the virus even though it harmed her and
benefited no one.

Perhaps in light of this kind of counterintuitive implication,
many egalitarians oppose income inequality not because they value
equality for its own sake, but because they think that an unequal
society will be bad in other ways. Specifically, they claim that
it is unfair for some to have more than others, that low-income
workers in a society with a lot of economic inequality would lack
self-esteem, or that other people would treat low-income workers
badly.

Consider first the intuition that, if some people are very rich and
others are very poor, something unfair must have happened. An initial word of warning about this line of argument—it's important not
to think of an economy as a zero-sum game where someone loses
whenever someone else gains. This is sometimes called the fixed
pie fallacy as if the whole economy is a pie of fixed size and one
person's gain is another's loss. If the economy were like that then
more income for the rich would mean less income for the poor, and
vice versa. But thankfully the economy is not like that—everyone
can get richer:

REFRIGERATOR GENIUS

*An entrepreneur earns millions of dollars by figuring out how to make refrig-
erators $50 cheaper for the people in her state. She gets richer than every-
one else in her state by selling these refridgerators. The residents of her state
get richer too—everyone who buys her refrigerators has $50 more than they
would have had otherwise.*

Even though the entrepreneur ends up with a lot more money than
her customers, this inequality is not unfair; indeed, it results from a
series of transactions that made those customers better off.

The best argument for the claim that a society's economic system is unfair whenever it is unequal comes from a group of political philosophers who are sometimes called left-libertarians. They argue that while everyone owns their bodies and their labor, everyone equally owns the rest of the external world and everyone is equally entitled to compensation whenever someone uses the external world to make a profit. On the basis of this argument, some left-libertarians therefore end up endorsing the aforementioned land value tax. But others take this view to be supportive of more extensive redistributive taxation. For example, some left-libertarians argue that when public officials enforce economic policies, including capitalist rules for property acquisition and transfer, they violate people's natural rights against interference. According to this view, public officials cannot justify their role as the monopoly enforcer of property rules. And for this reason, when public officials do enforce a set of property rules, they should do it in a way that at least ensures that everyone gets an equal share of any given person's use of the external world.

This left-libertarian argument is similar to the earlier libertarian case for property rights, except that left-libertarians have a different interpretation of what people's rights to acquire and transfer external property should entail. Yet left-libertarians agree with other libertarians that it is presumptively wrong for public officials to tax people's labor or to compel people to provide life-sustaining assistance to those in need. Where they disagree is whether other kinds of taxes violate people's basic rights.

Another prominent argument for the claim that a society's economic system is unfair appeals to the intuition that low-wage workers are underpaid for the work they do. Think, for example, of people who claim that it's unfair that some corporate CEOs are paid 100× more than the medical assistants and daycare providers that care for our most vulnerable loved ones. This claim resonates with people because the value of high-quality medical help and daycare is important and obvious, and yet people who work in these industries are often paid a below-average salary. Implicitly, the people who make this claim are assuming that a fair wage is a wage that reflects the social utility of a person's labor, and they are also assuming that corporate CEOs don't add anything close to 100× the social value of excellent caregivers.

Let's grant for the sake of argument that a CEO's job is, in some way, less virtuous or praiseworthy than a caregiver's job. Does that mean that pay inequality between CEOs and caregivers is unfair? Corporate boards choose to pay a lot for CEOs because, even if most CEOs are comparably qualified, small differences in effectiveness can translate to big differences in a company's performance. At the same time, there aren't as many qualified CEOs as there are qualified care-givers. So even if caregivers do work that is more important and praiseworthy than CEOs, they aren't entitled to higher wages on these grounds.

People who claim that income inequality is unfair because it fails to reward socially useful and morally valuable work also cannot explain why it is permissible, and even good, for people to *volunteer* their productive labor, yet it is unacceptable for people to do morally important work for a low wage. Millions of parents throughout the world do productive but almost entirely uncompensated labor by raising their kids, for example, and yet few people fret about the fact that parenting doesn't pay.

Consider also that a wage is just a price for labor; it's not a reflection of the moral quality of the labor, but rather it's economic value. And if we view wages as the price of labor, then a theory of fairness which holds that people should be paid more for socially useful and morally good labor would have surprising implications in other markets. For example, drugs like acetaminophen and amoxicillin are extremely socially useful, so on this theory, people should pay more for these drugs than less useful drugs, such as Propecia, a drug that prevents hair loss. However, the people who are critical of the low wages that caregivers and service workers receive are often the same people who criticize high prices for beneficial drugs. A low price for a service or product doesn't signal or express that it's unimportant or that it's not beneficial. Rather, prices signal supply and demand. People should be glad when the price of socially valuable things is low because that means that there are plenty of resources available to help people in need.

Egalitarian critics of market prices mistakenly assume that there is a "just price" for goods or services, which corresponds to the moral value or social utility of the good or service. This assumption misunderstands the purpose of prices. Prices do two things. First, prices provide information. Second, prices provide incentives. When the price of copper skyrockets, it indicates that copper is scarce. This information is useful to even the most public-spirited humanitarian because prices provide people with the information they need to effectively promote the public interest. Moreover, prices incentivize those who are not humanitarian to supply more of that good. Consider a simple example to illustrate this point:

COPPER PRICES

The rising price of copper tells public officials and businesses to look for ways to either supply more copper or to find substitutes for copper. Prices also provide people with incentives. If there is a copper shortage, the price increases, which induces people to find new ways to supply copper.

The same points apply to labor:

BARISTA PRICES

The labor market for baristas has changed, and coffee shop managers can no longer find qualified baristas to work at the previous wage. The rising price of barista labor tells employers to either raise wages, change the kinds of people they hire, or find ways to automate some of the things that baristas do. Or, when baristas' wages increase, some higher-skilled or more efficient baristas decide to work more hours.

Now imagine that public officials mandated that people could not charge more for copper than they charged for tin. Such a policy would deprive people of the information they needed to know whether to conserve or produce more copper. A policy like this would also diminish the incentive to supply more copper relative to tin, resulting in shortages. Similarly, imagine that public officials mandated that baristas must be paid the same wages as fast-food workers. Such a policy would make it harder for employers to find the best baristas by offering higher wages to more productive workers, and it could discourage great baristas from joining the profession or working more hours.

Understanding a wage as a price for labor also clarifies why we can't determine the "correct" wage for a given job from the armchair. Ask yourself this: how much more should a gram of plutonium cost than a gram of coffee? If you're anything like us, you don't know the answer. The difference in price is determined by supply and demand—but the same goes for the price of the labor of CEOs and baristas.

Other critics of income inequality argue that an economic system that permits some people to make 100× more than others is bad because it undermines social equality. According to this view, everyone is entitled to equal standing and status within their political community. Economic inequality gives some people more influence, esteem, and power than others. So social egalitarians oppose economic inequality because they think that economic inequality threatens social equality.

Even if public officials should enforce policies that encourage people to treat each other as equals, would an argument like this support policies that aim to reduce income inequality? In part, this is an empirical question. We suspect that most social comparisons are more local. Most people are not affected by the fact that billionaires fly around the world on private jets. Or even if they are, it's far worse for their self-esteem to see their neighbor get a new truck and their friends buy name-brand yoga pants. Since people tend to live and associate with those who make a similar income, large-scale income inequality is unlikely to be especially detrimental to their sense of self-respect and equal standing in their communities.

Another reason to doubt the social egalitarian case against income inequality is that it seems to treat a hypothetical cause of social inequality rather than the inequality itself. If people are unkind or demeaning to low-income workers, or if poor people are stigmatized in a community, the remedy to this kind of behavior should not be to reduce income disparities. Rather, people should stop demeaning and stigmatizing poor people. Consider an analogy:

FAT STIGMA

Some members of a political community are thin and some are fat. The thin people disparage the fat people and being fat is highly stigmatized. To remedy this social inequality, public officials propose policies that aim to reduce body weight inequality.

If a policy like this seems misguided, the same is true for policies that aim to reduce income inequality for the sake of social egalitarianism. In both cases, reducing stigmatizing differences fails to address the primary harm of social inequality, which is that people with inegalitarian dispositions mistreat their fellow citizens.

Social egalitarian critics of income inequality also overlook the fact that any efforts to reduce income inequality are likely to heighten inequalities between ordinary citizens and public officials. Whenever public officials expand their authority to interfere with ordinary people's personal or economic affairs, they introduce inequalities of power between themselves and the people they govern. From a social egalitarian perspective, these inequalities can also be objectionable insofar as they enable public officials to further increase their standing, status, and power relative to their fellow citizens.

Another reason that a high degree of wage inequality could be a good thing, even by the lights of egalitarianism, is that some people make an extraordinary amount of money due to what economists call superstar effects. Consider:

TAYLOR SWIFT

Taylor made billions by making her music available on streaming platforms and through a long stadium tour where tens of thousands of people attended each concert.

Entertainers like Taylor Swift and LeBron James get ultra-rich because they work in an industry where they can expand their market at a relatively low cost. Taylor makes an album once, and then streaming services can provide it to an unlimited number of people. Everyone can tune in to watch the NBA championship.

In these markets, competitors such as Olivia Rodrigo or the FIBA basketball league cannot compete with superstars like Taylor or the NBA by offering a similar product at a lower price. And when customers can access their first choice for the same price as their second, that means that the first-choice entertainer is going to get far richer than all the also-rans. This result means that there is a high level of material inequality within the entertainment industry and within society more generally. On the other hand, it also means that even the poorest people are able to access what they judge to be the highest-quality entertainment option—no one has to settle for their second choice because they can't afford to listen to their favorite artist. So, somewhat surprisingly, what initially looks like a very inegalitarian industry may actually be better for the worst-off consumers.

A final, simple argument for the permissibility of income inequality circles back to an earlier argument for the libertarian theory of property ownership. Income inequality isn't objectionable when it arises from voluntary transfers. Inspired by a similar case from Robert Nozick, imagine the following payment scheme for an extraordinarily talented running back:

SAQUON BARKLEY

Saquon Barkley agrees to play for the Philadelphia Eagles. His contract specifies that he'll receive 25% of all ticket and merchandise sales. Hundreds of thousands of fans buy tickets and merchandise. Barkley becomes the richest person in town.

Although the resulting distribution of income in Philadelphia would be unequal, it would not be unjust as long as every step that led to an unequal distribution of income was a consequence of people's voluntary choices about how to use their property. Barkley is entitled to keep his earnings as long as each of his fans consented to the transactions that made Barkley rich. Fans consent to buy tickets and merchandise because they love watching him play. The team has an incentive to offer Barkley these terms because they want to sell more tickets and merchandise too. Barkley's income would not come at the expense of anyone's enforceable rights, so public officials would have no grounds to interfere with the resulting distribution.

WEALTH INEQUALITY

The standard argument for tolerating income inequality is that wages reflect the price of labor, and as long as employers and employees agree on the price, it is not unfair that some people can charge more for their labor than others. In part, this argument is also an argument for tolerating wealth inequality. People generally build wealth through their labor, including the labor of investing. So insofar as people are entitled to keep their income, they are also entitled to keep their wealth.

Yet a recent line of argument from the economist Thomas Piketty holds that wealth inequality is different from income inequality because, in societies with low population growth and slow economic growth, the economic returns to owning capital will outpace the economic returns to labor, causing an ever-widening divide between people who make their money from the assets they own and people who make money from wages. Considering this dynamic, Piketty argues that public officials should band together to enforce a global tax on all assets, as a way of preventing a class of super-rich owners from amassing resources at a rate that working for a wage could never deliver.

Piketty's argument rests on some questionable empirical assumptions. He assumes that the rates of return on capital will not diminish over time, and he also assumes that wage growth will not eventually catch up. And most of the recent increases in income inequality have been driven by a widening gap in wages, not returns from capital.

But even granting Piketty's empirical assumptions, his argument overlooks the benefits of a system that rewards people for investing their wealth. The people who make money from their investments are not buying ultra-safe treasury bonds or storing their money in savings accounts; they're investing in businesses, some of which may not succeed. Investment not only enables companies to innovate and grow but also helps people identify opportunities to provide valuable goods and services, which may have otherwise been overlooked. Consider the example of tech investment:

FACEBOOK INVESTORS

Mark built a social network for his friends, and they seemed to like it. Mark thinks his social network is something that other people would like to use too, but Mark cannot expand his social network unless he hires a lot more staff. Even then, the social network may fail. Mark finds investors, who give Mark enough money to aggressively expand his social network to new users. The social network eventually becomes profitable, and the investors and Mark make a lot of money.

Mark's investors took a risk on his company and it paid off. Tech investors also take risks on lots of other companies that never succeed. Investors have incentives to find and invest in new products when they can profit from their investments. Any policy that diminished the economic benefits of investing in new products would diminish the incentive to look for new products that people value.

Maybe the example of tech investors is unpersuasive to people who think that social media has not actually been beneficial to society. But investors also take risks on promising pharmaceutical innovations, such as mRNA vaccines and gene therapy. Investors take risks when they buy stock in electric vehicle companies or new retail businesses. And sometimes, people lose their wealth through poor investments or when the economy takes a downturn. The people who make their money through investing aren't as passive as the rhetorical distinction between labor income and capital income suggests.

Building wealth through investments, including individual stocks and mutual funds, is also one of the primary ways that people save for retirement (in addition to real estate investments.) Unlike Social Security, where public officials coercively appropriate young workers' wages and transfer the cash to elderly people, people's retirement accounts are funded through their own voluntary contributions or through a fund that their employer manages. Both of these ways of paying for retirement involve building wealth through investments, which means that they can contribute to wealth inequality when the economic benefit of investment outpaces growth in wages. But compared to Social Security, private retirement savings are a morally better way for people to save for retirement because they do not involve coercively taking money from their grandchildren's paychecks every month.

Some critics of wealth inequality may argue that the case for individual retirement accounts and investment misses the real problem, which is that wealth inequality persists across generations, meaning that people who are born into poorer families are unlikely to ever reach the same standard of living as people who are born into rich families, even if they are just as talented and hardworking. Here people's objection to inheritance is that it's unfair and inefficient. Why should someone get rich simply because they were lucky enough to be born to rich parents? In at least some cases of inheritance, there may be other potential recipients who are more deserving of the wealth or perhaps need it more.

For this reason, public officials occasionally propose increasing taxes on inherited wealth as a way of diminishing intergenerational economic inequality. People who support these policies call them estate taxes, and people who oppose them call them death taxes. For our purposes, let's just call them inheritance taxes. They apply to cases like this:

INHERITANCE

Scrooge McDuck is a billionaire who dies and leaves his estate to his three nephews—Huey, Dewey, and Louie. His nephews never worked a day in their lives, and now they are richer than anyone else in their town.

A standard libertarian reply redirects our attention away from those receiving an inheritance to those giving an inheritance. If Scrooge has the right to his money, he also has the right to transfer it to his nephews—even if they do not deserve it and do not need it. Scrooge could also, for instance, give a random server at a diner a million-dollar tip, even though they don't deserve that million.

Proponents of inheritance taxes also overlook that even though wealth compounds over time, it diminishes over generations. Scrooge had a lot of money, but Huey, Dewey, and Louie each only inherited a third of it. Their children are likely to inherit an even smaller share, and so on. Today, most of the wealthiest people in America amassed most of their wealth through their own labor and investments, not through their parents' or grandparents' efforts.

The argument for inheritance taxes also has counterintuitive implications in other cases. If public officials are entitled to take parent's property in order to ensure that their adult children will not gain an unfair advantage from it, then why wouldn't this same argument justify a policy that prohibited parents from paying for their adult children's education or health care? Yet not only are these kinds of support for adult children viewed as acceptable, public officials mandate that health insurance providers permit adult children to stay on their parent's policies well into their twenties. Public officials also provide tax incentives for parents to invest and build wealth in order to pay for their adult children to go to college or graduate school. These policies are inconsistent with support for an inheritance tax, which is just another way that some parents choose to support their children.

Not all wealth is created equal, however, and for libertarians, it matters how someone built their wealth. In some cases, people build wealth by exploiting inefficient government policies that protect them from competition or which artificially inflate the market value of their property. Think, for example, of a person who owns the intellectual property rights for a popular image or song. Or, in the late twentieth century, the children of taxi owners could inherit the valuable medallions that permitted them to operate a taxi business. Or, imagine a family that owns a home in a place that prohibits new construction and supports policies that constrain the supply of housing. Wealth inequality that results from these kinds of policies is objectionable, in a sense, because the beneficiaries of these policies are profiting from injustice and inefficiency. Nevertheless, even in these cases public officials should not correct for these injustices and inefficiencies by enforcing wealth or inheritance taxes. Rather, they should correct for the policies that enable people to get wealthy in an unjust or inefficient way. By analogy, the state shouldn't respond to the robbery of Fort Knox by taxing all gold.

EQUAL OPPORTUNITIES

Maybe what bothers people about wealth inequality isn't that rich people don't deserve all that they have, but rather that wealth gives people and their descendants unfair advantages. Many egalitarians endorse an ideal of equal opportunities instead of equal outcomes. The idea here is that it's not unfair if someone finishes a marathon before everyone else, as long as everyone begins at the same starting line. Correspondingly, some egalitarians argue that people compete for economic success in the way that athletes compete in a race, so they think that public officials should enforce property rules that place everyone at the same starting line.

As a first reply, libertarian critics of this view point out that society is not like a race. When people trade with each other, it's a positive-sum interaction. People only voluntarily choose to buy and sell their labor and property when they can see that they benefit from the exchange. The demand that everyone begin at the "same starting line" in life becomes less compelling when we realize that life is not a zero-sum marathon, where a competitor's win comes at the expense of others.

Libertarians are also skeptical of the importance of equal opportunities as opposed to good opportunities. That a billionaire has better opportunities to travel than middle-class Americans doesn't worsen their opportunities to travel. In fact, a billionaire who earned their billions by creating a discount airline *improves* middle-class Americans' opportunities to travel. And the key to ensuring that everyone has good opportunities is growing the economic pie so that there's enough for everyone.

In response to these lines of argument, critics of libertarianism reply that at least some aspects of society are in fact like a race. For example, they argue that education is primarily a positional good, meaning that people pursue education because it gives them advantages that less educated people lack. Education can give people advantages either by developing new skills or because educators rank and certify people on the basis of their cognitive ability, which is a useful signal to employers. Because some egalitarians think that education is primarily a positional good, they argue that public officials should prohibit rich people from paying for private schools, which in their view, would give rich children social and economic advantages that other people can't access. Egalitarians also favor prohibiting private schools because they suspect that the presence of private schools lowers the quality of public schools due to parental divestment from the public school system.

Libertarians reply that prohibiting private education would clearly violate people's freedom of association and, in some cases, their religious freedom to educate their children in accordance with their faith. The egalitarian case against private schools also overlooks the ways that a public education system can entrench socio-economic inequality just as much, if not more, than a school system that allows parents to send their children to private schools:

FANCY SCHOOLS

Tina sends her child to a private school that costs $30,000 per year in tuition. Treena sends her child to a public school in a district where the average house costs $700,000 and her property taxes and HOA fees cost $12,000 per year.

In this scenario, a law that prohibited private schooling would prevent Tina from purchasing educational advantages for her children, but it would not prevent Treena from doing the same. Yet Treena's decision to pay for a home in a high-income school district is also a form of divestment from lower-income schools. And if anything, Treena's decision might be less egalitarian because, by bundling her fancy school tuition with expensive countertops and HOA amenities, she also chooses to invest in a residential community that low-income families can't afford.

Instead of prohibiting private schools, libertarians argue that public officials should promote opportunities by letting all parents have a say in how their children learn. School choice policies would expand access to private schools, charter schools, and maybe even religious schools:

SCHOOL CHOICE

Leta lives in a low-income neighborhood. Lola lives in a high-income neighborhood. Instead of sending Leta and Lola to their neighborhood schools, they are both given a voucher that they can use to attend the public or private school of their families' choice.

School choice policies would give all children access to high-quality schools instead of banning those schools for everyone. Egalitarians who are concerned about educational inequality should support school choice because a system that gives all parents a bit of market power is one which incentivizes schools to compete for students by providing a safe and effective educational environment.

Though libertarians generally support school choice as an improvement on the current system (and as a better option than banning private schools!) they disagree about whether public officials should be in the business of providing public education in the first place. Some libertarians support public education as a public investment in economic growth and as a way of supporting some of the most vulnerable citizens. Others argue that parents should bear the cost of educating their kids, that it's unfair to ask child-free taxpayers to pay for services that they do not use, and that public education indoctrinates children into a culture that encourages unthinking obedience to the state.

SUMMARY

In this chapter, we've reviewed a range of topics related to distributive justice. The libertarian beat on this topic is usually that people are more likely to respect each other's rights and improve each other's well-being when they are free to trade in an open market. That's not to say that public officials don't have a role to play. State actors can facilitate a voluntary and efficient distribution of resources by enforcing property rights and contracts and upholding a free market. And some libertarians even support some kinds of government spending that go beyond property rights enforcement, for example, basic income programs and school vouchers. Yet for lots of other kinds of redistribution, libertarians are skeptical that government programs are the best way to help people. Instead, libertarians argue that programs like public health care, progressive wealth and income taxes, and Social Security are often wasteful and inefficient. Redistributive tax policies can also violate people's rights to control the terms and conditions of their labor.

FURTHER READING

- Arnold, Samuel, Jason Brennan, Richard Yetter Chappell, and Ryan Davis. 2025. *Questioning Beneficence*. Routledge Press.
- Brighouse, Harry, and David Schmidtz. 2019. *Debating Education: Is There a Role for Markets?* New York, NY: Oxford University Press.
- Chartier, Gary. 2020. "Intellectual Property and Natural Law." *Australasian Journal of Legal Philosophy* 36 (2011): 58–88. https://doi.org/10.3316/ielapa.201112972.
- Christmas, Billy. 2021. *Property and Justice: A Liberal Theory of Natural Rights.* Routledge.
- Christmas, Billy. 2023. "Pollution and Natural Rights." In *Climate Liberalism: Perspectives on Liberty, Property and Pollution*, edited by Jonathan H. Adler, 25–52. Cham: Springer International Publishing. https://doi.org/10.1007/978-3-031-21108-9_2.
- Christmas, Billy. n.d. "Free to Build: Liberty and Urban Housing." *Philosophy & Public Affairs* n/a (n/a). https://doi.org/10.1111/papa.12281.
- DeAngelis, Corey A., and Neal P. McCluskey. 2020. *School Choice Myths: Setting the Record Straight on Education Freedom*. Cato Institute.
- Gaus, Gerald F. 1994. "Property, Rights, and Freedom." *Social Philosophy and Policy* 11 (2): 209–240. https://doi.org/10.1017/S0265052500004490.
- George, Henry. 1871. *Our Land and Land Policy*.
- Griswold v. Connecticut. 496AD, 381 US 479. Supreme Court.
- Hart, David M., Gary Chartier, Ross Miller Kenyon, and Roderick T. Long. 2018. "Benjamin R. Tucker, 'The Four Monopolies: Money, Land, Tariffs, and Patents' (1888)." In *Social Class and State Power: Exploring an Alternative Radical Tradition*, edited by David M. Hart, Gary Chartier, Ross Miller Kenyon, and Roderick T. Long, 179–187. Cham: Springer International Publishing. https://doi.org/10.1007/978-3-319-64894-1_27.
- Kelo v. New London. 2005, 545 US 469. Supreme Court.
- Mack, Eric. 2006. "Non-Absolute Rights and Libertarian Taxation." *Social Philosophy and Policy* 23 (2): 109–141. https://doi.org/10.1017/S0265052506060195.
- McFall v. Shimp. 1978, 10 Pa. D. & C. 3d 90. Court of Common Pleas.
- Nozick, Robert. 1974. *Anarchy, State, and Utopia*. Basic Books.
- Otsuka, Michael. 2005. *Libertarianism without Inequality*. Clarendon Press.
- Paine, Thomas. 1797. *Agrarian Justice*.

- Parijs, Philippe Van. 1998. *Real Freedom for All: What*. Oxford and New York: Clarendon Press.
- Schmidtz, David. 1994. "The Institution of Property." *Social Philosophy and Policy* 11 (1994): 42–62.
- Singer, Peter. 1972. "Famine, Affluence, and Morality." *Philosophy and Public Affairs* 1 (1).
- Spafford, Jesse. 2023. *Social Anarchism and the Rejection of Moral Tyranny*. Cambridge University Press.
- Stiglitz, Joseph E. 2015. "The Origins of Inequality and Policies to Contain It." *National Tax Journal* 68 (2): 425–448. https://doi.org/10.17310/ntj.2015.2.09.
- Thomson, Judith Jarvis. 1971. "A Defense of Abortion." *Philosophy & Public Affairs* 1 (1): 47–66. https://doi.org/10.2307/2265091.
- Widerquist, Karl, and Grant S. McCall. 2017. *Prehistoric Myths in Modern Political Philosophy: Challenging Stone Age Stories*. Edinburgh University Press.
- Wilkinson, Will. 2005. "Noble Lies, Liberal Purposes, and Personal Retirement Accounts." Social Security Choice Paper No. 34. Cato Institute.

5

ECONOMIC FREEDOM

Nearly everyone agrees that public officials should respect people's rights to own at least some personal property, such as toothbrushes, clothes, cars, and houses. Libertarians argue that public officials should also respect people's rights to own productive property, such as toothbrush factories, dry cleaners, car dealerships, and apartment complexes. And nearly everyone agrees that people should have occupational freedom, meaning that they should be allowed to choose the terms and conditions of their employment. Libertarians argue that a similar right applies to employers too, meaning that public officials shouldn't interfere with workers' and employers' rights to set their own wages, hours, and working conditions. Most people agree that consumers are generally better than anyone else at determining which products make the most sense for them, given their budgets and values. Libertarians argue that, for this reason, public officials shouldn't interfere with consumer choices by imposing restrictions on prices and financial services or by breaking up large firms.

In this chapter, we describe the libertarian case for an expansive view of economic freedom. Libertarians support economic freedom even in controversial cases like price gouging and tech monopolies. Even in dire circumstances, libertarians argue that public officials should respect unregulated markets. We conclude with a discussion

DOI: 10.4324/9781003270720-5

of how markets enable people to utilize their economic freedom for moral aims via ethical consumerism.

CONTRACTS

Freedom of contract is the freedom to make an enforceable promise to another person. The most straightforward justification for freedom of contract is that it is the foundation of trade. Because people can make binding contracts with each other, employers can hire workers by assuring the workers that they will be paid at the end of the week. Vendors produce products with the foreknowledge that a buyer will pay for them when they're ready. Freedom of contract has good consequences because it makes a lot of win-win exchanges possible. You probably wouldn't agree to sell someone a car in exchange for future payment if you couldn't count on them actually making that future payment. A contract solves this problem and makes both parties better off. Freedom of contract also enables people to pursue their own way of life by enabling them to make financial commitments and employment arrangements that reflect their preferences, values, and tolerance for risk.

Other justifications for freedom of contract follow from the premise that people have enforceable rights against being deceived. In virtue of these rights, people who make promises are liable to be interfered with when they fail to uphold their previous commitments. Another rights-based justification for freedom of contract is that promising is a normative power that all people are entitled to use so that they can pursue their plans and projects. According to this view, the right to make promises is similar to the right to alter the moral status of an action by giving consent. When a person consents to let you give her a shoulder massage, she transforms an act that would otherwise be impermissible and creepy into an act that is permissible and nice. Similarly, when a person promises to give you a shoulder massage, she transforms an act that would have been morally prohibited or optional into an obligation.

The case for freedom of contract only applies to contracts that adequately informed people voluntarily agree to. Libertarians do not claim that public officials should uphold and enforce misleading contracts, contracts that people made because they were threatened with violence, or contracts that people make on behalf of people who are incapable of giving consent. Sometimes the terms of a contract are unclear. In these cases, because contracts are legal documents that public officials have the authority to enforce, public officials have some discretion in resolving ambiguities in the initial terms of the contract.

Freedom of contract is also constrained by other enforceable moral requirements. For example, if someone hires a hitman or a car thief, public officials should not uphold the contract because people cannot have enforceable rights or obligations to violate other people's enforceable rights. Another potential limit on people's freedom of contract concerns very long-term contracts. Whether public officials should uphold very long-term contracts depends on whether people have the right to make decisions that constrain their future selves' autonomy.

Public officials are only required to enforce or uphold contracts when someone breaks their promise. In these cases, enforcing contracts might involve legally requiring that the promise-breaker keep their promise, which is called specific performance. Or, public officials can uphold a contract by requiring that the promise breaker compensate the other party to the contract.

The case against freedom of contract appeals to the idea that, in some cases, public officials should prevent people from making binding contracts by refusing to uphold contracts that are especially one-sided or burdensome. The unconscionability doctrine is a legal principle which empowers judges to refuse to enforce some kinds of contracts even if the people who make these contracts understand and consent to the terms. For example, officials may prohibit or refuse to uphold title loans and payday lending agreements:

TITLE LOAN

Seth takes out a high-interest loan from Molly. He gives Molly the legal title to his car as collateral. The terms of the loan state that if he doesn't pay the loan on time, Molly will take his car. Seth defaults on the loan, so Molly asks public officials to transfer the title for Seth's car to Molly.

Proponents of the unconscionability doctrine argue that title loans are unfair toward people like Seth because the interest rates are very high and the value of Seth's car might exceed the amount that Seth borrows. However, borrowers like Seth know that the terms of the loan are very favorable to the lender. (Insofar as you're concerned that borrowers don't know the terms of the loan, that problem can be solved by institutionalizing stricter requirements to ensure that borrowers are informed rather than banning or refusing to enforce the loan.) They nevertheless choose to take out title loans because they need money and no one else will lend to them with more favorable terms because they have reason to think that Seth will not repay the loan. Given the high chances of default, lenders like Molly are only incentivized to lend to Seth if they can secure a high return on the loans that are repaid and if they have some collateral to offset the costs of default.

Libertarians are critical of the unconscionability doctrine because it paternalistically limits Seth's and Molly's freedom of contract. A legal system that does not uphold title loan agreements would prevent potential borrowers and lenders from making financial decisions that they judge to be in their interest. Generally speaking, Seth is in a better position than anyone else to decide whether taking out the loan would be good from him. Worse, libertarians point out that taking away Seth's ability to get a title loan doesn't meaningfully improve his circumstances, it only limits his options more. Seth's basic problem is that he lacks good options, so the state shouldn't try to "solve" this problem by removing an option—indeed, the option that Seth himself regards as his best one.

Some philosophers and legal theorists have defended the unconscionability doctrine by claiming that it isn't paternalistic. They argue that no one has a right to demand that the government uphold and enforce their private agreements, so public officials are entitled to decline to uphold seemingly unconscionable contracts. This non-paternalistic defense of the unconscionability doctrine would be consistent with the libertarian case for freedom of contract if public officials did not also prohibit private enforcement of contracts:

TITLE LOAN, PART 2

Seth takes out a high-interest loan from Molly. He gives Molly the legal title to his car as collateral. The terms of the loan state that if he doesn't pay the loan on time, Molly's brother Murph will tow and resell Seth's car.

If public officials prohibit Murph from towing and reselling Seth's car, then they cannot claim that they're merely refusing to get involved. Rather, they'd be forcibly (and paternalistically) interfering with freedom of contract.

Just as freedom of speech also includes rights against compelled speech, freedom of contract also includes rights against compelled contractual terms. This means that people have the right to make contracts that leave out terms and conditions that neither party to the contract wants to include. To see how public officials sometimes compel people to include unwanted terms and conditions in their contractual agreements, consider regulations that constrain people's employment agreements:

EMPLOYER-PROVIDED HEALTHCARE

Greg owns a business with 200 employees. Public officials tell Greg that he must pay for his employees' health insurance, in addition to their wages. Greg's employees would rather have higher wages than health insurance and Greg would rather invest in growing his businesses. Instead, employees do not receive a bonus and Greg ultimately reduces the size of his workforce and raises prices.

In cases like this, public officials violate employers' and workers' freedom of contract by preventing them from freely choosing the terms and conditions of their labor agreement. Greg is happy to offer a job that pays workers in cash rather than health insurance and Greg's workers are happy to accept the job, but public officials violate their rights by requiring that their labor agreement include a benefit that neither party would choose on their own.

OCCUPATIONAL FREEDOM

The right to choose the terms and conditions of one's labor is entailed by freedom of contract. This right is sometimes called occupational freedom. It includes the right to choose a profession, to choose an employer, or to choose to be self-employed instead. Policies that violate people's occupational freedom include laws that prohibit people from doing certain jobs without first getting a permission slip from the government, as well as policies that prohibit people from owning their own businesses.

Just as personal property rights enable people to pursue their own plans and projects, the right to own productive property can be just as important for some people. Consider an example originally developed by John Tomasi:

PRODUCTIVE PROPERTY

Amy loves working with animals, so she saved for years to open her own pet grooming business, Amy's Pup in a Tub. Now she has her dream job and she employs half a dozen workers.

With the exception of communists, few people deny Amy's right to privately own a building, a bathtub, a dog crate, and a blow dryer. Libertarians argue that these rights don't change when Amy decides to use her property to provide dog-grooming services to people in her community, even if she charges them for the service. After all, if Amy acquired the resources needed to start her pet grooming businesses via permissible steps (say, saving a portion of the money that was given to her over a series of voluntary exchanges) and employed her workers on mutually agreed upon terms, then no one involved in the creation of Amy's Pup in a Tub has any claim against her decision to start a business.

Another reason to think that people have rights to own productive property is that there simply isn't a clear moral line dividing personal property from productive property:

CARLA'S CADILLAC

Carla owns a Cadillac that she rarely drives. Her neighbor Drew is looking for a part time job with flexible hours. Carla agrees to let Drew drive paying passengers in her Cadillac in exchange for a 20% cut of his earnings.

In this case, Carla's initial ownership over the Cadillac entitles her to drive it herself and allow Drew to drive it. The fact that Drew charges money for car services and gives some of the proceeds to

Carla doesn't invalidate the fact that Carla owns the Cadillac. If Carla is the owner of the car, then she has a right to use the car however she likes or to lend it out as she sees fit. And just as Drew has a right to use Carla's Cadillac with her permission, he also has a right to collect money from paying passengers.

Not everyone wants to be their own boss, however. Another aspect of occupational freedom is the right to choose the terms and conditions of one's employment. Conscription clearly violates this right, as do any national service programs that require young people to work for the government for a few years. But public officials can also limit people's occupational freedom in more targeted ways. Political philosophers sometimes defend regulations that would limit people's occupational freedom in specific professions. For example:

PATRICK THE PHYSICIAN

Patrick has studied for years to become a physician. He would like to work as a cosmetic dermatologist, but public officials tell him that he must first work for 4 years as a primary care provider to underserved populations or he will be legally prohibited from practicing medicine going forward.

A policy like this is like conscription or national service, but only for doctors. Unlike programs that offer loan forgiveness and other incentives for health workers to provide primary care in underserved areas, this policy prevents physicians from choosing where they work and what they do by threatening them with legal penalties.

In Patrick's case, public officials could also violate his occupational freedom to become a cosmetic dermatologist through the occupational licensing and scope of practice regulations that we described in the second chapter. Not only do these regulations violate patients' rights to choose their healthcare providers, they also violate providers' rights to choose their professions.

Licensing standards don't just apply to health workers. In lots of places, public officials require workers to get a permission slip from the government in order to work as a funeral director, florist, accountant, food truck owner, hair braider, interior decorator, teacher, gas station attendant, lawyer, upholsterer, travel agent, or manicurist. Often, these regulations prohibit people from making money from activities that anyone would be allowed to do for free:

EYEBROW WAXER

Elvira has a gift for shaping people's eyebrows in ways that make their faces look more harmonious and beautiful. She has waxed her friends' and family members' eyebrows for years. Elvira would like to work as a wax technician at her local salon, but before she can get the job she must attain a high school diploma or equivalency, pass a course in eyebrow waxing, take an exam, and complete weeks of supervised waxing. If Elvira doesn't do these things, public officials will legally prohibit the local salon from hiring her and they will also prohibit her from accepting people's money for eyebrow waxing services.

Even if Elvira's eyebrow waxing were really a danger to the people she waxed, Elvira would still be entitled to wax people's eyebrows as long as she disclosed all the known risks of the service. However, obviously, Elvira's eyebrow waxing is not a public menace, which is why even the most safety-conscious public officials would not support prohibiting Elvira from waxing her own eyebrows or her friends and family's eyebrows for free. The fact that personal eyebrow waxing is observationally identical to professional eyebrow waxing reveals that prohibitions on unlicensed eyebrow waxing aren't necessary to protect public health or safety.

Insofar as consumers have an interest in accessing qualified service providers, people who work in service industries can attain private certifications that signal their experience or quality. If public officials think that it's important to certify the quality of service providers, they can offer a voluntary public certification too, without making uncertified work illegal. Consumers can decide whether it's worth it to pay more for a certified service provider, based on their knowledge of the industry and their tolerance for risk. Because service workers can choose to attain voluntary third-party or public certifications, a policy that prohibits people from paying for uncertified work doesn't benefit consumers but just limits their options and raises the price of services.

So while people often say that licensing standards are necessary to protect consumers' health and safety, it makes sense that the most vocal and effective proponents of occupational licensing laws usually aren't safety-minded consumers. Rather, the people who are already licensed to work in industries are usually the most influential proponents of occupational licensing. In this way, occupational licensing is a form of rent-seeking. Incumbent workers convince public officials to regulate their profession. These regulations impose legal barriers to competition in the industry, thereby inflating incumbents' wages and imposing higher costs on consumers.

Other kinds of regulations that limit people's occupational freedom and harm consumers can also be explained by rent-seeking. Earlier we noted that, in some places, public officials grant groups of hospital executives the legal authority to decide whether someone can build a new hospital within their jurisdiction. These certificate of need laws empower incumbent stakeholders to limit newcomers' rights to open new businesses in places where the incumbents claim that people already have sufficient access to medical services. But incumbents are not in a good position to unbiasedly determine whether there is insufficient demand for a new hospital in an area because they have incentives to limit competition. And even if there isn't enough demand for two hospitals in an area, it doesn't follow that they should prohibit a new hospital from opening and competing with the old one.

WORKPLACE REGULATIONS

In the previous chapter, we argued that people should not object to an economic system on the grounds that it results in income and wealth inequality, and we explained why redistributive taxation that aims to remedy these kinds of inequality is usually unjustified. In this section, we'll argue further that other remedies to income and wealth inequality, such as minimum wage laws, not only violate people's rights but also are counterproductive. We also argue against other restrictions on workers' economic freedom, such as occupational health and safety requirements.

Consider first a landmark court case that set the legal foundation for safety and wage regulation:

LOCHNER

There were two kinds of competing bakeries—small immigrant bake shops where the employees lived at the store and worked around the clock to make bread and pastries, and large, established bakeries where the employees worked in shifts. The established bakers lobbied state officials to pass "the Bakeshop Act," which imposed limits on the maximum number of hours that a baker could work. This legislation did not affect the established bakeries, but smaller immigrant bakeries were in violation of the policy.

The US Supreme Court sided with the small immigrant bakeries, arguing that there was not a compelling health or safety reason to restrict the number of hours that a baker could work. But this ruling was later overturned during the Great Depression when public officials threatened to expand the Supreme Court unless the Justices reversed their prior stance to uphold New Deal legislation that expanded the American welfare state and limited workers' freedom of contract. As part of this reversal, the Court upheld minimum wage regulations:

MINIMUM WAGE

Bess is the manager at a large grocery store. She already has a lot of staff, but she suspects that she could sell more groceries if she hired people to bag groceries and take groceries to customers' cars. The expected economic benefit of hiring baggers is modest. If the bagger program is going to be profitable to her store, she can only pay baggers $5 per hour. She advertises the position and receives dozens of applicants. She hires Emily and six other people to work as baggers during times when the store is especially busy.

Bess pays the baggers a low wage. But should this be illegal?

A standard argument for minimum wage laws asserts that they prevent employers from exploiting some workers' lack of job options. Maybe Emily only has two options: bag groceries for Bess or not work at all. The worry, then, is that Bess will take advantage of Emily's situation and offer her low pay. Since the alternative is not working at all, Emily is, in effect, *forced* to take the bad job.

But even if Emily doesn't have a realistic alternative to taking the job offered by Bess, that doesn't mean that agreeing to the job should be made illegal. Here's a parallel case inspired by Robert Nozick:

EVAN'S MARRIAGE

Evan's top priority in life is getting married. However, no one has ever proposed to him and all of his marriage proposals have been rejected. Belle proposes to him. While Belle is literally the last woman on Earth that Evan would agree to marry, he realizes he would rather be married to Belle than spend the rest of his life alone. He accepts the proposal.

The state would, and should, enforce this marriage contract even though Evan only agrees because he lacks a better option. The same goes for employees like Emily who (let's assume) only agree to their labor contract because they lack a better option. In the marriage case, Evan also retained the right to spend his life alone. By analogy, workers always retain the right to spend their working life on their own, and in these cases, minimum wage laws don't apply to *self*-employment. Here's a case inspired by the philosopher Bas van der Vossen:

EMILY'S PRODUCE STAND

Emily goes into business for herself and runs a small produce stand. She works about 40 hours per week at the stand and earns $5 per hour.

Even if Emily is making a mistake by working for herself at a rate of $5 per hour, the state should not forcibly prevent her from making this choice and shut down her stand. We don't need to agree with someone's occupational choice to recognize that the choice is nevertheless theirs to make.

Emily is also free to volunteer and it would, for similar reasons, be wrong for a state actor to prohibit Emily from helping people in her community without collecting a wage in return. It is striking that some socialist critics of libertarianism argue that the ideal form of labor involves unconditional, uncompensated exchanges, where people assist each other out of solidarity, ideology, or sympathy. Yet when a person labors for a low wage rather than no wage, socialist critics view these exchanges as presumptively exploitative.

It's worth highlighting that Emily only accepted Bess's job offer because no other employer made her a better one. After all, if another employer had made her an offer that was better than Bess's, then presumably Emily would have accepted that one. So even if Bess is taking advantage of Emily's unemployment, she's still benefiting Emily more than every employer who offered Emily an even worse job or offered nothing at all. To put the point another way, Emily might say that Bess is the worst employer—except for all the others. Bess made the best offer, so it seems like she should receive the least blame. But critics of libertarianism criticize Bess for offering low pay while overlooking all the other people who didn't offer Emily anything at all. The "non-worseness claim"—roughly, the claim that a voluntary, mutually beneficial interaction is no worse than not interacting at all—helps us see where proponents of minimum wage laws go wrong. How could giving someone a job that they regard as better than no job be worse than not giving them a job at all?

Here's another way of getting at the same sort of idea: the state shouldn't criminalize *offers*. The recipient of the offer isn't forced to take it, so worst case scenario, they can simply reject it. This idea is intuitive in its own right, but we can spell it out more carefully in the case of low-paying job offers:

> If someone may make an offer of no job, they may make an offer of a low-paying job.
> Someone may make an offer of no job.
> So they may make an offer of a low-paying job.

Let's start with the first premise. It's hard to see how an offer of a low-paying job is worse for a prospective worker than an offer of no job. After all, if the low-paying job is worse (or no better) than nothing, she can simply decline the offer. So she's no worse off for having that offer. On the other hand, if the low-paying job is *better* than nothing, she can take it and thereby become better off.

It also seems clear there that someone may make an offer of no job. To put that point differently, there is no general, enforceable duty to give people jobs. For instance, if someone knocks on your door and offers to shovel your driveway after a snowstorm, you're not obligated to accept. Thus, we arrive at the conclusion that someone may make an offer of a low-paying job.

Returning to our case above, we should also be careful to not simply assume that Emily works for Bess because that she can't find a higher-paying option. Maybe Emily is rich, but she just wants to get out of the house and meet new people. Maybe she loves bagging groceries and she appreciates that she can walk to the grocery store on sunny days. Every worker has their own reasons for choosing a job. Most workers do not try to maximize their wages—other things matter too. People accept lower wages for the opportunity to work from home, or to do work they find meaningful, or to work with people they like, or to work for themselves. Some people choose to volunteer, or they take unpaid internships. If people can voluntarily work for a company at the rate of $0/hour, why should it be illegal for people to work for $5/hour?

A proponent of minimum wage regulations may argue that Bess has a duty to ensure that all of her employees make enough money to at least meet their basic needs. People sometimes criticize big box retailers on these grounds when they point out that these large employers pay people so little that their employees require public assistance to afford food and housing.

To evaluate this claim, let's first remember that employers are buyers of labor. An employee sells their labor to their employer just as a car dealer sells their cars to their customers. Consider an analogy:

DESPERATE DEALERSHIP

Irene plans to buy a car from a Doug, a car salesman who is losing so much business that he has fallen below a decent standard of living. Doug cannot afford to pay his rent or to buy enough food for the week.

Does Irene have an enforceable duty to pay Doug an extra, say, $2,000 for the car? Probably not. The mere fact that Irene is buying something from Doug doesn't generate an enforceable duty for her to pay even more to help him pay his rent.

Let's return to the case of employment. Suppose Bess buys Emily's labor, but Emily remains below an acceptable standard of living. Bess does not have an enforceable duty to pay Emily more simply by virtue of buying her labor. If anything, Bess has *less* of an obligation to help Emily than anyone else because she's already paying Emily $5/hour whereas other people aren't helping Emily at all. Libertarians reject the idea that a business owner who is already providing *some* benefit to someone thereby incurs an *additional* obligation to provide them with even more benefits. Furthermore, implementing this idea would disincentivize providing benefits to others in the first place. If you know that you'll be obligated—indeed, *forced*—to shovel your neighbor's driveway in the winter if you mow their lawn in the summer, you have a weaker incentive to mow their lawn in the summer. But now your neighbor is without a mowed lawn or a clear driveway.

Now maybe you think people *do* have an enforceable obligation to ensure that others can meet their basic needs. Consider, though, that this view doesn't establish that employers in particular shoulder an unequal share of this obligation. Rather, the most plausible version of this view is that everyone who can afford it has this duty, which speaks in favor of a universal basic income rather than a state-enforced living wage. (Note here the similarity between this argument and our argument about special accommodations.)

There is also an economic reason, in addition to the ethical reason sketched above, to address concerns about the material conditions of workers via cash transfers rather than compensation regulations. Legislation that pushes the wages that employers must pay employees above the employees' marginal products will not sustainably help those employees. Why? Because the legislation would require employers to take a loss whenever it hires one of those employees. Suppose that Bess will make an extra $6 per hour by hiring Emily. If the state mandates that Bess must pay Emily $10 per hour, she simply won't hire her, just as she won't exchange a $10 bill for $6. This outcome would be bad for customers who would like some help with their bags, bad for potential workers who no longer have the opportunity to work at Bess's store, and bad for Bess because she could have increased sales if only she didn't have to pay baggers a high wage. And, again, to say that minimum wage laws are unjustified isn't to say that there is nothing that can be done to help low-wage workers. If there is a general obligation to help them rather than an obligation that falls on employers alone, the state could supplement low wages with tax-funded cash transfers.

People who criticize employers for offering low wages also overlook the potential downsides of paying a higher wage. Imagine an employer who could offer a higher wage, but chooses not to:

RICH BOSS

Andrea is a rich entrepreneur who starts a new business. Emma agrees to be her employee, accepting a wage of $15 per hour. Andrea could, however, afford to pay Emma $20 per hour.

Libertarians deny that Andrea acts impermissibly when she offers Emma a lower wage than what she can afford. The mere fact that someone can afford to pay a higher price for something does not obligate them to pay that higher price. For example, if your local coffee shop charges $2.50 for a cup of coffee but you could afford to pay more than that, you still aren't morally obligated to pay $10.00 for a cup of coffee instead. Few, if any, people think you're obligated to pay $10.00 for the coffee simply because you can.

Not only is Andrea's decision to pay $15 permissible though; in principle, it's just as praiseworthy as the decision to pay $20. The money that Andrea could have given Emma doesn't vanish—she still has it. Maybe she'll spend it on an Uber ride, which would benefit the Uber driver. Or maybe she'll invest it in another business, which would benefit customers and employees. Think back to the coffee shop. The extra $7.50 you could have spent on the coffee doesn't disappear. You'll put it to a different use that will benefit someone else. The case of an employer is no different.

It might even be more praiseworthy for Andrea to offer a lower wage because, by doing so, Andrea can ensure that the people she hires are the people who benefit the most from taking the job. When employers offer higher wages, they are still likely to hire the people who they think are the most qualified people for the job. This means that they are likely to end up hiring people who are more skilled, experienced, or productive, because the higher wage will induce these higher-skilled workers to apply for a job that they would not otherwise consider.

Relatedly, one of libertarians' least popular policy views (and that's a fierce competition) is that officials shouldn't mandate occupational safety regulations, for the same reason that they shouldn't regulate people's wages or hours. But this view isn't as counterintuitive as it seems as at first blush. Because complying with these rules comes at a cost for employers, libertarians contend that they should be permitted to bypass some or all of these rules and pass the savings onto their employees in the form of higher wages. Consider a similar case:

KURT THE QUARTERBACK

Kurt bags groceries for a living. An arena football team offers him more money to be their quarterback. Kurt accepts the money even though playing football is riskier than bagging groceries.

The state shouldn't coercively prevent Kurt from taking on this new risk in exchange for more money. As long as he is informed about those risks, he should be permitted to make his own decisions about how to make the trade-off between safety and salary. And this point applies to *any* worker—as long as they are informed about the risks, the state should permit them to accept greater risk in exchange for more money.

WORKPLACE EMPOWERMENT

Socialists oppose the private ownership of productive property because they claim, among other things, that powerful business owners would have too much power to control and oppress their workers. Although you might have some choice while you're on the clock, your boss typically tells you what hours to work, what tasks to perform, what sort of clothes to wear, and so on. Thus, the argument goes, a concern for workers' freedom provides a reason to oppose capitalism.

This argument looks particularly worrisome for libertarians who defend capitalism on the grounds that it's the only economic arrangement consistent with respect for people's freedom. However, to the extent the economy is characterized by consumer sovereignty, it's not clear that the socialist claim that workers are uniquely unfree lands:

BARRY'S CAFE

Barry owns and operates a cafe. Because he wants to make money, his freedom to determine the hours he works, the tasks he performs, and the products he sells is severely limited. If Barry decided to sell anchovy muffins and open the cafe at noon, he could not stay in business for long. The same can be said if he scowled rather than smiled at his customers, or if he wore a filthy, tattered Metallica t-shirt instead of clean clothes. Barry's freedom to work as he pleases is not limited by a boss but rather by prospective customers.

Maybe Barry still has more freedom than a typical worker, although that's partly an empirical question. Plus, it's not clear whether that's a difference in kind or a difference in degree. In both cases, the demands of others set significant constraints on someone's freedom to work as they please (at least insofar as they want those others to provide them with income in exchange for their work). If Barry wants his customers to give him their money, he needs to accommodate their preferences. If Barry is thinking about hiring an employee, that employee needs to accommodate Barry's preferences (which are likely a reflection of his customers' preferences) if he wants Barry to give him the job and the wages that come with it.

Plus, worker (un)freedom isn't just an issue under capitalism. It arises under any system where one's income depends on giving others what they want. Take a socialist system where all businesses are democratically-operated, worker-owned cooperatives. If you worked in a society like this, the other members of your cooperative would be able to set significant constraints on your freedom to work as you please:

WORKER COOPERATIVES

Ned is a member of a democratically-run worker cooperative. His coworker, Matt, recently started wearing makeup and nail polish to work. Ned doesn't Matt's new look. He thinks it is ugly and embarrassing for the company brand, and he knows that a lot of the other employees agree. At the next employee meeting, Ned proposes a company code for makeup and nail polish. Matt votes against the code but it passes, and Matt is required to stop wearing makeup and nail polish to work.

It's a mistake to claim that workers in a cooperative don't have a boss—they actually have *many* bosses, namely, all of their coworkers. Workplace democracy doesn't empower the worker any more than citizens are empowered by having the right to vote. If a person's vote doesn't meaningfully expand their freedom or improve their material circumstances in other ways, then any seeming empowerment that comes with voting rights is functionally useless. At least an undemocratic workplace has fewer meetings.

A related criticism of libertarianism is that respecting employers' economic freedom is bad for workers since employers in a market economy employ workers at will. A worker is employed "at will" when their employer may fire them at any point and for any reason they choose. Critics of capitalism claim that at-will employment gives employers the power to arbitrarily dismiss employees and thus dramatically worsen their lives. Even the workers who aren't fired can suffer under this system because they preemptively change their behavior to curry favor with the bosses out of fear that they could be fired at any time.

It's true that libertarians do think that public officials should not limit workers' or employers' freedom to make at-will employment agreements. Notice, though, that workers have a parallel freedom— in the absence of a contract that says otherwise, they can also quit at any time for any reason. Employers and workers both benefit from this sort of freedom, even though both can be harmed if the other suddenly ends the relationship. Although this claim is counterintuitive, permitting at-will employment actually has advantages for workers because imposing restrictions on employers' ability to dismiss workers that may turn out to be unsuitable for the job reduces employers' incentive to hire more workers in the first place. Any policy that makes it costly to hire workers would have a negative effect on employment, thus diminishing the bargaining power of all workers because it would reduce the supply of jobs and make the labor market more competitive for them.

Think of it this way: if you were legally obligated to stay in a job for at least two years after accepting the job offer, you'd be more reluctant to take a job. This is not to say that employers or workers should carelessly fire people or quit without considering how their choices affect other people. Many workers are often devastated when they lose their jobs, and when good employees quit, it can be enormously disruptive to an employer's business. But even if some people are objectionably callous when they downsize their workforce or quit, this fact doesn't entail the state should prohibit people from ending employment relationships.

Consider an analogy to romantic breakups (with apologies to Seinfeld):

JOHN AND EVE'S BREAKUP

Despite being together for 30 years, John and Eve eat peas together for the first time. Eve notices that John eats peas one at a time instead of scooping them. She is appalled by this and breaks up with him.

How someone eats peas is a bad reason for breaking up with a long-term boyfriend. Nevertheless, it would be wrong for public officials to prohibit Eve from breaking up with John in this case, even though she doesn't have a good reason to do it. The fact that Eve doesn't want to be with John anymore, for whatever reason, is sufficient grounds for her to end the relationship and lawmakers should respect Eve's choice. For the same reasons, it would be callous and insensitive for an employer to fire someone because they don't scoop the peas they eat for lunch, but it shouldn't be illegal.

Another libertarian defense of at-will employment appeals to an idea we discussed earlier: even bad job offers leave prospective employees no worse off than they'd be if they never received an offer in the first place. And bad offers potentially leave people better off when they are the best bad option someone has. So, the state shouldn't prevent employers from making bad job offers.

All that said, if workers can secure more favorable terms for their employment, that's also a permissible exercise of their economic freedom. Tenured professors, for example, have labor agreements with their employers that prevent at-will termination. Instead, they can only be fired if they violate specific, pre-specified rules. Just as public officials should permit at-will employment arrangements, they should also enforce labor contracts that constrain employers' options. In these cases, even employers benefit from the freedom to make these more restrictive contracts because they can offer potential workers job security in exchange for lower wages and the ability to offer more stability can enable them to recruit and retain better workers than they would otherwise attract.

Workers can collectively advocate for better employment terms by forming a union and organizing a strike:

UNIONS

Most of the skilled workers at the factory think they are underpaid and overworked. When any given worker negotiates with the boss individually, the boss tells her that if she doesn't like it she can quit. The workers know that the boss cannot re-hire the same number and quality of workers he currently employs, so they decide to coordinate with each other to strike for higher wages and fewer hours. Each of the striking workers refuses to negotiate with the boss individually. In order to induce the workers to return to the factory, the boss agrees to terms that the workers collectively endorsed.

Because libertarians support freedom of association and freedom of contract, they support people's right to form unions and their right to strike. Workers have the right to enter and exit unions just as they have the right to enter and exit religious congregations and fantasy football leagues. In each of these cases, state actors should neither encourage nor discourage groups that unite people on the basis of their shared interest.

Although libertarians support the right to unionize, they are often skeptical that unionization will dramatically improve the material condition of workers. To see why, suppose that baristas are paid $15 per hour, but they produce $20 per hour for their employer. They go on strike, sustain themselves with the union's strike fund, and win a higher wage. That's an improvement for the workers, but their productivity sets a hard limit on their wages. They won't win a $25 per hour wage because that would result in their employer losing money on each employee.

The barista union is also unlikely to succeed if their employer can easily hire new people who are willing to work for $15 per hour. In order to avoid this outcome, union leaders often advocate for favorable treatment from the state to prohibit competition from ununionized workers. Policies that prevent employers from hiring ununionized workers might drive up the wages of union members, but they impose costs on consumers, employers, and unemployed people. For similar reasons, unions have also historically advocated for trade restrictions, immigration restrictions, or restrictions on automation. Each of these restrictive policies were impediments to productivity that harmed shareholders and consumers by driving up prices. Libertarians take no issue with unions per se, but they object to unions' support for legislation that prevents people from competing on fair terms.

The economist Milton Friedman argued that a worker's best protection isn't a union but rather the presence of many employers who are willing to compete to hire her. Consider:

BAD PIZZA

Milton tries out a new pizzeria that opened in his neighborhood. But the staff was rude, the pizza was subpar, and the price was too high. Milton vows never to return.

Milton was subject to a bad pizzeria. So what's his protection against bad pizzerias going forward? The answer is simple: the existence of other pizzerias. He can shop around for a better one and eat there. Similarly, the existence of other employers protects workers against bad employers because those other employers enable them to shop around for a better option.

Of course, there are limits to this analogy. Most importantly, it's a lot easier to change pizzerias than to change jobs. Still, the basic insight remains—workers are well served by robust competition for their work. So to protect workers, the state should remove obstacles that make it difficult for people to start new businesses and to offer and take jobs, instead of enforcing burdensome regulations that increase the legal risks and other costs of employing people.

Does capitalism require workers to spend too much time on the clock? Critics allege that capitalism is bad for workers in virtue of depriving them of leisure time. But in fact capitalism has radically *reduced* the number of hours people have to work in virtue of accelerating economic growth. In the past, people had to spend a lot of time working just to afford basic necessities. Now an hour of work is far more productive, meaning that people can work less and buy as much—and typically, much *more*—than they could before. Today, most workers can buy an entire day's worth of calories in under an hour of work.

This is why if you hate your job, you should love capitalism. It's never been easier to spend a majority of your life doing things other than work, especially if you dramatically cut back on your consumption to pile up a retirement fund:

FIRE

Danielle and Kyle started working at age 22. For the next 20 years, they lived together on Kyle's income in order to achieve financial independence and retire early (FIRE). At age 27, they bought a house with a large down payment and a 15 year fixed-rate mortgage, which they paid off with Kyle's earnings. By the time Danielle and Kyle turned 42 they were homeowners who had saved enough to retire early.

Granted, Danielle and Kyle's lifestyle isn't for everyone. But it's an option that's available to many people thanks to the abundance that is associated with free markets.

We also shouldn't overlook how capitalism has reduced the amount of time people spend toiling *outside* of their jobs by driving down the price of labor-saving devices:

TYRA THE TIME SAVER

Tyra pops a pod in the Keurig to get her morning coffee after she drops a bagel into her toaster. When she's done eating, she puts her dishes in the dishwasher instead of washing them by hand. She grabs some clothes out of the dryer that she had previously tossed in a washing machine instead of cleaning them with a washboard and hanging them to dry on a clothesline. Before heading out of her house, Tyra turns on her Roomba to clean her floors while she's away. Tyra then orders a self-driving Waymo to take her to work—while on the way, she sends out a few emails instead of writing letters by hand. While taking a walk during her lunch break, Tyra takes a digital photo that doesn't need to be developed. After work, she asks Alexa to play some music while she takes a few minutes to microwave dinner. She remembers that she needs to make a poster for her kids' school fundraiser and so she enlists AI to do it for her. Tyra finds a movie for the family to watch by browsing Netflix from her couch instead of driving to a video rental store.

We take it that Tyra's day looks familiar—most of these labor-saving devices are widely available. Of course, you might prefer not to use *all* of these labor-saving alternatives—maybe you'd rather cook a meal from scratch than microwave something from the freezer. Fair enough (although we'll note you'll have more time to cook if you don't have to wash the dishes by hand). But the key point is that capitalism makes this extra discretionary time available to us, whether or not we want to take advantage of it in any particular case.

MONOPOLIES

A monopoly occurs when a supplier has so much market power that competition does not affect their ability to set prices. Monopolies are considered market failures because the supplier in a monopoly market doesn't have incentives to provide goods or services to consumers efficiently because no one is competing for their business by offering the same or substitute goods or services at a lower price.

Government officials sometimes interfere with businesses when they think they wield so much market power that they are able to engage in monopoly pricing. For example:

STANDARD OIL

John D. Rockefeller founded the Standard Oil company in the late 1800's. The company grew as the country continued to industrialize and the company bought other energy companies. After a few decades, the US Supreme Court ordered the company to break itself up on the grounds that it was an illegal monopoly that imposed "unreasonable restrictions on trade" in the oil industry.

The Standard Oil case is the textbook example of anti-monopolistic regulation. But the case isn't as favorable to regulation as critics of free markets claim. Rockefeller paid Standard Oil workers a higher wage than competitors. And as the energy market expanded, Rockefeller's share of the market decreased even as the size of his company grew. During the time that Standard Oil was being accused of monopoly behavior, the price of oil actually fell due to more efficient production methods. That's actually what got them into trouble because federal authorities claimed that Standard Oil engaged in "predatory pricing" by charging less, thus making it harder for other energy companies to compete.

This case shows how antitrust regulations empower state actors to arbitrarily interfere with private businesses, even when they aren't acting in ways that harm workers or consumers. Even if these regulations are rarely enforced, the mere threat of expensive litigation can deter a company from growing and investing in innovative new ways to attract customers. After all, state actors are empowered to break up businesses for charging too much or too little, so a company in Standard Oil's position has no assurance that public officials will respect their freedom to grow their business.

Another problem with antitrust regulations that empower judges to break up large companies is that these regulations rarely if ever target true monopolies. That's because there aren't many private businesses that would qualify as true monopolies. Even though

Amazon is a huge company, if it used its market power to charge more for books and diapers and video content and web services, consumers who wanted to take their business elsewhere would have lots of other options. Nevertheless, officials today are trying to give Amazon the Standard Oil treatment. And here again, there is little evidence that Amazon is charging higher prices or paying their workers below market rate:

AMAZON

Jeff Bezos founded Amazon, an online retailer, in the 1990s. The company grew as Americans purchasing power increased, and the company expanded to other industries such as web hosting services and entertainment. After a few decades, the Federal Trade Commission sued Amazon for using its market power to give advantages to its preferred suppliers.

As in the Standard Oil case, officials claimed that Amazon's market power was a problem because smaller businesses that were not affiliated with Amazon had a hard time competing with suppliers that worked with Amazon. When regulators sue Amazon for placing other businesses at a disadvantage, they aren't standing up for customers or workers; they're using public resources to harm an unpopular company for the benefit of more favored businesses. It's not consumer protection, it's crony capitalism.

To this line of argument, critics of large companies say that officials should stand up for smaller retailers because it's not fair that big corporations like Walmart have the power to put so many small retailers out of business. But libertarians reply that the only reason Walmart puts smaller retailers out of business is that they provide goods and services to consumers at a lower price:

WALMART

Most of the people in a small rural town purchase their food, hardware, and clothes on Main Street. The business owners on Main Street charge high prices because they are too small to negotiate for lower prices from their wholesalers and because they have little competition, since is inconvenient for the townspeople to go anywhere else. When Walmart comes to town, the

> *townspeople can purchase similar goods from Walmart for a lower price. Few*
> *people shop on Main Street anymore, and the businesses close.*

Main Street retailers aren't entitled to their neighbor's paychecks. When people in a town start shopping at Walmart, they are able to save money or buy more things that they want. Other small local businesses benefit from cheaper access to retail goods. Walmart is also a very large buyer that supports more small manufacturers than smaller retailers ever could. So small retailers that criticize Walmart are basically saying that it would be better if their neighbors and other local businesses had less purchasing power and fewer options, just so that their business could remain in town. In cases like these, if public officials were to prevent Walmart from opening in their town, they would effectively be imposing a tax on all shoppers, including some local businesses, paid to incumbent retailers who provide a less efficient and more expensive product.

PRICE GOUGING

One of libertarians' most controversial views is that businesses may engage in "price gouging"—that is, charging extremely high prices for goods and services when demand is unusually high and supply is unusually low:

EMERGENCY SUPPLIES

After a hurricane, the roads were covered in debris and many people in a small mountain community were without power. A few entrepreneurial young men decided to rent a refrigerated truck, fill it with ice, and use chainsaws to clear the roads as they drove into town to sell ice for $40 per bag. People who needed to refrigerate medicine or food were happy to pay for the expensive ice.

Critics of price gouging would argue that the entrepreneurs who charged high prices for ice treated all potential consumers unfairly because they exploited an emergency to make a profit.

Libertarians tend to offer two kinds of arguments in defense of price gouging. First, permitting price gouging has good consequences—it provides incentives to conserve the existing supply of the good and to bring about new supply. For instance, if a bag of ice is $40, you'll buy enough to chill your medicine but not your beer (thereby sparing a bag for someone else who needs to chill their medicine). Plus, if you can buy a bag of ice for $5 at Walmart and then drive it to a disaster site where you can resell it for $40, you're more likely to get off your couch and bring some ice to those who need it than if you can only sell each bag for $6.

Another argument against price gouging regulation resembles an argument we made against the minimum wage. Giving people the option to buy expensive ice doesn't make them worse off because they retain the freedom to just not buy any ice at all. But giving someone the option to buy expensive ice might make them better off if they judge that the price is worth it.

A critic of price gouging might reply that this argument is too quick because it rules out the possibility that people can have enforceable duties to provide uncompensated assistance to people in need, especially during emergencies. Even if this were true, it wouldn't justify legal restrictions on price gouging because if people did have duties to provide free ice to people in need during emergencies (and they fulfilled those duties), then price gouging would not occur in the first place. Who is going to buy a bag of ice for $40 when they can get one for free or maybe 50 cents? There is a reason why you don't see price gougers attempt to sell a bottle of soda for $10 in front of a fully stocked vending machine.

Similar arguments support the unpopular practice of offering high-interest short-term loans to high-risk borrowers:

PAYDAY LENDING

Tammy's rent is overdue because her car broke down and she needed to pay for repairs so she could get to work. If she doesn't pay her landlord $900 by Friday she will be evicted from her home. Tammy gets paid next Wednesday. She takes out a payday loan that has a very high interest rate, pays her rent, and then quickly repays the loan when her paycheck hits her bank account.

Payday lenders do not make borrowers worse off; they merely give people the option to borrow at a high interest rate in circumstances where they'd otherwise lack access to any sources of credit. Meanwhile, restrictions on payday loans just limit borrowers' options even more, and in the absence of the option to take out a payday loan, desperate borrowers might turn to even worse options, such as stealing from people or borrowing from violent loan sharks.

Laws that control prices can also have devastating consequences when they disincentivize investment and innovation:

PHARMACEUTICALS

Most countries limit how much a drug manufacturer can charge patients for their products. In the United States, manufacturers can freely set the prices for their products and they can negotiate drug prices with large purchasers, such as insurance companies. As a result, drugs are generally more expensive in the United States, but American patients also have more treatment options and they can access new drugs earlier than people in other countries. People all around the world travel to the United States for treatment.

When public officials uphold patents but do not set a ceiling on the price of drugs, drugmakers can charge very high prices for new drugs that dramatically improve or extend people's lives. The pharmaceutical market in the United States is so profitable because public officials give drugmakers property rights in new drug discoveries and they let manufacturers set their own prices. This system incentivizes drug innovation and discovery far more than other countries, and when a drug is created for the US market, the whole world ultimately benefits, as do generations of patients to come.

People support price controls because they see the high price of pharmaceuticals and worry that not everyone will be able to afford the high price of treatment. Or, they think that greedy businesspeople are profiting off of sick people's misfortune. What supporters of price controls fail to see is that drugmakers are helping patients more than anyone else and that a system that permits high prices for pharmaceuticals ultimately benefits all sick people more than any alternative way of incentivizing drug discovery and development.

The same considerations apply to other cases too. People may object to a payday lender's character, but they fail to see that the payday lender is doing more for a desperate borrower than anyone else. People object to vendors who raise their prices during an emergency, but they overlook the harm caused by vendors who refuse to raise prices and rapidly exhaust their supplies.

ETHICAL CONSUMERISM

Libertarians argue that markets don't mistreat consumers; they empower consumers. For example, when people act as consumers they have social power because companies are competing for their business. Consumers can therefore exert influence by choosing to support businesses that share their values. Or alternatively, consumers can punish businesses that act immorally through boycotts and divestment:

CONSUMER BOYCOTT

A company makes some of its products in a country that violates human rights. The company has close ties to the country's government. Critics of that country express their disapproval of its policies by refusing to buy products from the company.

If only a few consumers boycott an unethical company it is unlikely to be effective. But if enough consumers use their market power to support a company's competitors instead, the leaders of the company might reform their production methods or policies so that they can stay in business.

Yet in order for consumers to use their market power for good, they must also be willing to pay the price of a boycott. When people say that they disapprove of a large tech company's labor practices, or that they think that sweatshop labor is abhorrent, or that they are opposed to animal testing, or that they think it's important to buy local, these words are cheap talk if they are unwilling to pay more for products that are sold by small local retailers and made by highly paid workers.

Often, consumers are unwilling to pay more for a product that aligns with their values, but they do have an interest in purchasing goods that signal the company's alignment with their values. This is why businesses often appeal to consumers' moral sensibilities in symbolic ways even if their business model is otherwise in tension with those values. Cases of greenwashing and grandstanding reflect this dynamic:

GRANDSTANDING

A fast food restaurant on the highway is very profitable, due to all the drivers who pass their exit. The restaurant mainly sells burgers, fries, and soda. To signal their commitment to environmental sustainability, the restaurant places recycling bins in the parking lot and switches from plastic straws to paper straws.

In this case, the restaurant's business model is, overall, bad for the environment. The company is making it easier for people to commute by car, profiting from car commuters, and selling food that is worse for the environment than other kinds of food. Some consumers think of themselves as people who care about the environment, but they also want to drive their cars and eat hamburgers. The restaurant has found a way to satisfy both of these consumer preferences by offering them a product that is not especially eco-friendly while signaling that they share their environmentalist customers' values. This is an example of markets giving people what they really want, even if that looks different from what people say they want.

For consumers who are really serious about using their economic power to express disapproval of immoral businesses, divestment is another option:

DIVESTMENT

A large university's endowment includes some investments in fossil fuel companies. People at the university claim that climate change is the greatest injustice of our time, and demand that the university's endowment managers sell all their stock in fossil fuel companies.

Here again, libertarians support a private investor's right to divest as they see fit, although they might doubt its effectiveness because it's difficult for a politically motivated group of investors to wield so much market power that they can meaningfully diminish the share price of a company that they disapprove of when there are many others willing to invest. Very large institutional investors can sometimes influence how companies do business, but even in these cases, they are often reluctant to do so if socially responsible investing would compromise the return on their clients' investments.

TECH REGULATION

Libertarian principles extend to what people do online. For example, people say pretty messed up things on social media platforms, but it would be wrong for state actors to censor them:

SOCIAL MEDIA

People on social media make false claims, bully each other, encourage disordered eating, and post content that can make people suicidal. They also watch pornography and violent content and talk about using illegal drugs. Some people form communities around common interests, such as mommy bloggers and the Pittsburgh Steelers.

The terrible things that people say on social media platforms should be protected by the same legal standards that apply to speech in other contexts. That said, social media platforms are private companies, not public utilities. For this reason, social media companies should also have the legal right to privately censor content that they find distasteful, harmful, or just bad for their brand. And if people notice that a social media platform has a lot of negative or immoral content, they can delete their accounts. This should be an incentive for platforms to curate their content in ways that discourage harmful speech. So when social media companies are unwilling to deplatform negative content, it's likely not the company that is to blame but rather, the users are engaging with the negative content despite their professed disapproval of it.

Libertarian principles of freedom of contract apply online too. Often, consumers order things or agree to things online that they would not have signed up for in person. Consider, for example, notices of terms and conditions for apps and services:

Libertarians argue that people are entitled to make voluntary contracts as long as they are fully informed of the terms. So as long as the terms and conditions of using a puzzle app were accurately disclosed, Nancy has no complaint against the app maker for tracking her. On the other hand, when tech companies mislead consumers about the terms and conditions of using their products, libertarians agree with proponents of tech regulation that consumers can reasonably hold tech companies liable in these cases.

Recent technological innovations have also enabled people to create cryptocurrencies, which are another kind of property that people can own and use as money:

CRYPTO

Investors created new asset class consisting in fungible tokens. People can use these tokens to make transactions that are recorded in an anonymous public ledger. People can acquire these tokens through trade, or by running complex computer algorithms that validate other people's transactions.

From a libertarian perspective, cryptocurrency is appealing because the value of the tokens is not determined by a central bank or political authority. This means that people can make transactions without government surveillance and they can retain assets without the threat of taxation or government seizure.

In response to the increasing prevalence of cryptocurrency, public officials worldwide have proposed and passed regulations for cryptocurrencies and exchanges. For example, regulators in the United States treat cryptocurrencies as securities, commodities, and as a form of property. This means that companies that issue and trade digital assets are legally required to register for a license and they are subject to the same kinds of regulations that apply to other kinds of financial investments. Public officials also tax digital assets like cryptocurrencies in the same way that they tax other sources of capital gains. Libertarians typically oppose these regulations, just as they object to comparable regulations that apply to other kinds of contracts and property.

SUMMARY

The best way for public officials to help workers is for them to allow employers to compete and to allow workers to make their own choices. Many of the regulations that paternalistically limit worker's economic freedom end up backfiring anyhow because they disadvantage low-skilled workers and make it more costly for employers to hire people. If consumers want to support businesses that they view as being better for workers, they are of course entitled to use their own economic freedom to advance their moral and political ideology. Yet even the workplaces that would strike many people as the most dangerous or exploitative generally employ people who are there because they view it as their best option.

Other justifications for economic regulations are similarly dubious. In a market economy, there are rarely if ever monopolies that require regulation for the sake of consumer protection. More often, lawmakers support policies that aim to regulate large businesses as a way of protecting smaller companies from competition, and they pass the costs of their intervention onto consumers. For reasons like these, libertarians are also generally skeptical of proposals to regulate new technologies and cryptocurrencies.

FURTHER READING

- Anderson, Elizabeth. 2017. *Private Government: How Employers Rule Our Lives (and Why We Don't Talk about It)*. Princeton University Press.
- Bernstein, David E. 2012. *Rehabilitating Lochner: Defending Individual Rights against Progressive Reform*. Chicago, IL: University of Chicago Press.
- Dierksmeier, Claus, and Peter Seele. 2018. "Cryptocurrencies and Business Ethics." *Journal of Business Ethics* 152 (1): 1–14. https://doi.org/10.1007/s10551-016-3298-0.

- Friedman, Milton. 2002. *Capitalism and Freedom*. University of Chicago Press.
- Gourevitch, Alex. 2014. *From Slavery to the Cooperative Commonwealth: Labor and Republican Liberty in the Nineteenth Century*. Cambridge University Press.
- Hodgkinson, Tom. 2006. *How to Be Free*. London, UK: Hamish Hamilton.
- Hussain, Waheed. 2012. "Is Ethical Consumerism an Impermissible Form of Vigilantism?" *Philosophy & Public Affairs* 40 (2): 111–143. https://doi.org/10.1111/j.1088-4963.2012.01218.x.
- Khan, Lina M. 2016. "Amazon's Antitrust Paradox." *Yale Law Journal* 126: 710.
- Lochner v. New York. 292AD, 198 US 45. Supreme Court.
- Munger, Michael. 2007. "They Clapped: Can Price-Gouging Laws Prohibit Scarcity?" *The Library of Economics and Liberty* (blog), January 8. www.econlib.org/library/Columns/y2007/Mungergouging.html.
- Plemmons, Alicia, and Edward Timmons. 2025. "Occupational Licensing: A Barrier to Opportunity and Prosperity." The Center for Growth and Opportunity, March.
- Radin, Margaret Jane. 2013. *Boilerplate: The Fine Print, Vanishing Rights, and the Rule of Law*. Princeton: Princeton University Press. https://doi.org/10.1515/9781400844838.
- Sotirakopoulos, Nikos. 2018. "Cryptomarkets as a Libertarian Counter-Conduct of Resistance." *European Journal of Social Theory* 21 (2): 189–206. https://doi.org/10.1177/1368431017718534.
- Standard Oil Co. of NJ v. United Sates. 1910, 221 US 1. Supreme Court.
- Tomasi, John. 2012. *Free Market Fairness*. Princeton: Princeton University Press.
- Tosi, Justin, and Brandon Warmke. 2020. *Grandstanding: The Use and Abuse of Moral Talk*. New York, NY: Oxford University Press.
- Zwolinski, Matt. 2008. "The Ethics of Price Gouging." *Business Ethics Quarterly* 18 (3): 347–378.

6

CRIMINAL JUSTICE

Libertarians have long opposed overcriminalization, most notably in their support of ending drug prohibition. This chapter explores this issue, along with libertarian analyses of police reform, prison abolition, and prosecutorial discretion. We make the case for a restorative rather than punitive approach to criminal justice, and we explain why public officials often have incentives to enforce laws that violate people's rights and exacerbate social and economic inequality.

CRIME

Libertarians agree with most everyone else that public officials are entitled to prevent and punish some kinds of anti-social behavior. Specifically, police, prosecutors, judges, and prison guards are entitled to interfere with violent criminals who threaten or violate other people's enforceable rights. Throughout human history, a shocking large percentage of people were violently killed, in either interpersonal disputes or genocidal warfare. Interpersonal violence decreased as political communities' state capacity grew. Rates of random violence went down as the pervasiveness of state violence increased.

DOI: 10.4324/9781003270720-6

Today, most people live in states where public officials protect people's safety by enforcing laws against assault and murder. Consider the alternative:

PRIVATE ENFORCEMENT

Jake lives in a society where public officials do not provide citizens with police protection. Instead, people pay bodyguards to protect them. When someone is assaulted or killed, the victim or the family of the victim can pay a private enforcement agency to capture, prosecute, sentence, and punish the offender. If the offender doesn't participate in the private enforcement process, he loses his right to use private enforcement agencies in the future, making him vulnerable to revenge from the victim or the victim's family.

Because the state isn't special, private enforcement agencies are just as entitled as anyone else to investigate and punish violent criminals. And an advantage of private enforcement agencies is that they are funded through people's voluntary contributions rather than through coercion. But a system like this really only makes sense in a stateless society because states provide the same services that a private enforcement agency does. So insofar as some kind of public agency exists that coercively confiscates some people's property in order to fund the enforcement of property rules and contracts, that agency can also protect people's safety. If states are justified for any reason, it is to secure people's rights against violence and threats of violence.

Some people argue that states are necessary because people disagree about the scope and strength of people's enforceable rights, especially property rights. For this reason, some political philosophers argue that the state is morally special because public officials have the sole authority to pass and publicize laws that specify the boundaries of everyone's entitlements as a way of preempting disputes. Libertarians reply that forming a state can't solve this problem, since it's clear that public officials can do a better or worse job at specifying the boundaries of people's property rights, which indicates that their moral authority to enforce property rules doesn't derive from the role they play in preempting disputes but from their ability to reliably identify people's actual entitlements. Public officials can permissibly enforce whatever property rights people *do* have, but they have no special insight into the scope or strength of people's rights.

Assuming that people have some enforceable property rights, public officials are entitled to enforce laws that prohibit theft, trespassing, and vandalism:

PROPERTY CRIME

Leticia sells baskets that she made from seagrass. One day, Vincent breaks into Leticia's house and steals her baskets with the intention of selling them. Leticia calls the police. The police break into Vincent's house and take back the baskets. They also force Vincent to compensate Leticia for the trouble he caused by preventing her from selling her baskets earlier.

In this case, Vincent has no legitimate complaint against Leticia or the police. If it's possible for anyone to have an enforceable property right to seagrass baskets, the baskets belong to Leticia. So the police do not violate Vincent's rights by forcing him to return them because he never had a right to them in the first place. This is another example of law enforcement that is consistent with libertarian values.

Though libertarians support law enforcement when it comes to assault and property crime, they are critical of other forms of law enforcement which threaten and punish people who are not liable to be interfered with. Specifically, libertarians hold that victimless crimes shouldn't be crimes at all. It shouldn't be a crime to sell sex, do drugs, work without a license, cross a border, sell loose cigarettes, employ someone at a low wage, charge a high price for toilet paper during a natural disaster, decline to buy health insurance, choose medical aid in dying, practice an unpopular religion, write an obscene book, homeschool children, or to do any of the thousands of other voluntary, permissible things that public officials nevertheless prohibit and public people from doing in most states. When libertarians talk about overcriminalization, they are referring to cases like these, where law enforcement interferes with people who are acting entirely within their rights and who are not liable to be threatened, fined, or incarcerated.

When victimless criminals can resist or evade law enforcement, they have every right to do so. Resisting unjust laws in minor ways is often praiseworthy, in the way that we praise and admire the victims of other kinds of injustices who resist mistreatment. The social theorist James Scott coined the term "anarchist calisthenics" to describe all the quotidian ways that people can undermine unnecessary and unjust laws by resisting and refusing to comply. For example:

ANARCHIST CALISTHENICS

Sasha notices that she often has the opportunity to break laws that she thinks are misguided and unjust. She jaywalks, fails to report tipped income on her taxes, illegally downloads movies, and hires undocumented immigrants.

Everyone agrees that Sasha is cool. She's not doing anything wrong, and she is subtly undermining a culture of mindless conformity and rule-worship. The only squares who wouldn't appreciate Sasha are professional political philosophers who believe in political legitimacy (Dan Layman—this is a callout!).

An even more extreme way to resist overcriminalization involves forcibly evading law enforcement and legal penalties:

JUSTIFIED RESISTANCE

Trae is wearing a psychedelic inspired t-shirt. A police officer approaches him in a public park and says that he believes that Trae may be trying to sell drugs in the park. The officer demands that Trae consent to a quick pat-down of his clothing to look for drugs. Trae refuses to be searched, and the officer tries to detain him. Trae shoves the officer to the ground and runs away.

Trae acts within his rights when he resists and evades the officer because the officer had no right to search him in the first place. Even if the officer reasonably believed that Trae was breaking the law, Trae wasn't breaking a just law, so he wasn't liable to be searched or detained. (Of course, it may be *unwise* for Trae to resist the officer if doing so puts him at risk.)

SELF-DEFENSE

Even though public officials are entitled to use force and threats of force to protect people's enforceable rights, they aren't legally obligated to protect anyone's safety. Even when a person is in imminent danger, police in the United States cannot be held accountable for failing to show up. Consider a horrific case:

DUTY TO PROTECT?

Jessica Gonzales had a protective order against her estranged husband, Simon. The order required Simon to stay away from her and their children. Simon kidnapped the children. Jessica called the police five times and visited the police station, but they took no action to find her children. Simon murdered the children and then showed up at the police station where he was killed in a shoot-out with the officers.

In this case, the US Supreme Court ruled that the police had no legal duty to respond to Jessica's calls and visits, even though she had a restraining order against her estranged husband and her children were in imminent danger. Though the police justify their power on the grounds that they are protecting public safety, citizens cannot count on the police to protect them because officers have no legal duty to protect specific people and they are given a lot of discretion in deciding whether to respond to reports of violence.

Because people have enforceable rights against violence, they also have rights to defend themselves against violent threats. This is one of the main reasons that libertarians support people's right to own guns. Though people commit violent crimes with guns, they also deter violent crime with guns. Consider an example that is inspired by a country song:

DOMESTIC VIOLENCE

Jane is worried that when her ex-husband is released from prison, he will return to their home to assault or kill her. To protect herself, she obtains a restraining order. She lives in a rural area, so she knows that if he returns, the police will be too far away to arrive in time to protect her, so she also purchases a shotgun. When he hears him approaching her house, she appears in the driveway holding the gun. Her ex-husband leaves the property.

Women are generally smaller and physically weaker than men, so they are unable to effectively defend themselves in unarmed fights. Firearms level the playing field, prevent men from using their physical advantages to terrorize and assault women. To paraphrase an old slogan, "God made men and women; Sam Colt made them equal."

Guns also played an important role in the civil rights movement by equipping even non-violent civil rights leaders with the means to defend themselves against violent racist hate groups. In the twentieth century, Black civil rights leaders would openly display firearms to protest the mistreatment of Black Americans and to signal that Black people were capable of defending themselves against white aggression. These open-carry demonstrations motivated white politicians to pass restrictions on gun ownership.

Even today, the right to own a gun can enable people to defend their rights when public officials fall short:

SELF-DEFENSE

Martin is a Black man living in a predominantly Black neighborhood where the police refuse to deter, investigate, or punish violent crime and property crime. Martin purchases a gun so that he can protect his family if people show up at his home to threaten him.

Martin represents one of the many Black Americans who live in areas that are under-policed when it comes to violent crime. Because the police do not have a legal duty to protect the people in his neighborhood, they decide to protect each other and themselves. A policy that prohibited people like Martin from purchasing the necessary means to protect their own lives and property would violate Martin's rights of self-defense.

PUNISHMENT

There are many different moral justifications for punishment. According to one view, people who violate other people's enforceable rights deserve to be punished. Another justification for punishment claims that it benefits victims and bystanders because people think that wrongdoers should suffer. Others argue that punishment enables public officials to express the community's values by publicly condemning people and excluding them from social life. Some people think that punishment is justified because certain criminals are so dangerous that they need to be incarcerated in order to prevent them from harming more innocent people. Or, punishment can be a way to deter other people from committing crimes. Punishment can also be educational or rehabilitative for criminals.

Whatever moral reasons justify punishment, there are also moral limits on public officials' authority to punish. Punishment should be proportionate to the crime, for example. Stealing a candy bar merits less than life in prison; murder merits more than a month of community service. Some people think that punishment should not last a lifetime because people can change so much over the course of a few decades that it would be unfair to hold a person responsible for his youthful choices throughout his entire life. Capital punishment is also controversial:

THE DEATH PENALTY

Ted killed many people. When he is finally caught, members of a jury deliberate about how the state should punish him. People on the jury agree that Ted is liable to be killed, but they disagree about whether he ought to be killed.

Some people oppose the death penalty for religious reasons, or because they are pacifists, or because they think that it is hypocritical for the state to kill people in order to demonstrate that killing is wrong. Others oppose the death penalty because they suspect that public officials and juries cannot be trusted to make such a high-stakes decision in light of the possibility of inequitable enforcement or wrongful conviction. On the other hand, supporters of the death penalty argue that some people are so bad that they have fully forfeited their right to life and the state should not be required to pay for them to live out their days in prison. Still others believe that the punishment of death is the proportionate response to the crime of murder.

Libertarians can consistently hold any of these views of capital punishment, depending on their views about the moral justification for punishment. Libertarians offer a more distinctive perspective on punishment when it comes to non-punitive approaches to deterrence. In general, libertarians argue that civil courts can effectively deter impermissible conduct and resolve disputes without getting the criminal justice system involved:

RESTITUTION VS. INCARCERATION

Grayden defrauded his investors, and he cannot pay back their investments. Public officials could either garnish Grayden wages for the rest of his life, or they could incarcerate him.

In this case, it would be better for everyone if public officials required Grayden to repay his investors instead of locking Grayden in a cage and preventing him from productively contributing to society. Though fraud should be a crime, private remedies can adequately punish and deter some kinds of crimes—requiring that criminals pay restitution raises the cost of committing crimes and thus disincentivizes crime. And even the victims of crimes may have reason to prefer non-carceral responses to crime in some cases; for instance, when such responses provide them with adequate compensation. Restitution and compensation-based remedies are also better for taxpayers who would otherwise foot the bill for Grayden's incarceration. And if it turns out that Grayden was wrongly convicted, it is easier to repay him whatever restitution he was required to pay than it is to adequately compensate him for the years he would have spent in prison.

All else being equal, less punitive sentencing is likely to emerge from a legal system that primarily enables victims to seek restitution for mistreatment, compared to a legal system where judges punish offenders on behalf of the political community. Still, a role for incarceration may remain. For example, some criminals might be "flight risks" who must be monitored until they pay restitution. Other criminals might simply be too dangerous to be released into the public. And for especially horrific crimes, victims and their families might prefer punishment to restitution. But for non-violent crime, property crime, and even some kinds of assault, a restitution-based approach to criminal justice could effectively deter wrongful conduct without unnecessarily limiting wrongdoers' freedom, and it would have the added benefit of improving victims' circumstances to a greater extent than incarceration.

Despite the availability of civil remedies, most people who commit crimes currently face criminal penalties that carry the possibility of incarceration. Mass incarceration occurs when a high percentage of a population lives behind bars. Mass incarceration is driven, in part, by high rates of violent crime. Some places are unusually violent. People in the United States, for example, are remarkably violent when compared to other developed countries. Comparatively high incidences of violent crime contribute to high rates of incarceration, which is not necessarily unjust because public officials are often entitled to incarcerate violent criminals. However, mass incarceration is morally objectionable when people are incarcerated for things that shouldn't be illegal in the first place, or when punishment is justified but unfairly applied, or when punishment is excessive.

Overcriminalization is one of the contributing factors to mass incarceration. Too many things are illegal, which means that law enforcement officers punish too many people for things that shouldn't be crimes in the first place The obvious remedy to this problem is that legislators should rescind laws that criminalize permissible conduct, executives should refuse to enforce bad laws, and judges should avoid sentencing people for violating unnecessary and unjustified laws. Failing these sweeping changes to the legal system though, ordinary citizens can do their part to undermine mass incarceration if they ever find themselves serving on a jury. The practice of jury nullification permits jurors to refuse to convict people for violating laws that shouldn't exist in the first place. Consider an example that is loosely based on a real case:

JURY NULLIFICATION

Ed was arrested for possession of marijuana in a place where it is illegal to carry large quantities of marijuana. During his trial, he represents himself. He tells the jury that marijuana prohibition is unjust, so even though he was in possession of marijuana at the time of his arrest, they nevertheless should not convict him of a crime.

In the United States, jury nullification is a legal way for citizens to prevent people from serving criminal penalties for illegal conduct when they judge that the law is unjust. If more people practiced jury nullification, fewer people would go to prison due to overcriminalization.

Mass incarceration is also morally objectionable when some people face harsher criminal penalties than others for reasons that are unrelated to the severity of their initial offence. In the United States, most of the people who are incarcerated in jails are awaiting sentencing. Pretrial detention policies are extremely disruptive for defendants. They cannot work or care for their children and jails are often dangerous places. What's worse, officials in some jurisdictions enforce pretrial detention policies that are far more burdensome to poor defendants than rich defendants:

CASH BAIL

Officials detain defendants who are charged with crimes before they appear in court. Officials release defendants who can pay cash bail, and if the defendant appears in court, they receive their money back. Defendants who cannot pay bail must remain in jail until their trial.

Cash bail policies are unfair because they effectively hold rich and poor defendants to different standards when it comes to punishment and incarceration. Most countries don't enforce cash bail policies because there are other, more egalitarian ways to ensure that people show up to their court dates. For example, public officials could release people based on pretrial risk assessments or they could impose financial penalties on people who don't come to court without requiring that they post bail as a condition of release.

Some critics of mass incarceration blame markets for the problem, at least in part. They argue that private prison companies have an incentive to lobby for policies that increase the prison population:

PRIVATE PRISONS

Harry and Marv are both convicted of burglary and assault and sentenced to 3–5 years of incarceration. Harry goes to a prison that is owned and managed by a private company. Marv goes to a prison that is owned and managed by the government. They have comparable experiences.

Here again, it's important to remember that the state isn't special. Those who run and work for public prisons are made of the same stuff as those who run and work for private prisons. There is little reason to think that private prisons are more likely to lobby for longer sentences compared to public prisons. Members of public sector unions also have professional incentives to increase the demand for prisons, public services for prisoners, and corrections officers. Politicians have incentives to support public and private prisons in their districts because prisons employ their constituents and both private prison firms and public sector unions contribute to local political campaigns. Most prisons in the United States are public prisons anyhow, so it is unlikely that prison privatization is a significant cause of mass incarceration.

PROSECUTORS

Public prosecutors also contribute to mass incarceration because they have the discretion to decide who to prosecute and they can influence criminal sentencing. Elected prosecutors' decisions are informed by voters' demands. This means that rates of incarceration often reflect citizens' own preferences about criminal justice.

Elected prosecutors contribute to mass incarceration when they have professional incentives to present themselves as being tough on crime:

TOUGH PROSECUTOR

Kendra is an elected prosecutor in a city where citizens value a tough on crime approach to law enforcement. She advocates for criminal penalties that include incarceration and long sentences so that she can say that she put a lot of bad guys behind bars.

The legal theorist John Pfaff argues that prosecutors are in part responsible for mass incarceration because their constituents are likely to punish them for failing to prosecute a criminal who then goes on to commit more crime, but are unlikely to punish them for advocating for longer sentences or for incarcerating a non-violent lawbreaker. For instance, news about an "under-punished" criminal who commits a violent crime has a greater impact on people's perception of crime and punishment than news about an over-punished criminal who remains in prison despite posing little risk to the public. Voters' preferences for public safety thereby discourage prosecutors from being lenient or merciful, especially when prosecutors have higher political ambitions that could be thwarted if they fail to prevent a violent criminal from reoffending.

In light of these electoral dynamics, one might wonder why some voters hold prosecutors accountable for mistaken leniency but not for excessive punitiveness. One reason is that some voters have false beliefs about public safety and the odds that they will be victims of a violent crime. Most voters don't look up crime statistics and calculate the costs and benefits of incarcerating more people for longer sentences. Moreover, a story about a particular violent crime tends to make more of an impression on voters than numbers on a page.

Voters' opinions about crime and policing are also part of their conceptions of themselves and their cultural group. For instance, "backing the blue" and "getting tough on crime" are, for many people, not just a policy stance but an expression of who they are.

PROGRESSIVE PROSECUTOR

Kelly is an elected prosecutor in a city where citizens value restorative justice. She advocates for non-carceral sentencing options and she declines to prosecute some criminal cases, so that she can say that she is making the city's justice system fairer.

Suppose that Kelly's approach turns out to be effective. Will more punitive voters update their beliefs and gravitate toward restorative justice? It's unlikely. Voters have little reason to investigate or correct their inaccurate beliefs about public safety because their individual votes almost certainly will not change the outcome of the election and therefore not change what public safety outcomes they actually get. So the benefit to them of correcting their beliefs is low. Moreover, it can come with a cost—the self-conception of someone who prides themselves on backing the blue can take a hit if they realize they've been on the wrong side all along.

POLICING

Libertarians have historically been at the forefront of police reform movements. Though police provide an important good when they enforce laws that promote public safety, they often use excessive and unnecessary force. In these cases, police threaten public safety in their own right:

SWAT RAID

Police suspect that Zaylen is selling illegal drugs, so they execute a no-knock raid on his house. They break down his door with a battering ram, throw flashbang grenades, enter the house carrying rifles, and shoot Zaylen's dog.

Even if drug prohibitions were just laws (which they are not!), this form of policing is clearly disproportionate and unnecessary. Police departments initially formed paramilitary SWAT teams to address rare, high-risk situations like hostage rescues or active shooter events. But in practice, police now use SWAT raids primarily for drug-related search warrants. These violent tactics are dangerous and unnecessary, since no evidence shows that using a SWAT team in non-emergency contexts makes law enforcement more effective.

More generally, law enforcement practices that give police officers wide discretion in deciding how to enforce the law can have a disparate impact on minority communities. Consider, for example, the practice of "stop and frisk," which empowers police officers to temporarily detain, question, and search people on the street, without first establishing any cause for suspicion of criminality. In some cities, police officers overwhelmingly used this authority to interfere with Black and Latino men. In these cases, a seemingly neutral policy that expanded officers' discretion to interfere with anyone was enforced in a way that primarily violated Black and Latino men's rights.

As critics of public employee unions, libertarians have consistently argued that indemnification provisions that protect police officers from civil liability unfairly require taxpayers to pay settlements for police misconduct against members of their own communities. Similarly, the legal doctrine of qualified immunity protects police and other public officials from being held personally liable for violating citizens' constitutional rights:

QUALIFIED IMMUNITY

Officer Oliver was called to a house to intervene in a domestic dispute. When the residents of the home don't answer the door, Oliver forcibly enters the property. He sees a large man, Roy, in the next room who appears to be running away. Panicked, Oliver draws his weapon. When Roy turns to face him, Oliver shoots Roy in the back, paralyzing him. Oliver then realizes that he entered the wrong house.

Plausibly, Oliver violated Roy's constitutional rights against being subject to an unreasonable search, and he also assaulted Roy. But the doctrine of qualified immunity protects officers like Oliver from legal punishment for unethical or risky behavior, In this way, qualified immunity weakens the incentives of officers to take care to avoid recklessly harming the people they are supposed to protect.

By analogy, if grocers were shielded from liability for selling tainted food, we'd expect to see an uptick in the amount of tainted food on grocery store shelves. For this reason, we suspect few people would support extending qualified immunity to private security guards, or business owners, or anyone else who uses force to protect their property and physical safety. In these other cases, well-intentioned people are still legally liable when they recklessly harm innocent bystanders in an attempt to prevent crime.

The fact that police work in the public sector does not ensure that they are more likely to work for the public interest. For instance, everyone's familiar with speed-trap towns where the speed limit on a country road abruptly goes from 60mph to 40mph. In these towns, police officers often have incentive to write lots of speeding tickets because the revenue from tickets directly finances the local police department. Consider also:

CIVIL ASSET FORFEITURE

Jonah was driving through a small town on his way to buy a boat. He was carrying $10,000 in cash, which he planned to use to pay for the boat. After a routine traffic stop, the local police seized Jonah's money, though they did not charge Jonah with a crime.

The proceeds from the seized assets in cases like that often go to the law enforcement agencies that do the seizing, which incentivizes unethical behavior. Here again, because public officials benefit from increasing the scope of law enforcement but do not suffer any disadvantages when they unjustly enforce the law, the system of institutional incentives does not effectively protect citizens from mistreatment by the police.

FELONS' RIGHTS

Because libertarians maintain that victimless criminals shouldn't be punished at all, there are a lot of formerly incarcerated people who shouldn't be classified as felons in the first place because their conduct should never have been a crime. That said, some well-intentioned political efforts to help felons, including wrongfully incarcerated victimless criminals, are likely to backfire or violate people's rights. For example, some felons' rights advocates argue that employers should not be legally allowed to ask whether an applicant has been convicted of a felony:

BAN THE BOX

After his release from prison, Tony is looking for a job. Many job applications ask Tony to reveal if he has ever been convicted of a felony. Tony checks the box, affirming that he has been convicted of a serious crime. These employers decide not to interview Tony for the job.

If Tony committed a victimless crime, then Tony should not have been convicted and incarcerated in the first place. Nevertheless, potential employers are entitled to ask if Tony was convicted and incarcerated. A policy that prohibited employers from asking applicants to disclose former felony convictions would violate their freedom of association rights by preventing people from choosing whom to hire based on the considerations that matter to them.

Ban the Box policies could also backfire by prompting employers to instead discriminate against all applicants from demographic groups that they associate with criminality, preventing non-felons from those groups from communicating this information to potential employers. And if applicants were also prohibited from disclosing their lack of felony convictions, an employment law like this would also curtail freedom of speech.

In contrast to private businesses, public officials cannot appeal to considerations of freedom of speech and association as grounds for limiting felons' opportunities to participate in politics and public life. That, in addition to the fact that some felons are victimless criminals, is why libertarian politicians and public intellectuals generally support restoring voting rights for people with felony convictions:

VOTING RIGHTS FOR FELONS

After her release from prison, Tina gets a job and starts a family. She is interested in politics because she is a taxpayer and a parent, and she would like to participate in the next election by casting a vote.

Assuming that Tina was liable to be incarcerated for committing a crime such as assault or theft, she forfeited rights such as freedom of movement, association, occupational freedom, and potentially voting rights during the time of her incarceration. But if she completed her sentence, public officials should then restore all her rights, including the right to vote. To do otherwise would be to indefinitely extend at least one aspect of Tina's sentence without any compelling justification from the state. After all, disenfranchising felons doesn't protect the public or express disapproval or facilitate rehabilitation; it doesn't satisfy any of the usual justifications for punishment. Rather, lawmakers are more likely to support felon disenfranchisement as a way of limiting the eligible electorate in favor of their party.

These remarks on felon enfranchisement may be surprising in light of libertarians' instrumentalist stance on political liberties, including the right to vote. But a commitment to felon enfranchisement follows from two libertarian principles. First, libertarians are especially attuned to the dangers of overcriminalization and excessive punishment, so they oppose any lifelong sentences on these grounds, especially for victimless criminals. Second, libertarians are always quick to point out when public officials limit people's entitlements and options without just cause, only in order to secure and expand their own political power. Felony disenfranchisement is yet another case where public officials constrain citizens' options in order to further their own electoral interests without considering the public interest.

REPARATIONS

When someone wrongfully interferes with another person, he should compensate his victim for any injuries and rights violations. The same goes for public officials:

WRONGFUL CONVICTION

Six years ago, Beth was sentenced to ten years in prison for burglary. New DNA evidence comes to light and exonerates her. Beth discovers that the prosecutors and police concealed this evidence at the time of her trial. She is released from prison and given compensation for being wrongfully deprived of her freedom by the state.

Beth is entitled to compensation because public officials caused her to go to prison even though she didn't belong in prison. Officials culpably manipulated the justice system to deprive an innocent person of her liberty.

Similarly, the public officials who enforce drug prohibitions wrongfully manipulate the justice system when they arrest and incarcerate drug dealers because drug prohibitions are unjust laws. As states increasingly revoke drug prohibitions, they should also compensate the victims of the drug war:

DRUG WAR REPARATIONS

Six years ago, Anders went to prison for two years after being convicted of various drug crimes associated with his illegal marijuana business. Three years ago, Anders's state legalized marijuana. Anders has had a hard time finding work since his incarceration.

In cases like these, public officials owe Anders compensation because, like Beth, public officials put him in prison even though he didn't belong in prison. Of course, there's a difference between the two cases. Beth didn't break the law, but Anders did. Nevertheless, if we're right that selling marijuana doesn't violate anyone's enforceable rights, then Anders wasn't doing anything unjust. Rather, Anders was a victimless criminal and yet police and prosecutors worked on behalf of the public to take Anders away from his family and lock him in a cage with potentially violent criminals for two years.

One objection to the claim that public officials should pay reparations for unjust law enforcement is that compensation is likely to be financed by taxpayers who were not themselves responsible for the injustice. Notice, though, that this point also applies to the case of Beth. So if this objection undermines, say, drug war reparations, it also undermines reparations for any wrongful conviction or for police misconduct and abuse. But this implication is implausible because people should be able to hold public officials accountable for mistreating them, even if taxpayers end up footing the bill. Additionally, someone will suffer an injustice regardless of whether or not reparations are paid. If reparations are paid, taxpayers will suffer an injustice; if reparations are not paid, the victim of wrongful conviction will suffer an injustice. Plausibly, failing to compensate a victim of a potentially life-ruining conviction is a greater evil than extracting slightly more tax revenue from taxpayers. Moreover, if taxpayers knew that they could be financially liable for unjust laws, they may be less supportive of politicians who support laws that would expand the state's liability for wrongful enforcement.

The libertarian case for reparations for state injustices is limited to instances where public officials violate people's rights by enforcing unjust laws. It does not necessarily extend to instances where public officials in the past violated people's rights by enforcing unjust laws decades or centuries ago. Consider unjust laws such as Jim Crow laws and the American slave trade. In these sorts of cases, the original victims of state injustices may no longer be able to be compensated. Whether compensation is warranted in these cases depends on whether public officials can identify a person who was made worse off by unjust law enforcement.

Consider a scenario in which Beth dies before finishing her prison sentence. In this scenario, Beth's children might have an entitlement to some of the compensation that would otherwise have gone to Beth, even though they were not themselves the direct victims of the injustice, because they were indirectly harmed by Beth's wrongful incarceration. Similarly, the children of people who were harmed by segregation and Jim Crow laws might have an entitlement to compensation.

In contrast, people who were born after historical injustices occurred, such as the descendants of enslaved people, have a less plausible claim to compensation for the enforcement of these unjust laws because, had history unfolded differently, they would not have existed at all. Different people would have existed. Since the prior enforcement of an unjust law was a necessary condition for the conception and subsequent existence of the descendants of enslaved people, it's tricky to explain how these laws made them materially worse-off, even though the laws were clearly a serious injustice against their ancestors. These comments reveal that there is far more to say about reparations for historical injustices than we have the space for here. But these arguments show, in broad strokes, the libertarian case for some kinds of redistribution aimed at addressing historical and enduring injustices.

SUMMARY

Libertarians are not against law enforcement as a matter of principle. Public officials are entitled to use coercive force to prevent violence and property crime, and the people who commit these crimes are liable to be punished in some way. Libertarians often express criticism of law enforcement because so many law enforcement agencies enforce unjust laws or enforce laws in ways that are excessively punitive or discriminatory. Libertarians are also mindful of the ways that public officials, including law enforcement, use the legal system to their advantage and avoid accountability for wrongdoing. These problems are exacerbated in contexts where law enforcement is subject to democratic oversight, because voters do not reliably support effective and proportionate law enforcement.

FURTHER READING

- Balko, Radley. 2021. *Rise of the Warrior Cop: The Militarization of America's Police Forces.* UK: Hachette.
- Brennan, Jason. 2018. *When All Else Fails: The Ethics of Resistance to State Injustice.* Princeton University Press.
- Flanigan, Jessica, and Christopher Freiman. 2020. "Drug War Reparations." *Res Philosophica* 97 (2): 141–168.
- Friedman, David, Peter Leeson, and David Skarbek. 2019. *Legal Systems Very Different from Ours.* Independently Published.
- Huemer, Michael. 2003. "Is There a Right to Own a Gun?" *Social Theory and Practice* 29 (2): 297–324.
- Huemer, Michael. 2018. "A Defense of Jury Nullification." In *The Palgrave Handbook of Philosophy and Public Policy*, edited by David Boonin, 39–50. Cham: Springer International Publishing. https://doi.org/10.1007/978-3-319-93907-0_4.
- Monaghan, Jake. 2023. *Just Policing.* Oxford University Press.
- Pfaff, John. 2017. *Locked in: The True Causes of Mass Incarceration-and How to Achieve Real Reform.* Basic Books.
- Scott, James C. 2012. *Two Cheers for Anarchism: Six Easy Pieces on Autonomy, Dignity, and Meaningful Work and Play.* Princeton University Press. https://doi.org/10.1515/9781400844623.
- Surprenant, Chris, and Jason Brennan. 2019. *Injustice for All: How Financial Incentives Corrupted and Can Fix the US Criminal Justice System.* Routledge.

7

ENVIRONMENTAL JUSTICE

Environmental justice refers to moral questions about how to equitably and efficiently manage natural resources. Often, the best way to manage natural resources is to enforce property rules that give people incentives to produce resources and to use them efficiently. But a persistent problem for libertarians is figuring out how to manage resources that cannot be effectively privatized, such as the atmosphere. In this chapter, we explain why libertarians of all ideological stripes can endorse policies like carbon taxes, which internalize the negative externalities of pollution-producing behavior. The chapter also explores the various ways in which state policies themselves have worsened environmental quality, including overzealous regulation of zero-carbon nuclear power.

CONSERVATION

The environmentalist movement began as a conservationist movement. As societies rapidly industrialized over the past few centuries, people began to worry that economic growth would coincide with the degradation of natural landscapes and the depletion of natural resources. In some cases, these concerns were justified. But these cases are the exceptions, not the rule. And for most natural resources,

DOI: 10.4324/9781003270720-7

the best thing that public officials can do to conserve and create natural resources is to uphold a market economy and enforce private property rights.

At first glance, the claim that private property rights are a force for conservation might seem counterintuitive. After all, if someone has the option to extract and sell a natural resource one might think that they would be more likely to diminish the supply of the resource. But as the supply of a given resource decreases, the price is likely to increase. When the price increases, it incentivizes consumers of that resource to use less of it. Price increases also incentivize producers to make more of it. And higher prices incentivize everyone to look for innovative substitutes:

COFFEE SHORTAGE

Due to a disastrous crop disease, there is a widespread shortage of coffee. Because the demand for coffee exceeds the supply, the price of coffee increases. In response, some people cut back on their coffee consumption, which preserves the remaining supply for the truly addicted night owls who just can't quit. Other people abandon coffee altogether and switch to tea or caffeine pills. A start-up creates a new product, Moffee, which tastes a lot like coffee but which is produced with artificial ingredients instead of beans. Coffee growers buy more land and plant more coffee beans than they previously did, so that they can restore the coffee supply to pre-disease levels while accounting for a higher rate of crop failure. Eventually, the price of coffee decreases and falls below pre-disease prices.

This case illustrates how markets can both conserve and create more natural resources. In the end, there were more coffee plants than before the crop disease not because of a centrally planned coffee restoration program but because the coffee drinkers of the world provided a market incentive to plant more beans.

The economist Julian Simon popularized this way of looking at the relationship between conservation and markets. Simon illustrated this point by describing how, in the 1600s, English people were worried that deforestation would cause a shortage of fuel for household heating and industrial ironworks. Anticipating energy scarcity, people developed coal as a new source of fuel. In the 1800s, the English worried that they were running out of coal, so entrepreneurs began investing in oil production as an alternative energy source. At each point, the conservationists who were worried about resource depletion failed to anticipate that entrepreneurs and innovators would develop sources of energy in response to anticipated scarcity.

Simon famously claimed that natural resources were infinite, because even though some objects in nature are in principle finite, people have an unlimited capacity to innovate by creating new resources and finding substitutes for existing resources. For this reason, the resources that are provided to us by the natural world are infinite, as long as we are free to find new ways to use them.

Paul Ehrlich was an environmentalist who argued that Simon was incorrect about conservation. Ehrlich predicted that the rising rate of human population growth was unsustainable, and that humanity would soon be unable to provide enough food and resources for everyone. If Ehrlich was right about conservation, then prices for raw materials would rise as they became more scarce due to population growth. If Simon was right about conservation, then people would innovate and find substitutes for raw materials and prices for raw materials would therefore stay stable or fall. To adjudicate this dispute, Simon bet Ehrlich that the prices for certain raw materials would fall as the population rose over a ten year period. Simon won the bet because prices fell over the course of the decade.

On its own, the Ehrlich-Simon bet couldn't settle who was right about population growth and resource conservation in the long run, because even Simon would predict that prices in raw materials would temporarily rise when they became more scarce. However, long-term trends in commodity prices also confirm Simon's view. As the population grows, prices in raw materials stay stable or fall even as people consume far more of them. This trend has remained true since the Industrial Revolution. Because there are markets in natural resources and raw materials, resource depletion is not a significant problem for humanity even though there are more people on Earth today than any other time in our history and even though today's people consume more than any previous generation.

ENDANGERED SPECIES

Even if we just focus on particular resources, such as minerals, it is unlikely that any given resource will ever be fully depleted because as a natural resource becomes scarce, it eventually becomes so costly to find and extract that people have incentives to use the existing supply more efficiently or to look for substitutes instead. Yet to claim that natural resources are infinite is not to say that every particular natural resource is immune to total depletion. Some kinds of plants and animals no longer exist in nature due to anthropogenic extinction:

PASSENGER PIGEON

Until the 19th century, there were billions of passenger pigeons in North America. By the 20th century, the passenger pigeon had gone extinct due to commercial hunting and habitat loss.

Though this example may seem to show that markets can lead to resource depletion, the extinction of the passenger pigeon does not discredit Simon's point. Rather, this case affirms Simon's broader point about the abundance of natural resources and further demonstrates his point about the importance of using markets for the management of natural resources. The passenger pigeon went extinct because no one had a property right in passenger pigeons, so hunters were free to kill them *en masse* and no one had an incentive to preserve the pigeon population long-term.

Consistent with Simon's argument, Americans who were eating pigeon quickly found substitutes as passenger pigeon populations declined. People don't eat pigeon anymore, but more chickens exist today than at any previous point in history. This kind of substitution shouldn't trouble conservationists any more than the natural turnover across generations of animals does, since the value of natural resources doesn't adhere to any specific natural object or object-type. Rather, the value of any given natural resource derives either from its contribution to overall welfare, to human well-being, or to ecological sustainability.

In any case, if anyone is especially concerned that passenger pigeons no longer exist, don't worry—the market offers a solution. Today, some entrepreneurs are developing genomic technology that could de-extinct the passenger pigeon in the next century. Here again, in market societies, people can find ways to prevent or even reverse resource depletion because markets incentivize conservation, substitution, and innovation.

The American bison almost met a similar fate as the passenger pigeon, but bison still exist today, in part because people could easily establish and maintain property rights in bison:

AMERICAN BISON

The American bison nearly went extinct during the nineteenth century because of over-hunting on public lands, driven by the market in bison hides. As bison populations dwindled, a few ranchers determined that the bison were so rare that it might make sense to raise a small number of wild bison on private ranches, primarily as an investment in their novelty value. When innovations in food production made it cheaper and easier to transport bison meat, ranchers had an incentive to create ever-larger commercial bison herds. Today, bison are no longer in danger of extinction.

Though it may sound counterintuitive, upholding property rights in endangered animals incentivizes conservation. To take another example, trophy hunting for endangered species is legal in parts of Africa, because local governments can use the revenue from tourism and the sale of hunting licenses to pay for conservation efforts, such as habitat preservation and wildlife management.

Some environmentalists claim that environmental conservation requires government intervention, such as laws that prohibit people from killing an endangered species, zoning regulations that prevent people from depleting natural habitats, or national parks programs. Yet libertarians often point out that non-governmental solutions can outperform a centrally-planned approach to resource conservation. Consider an influential case study by the economist Elinor Ostrom:

LOBSTERMEN

Lobstermen in Maine developed a complex system of customary rules and sanctions that prevented overfishing. "Lobster gangs" privately enforced traditional fishing norms, such as minimum lobster sizes and territorial limits for lobster harvesting. They also prevented newcomers from catching lobsters by cutting their traps and excluding them from their territory.

In this case, the lobstermen developed and enforced a system of property rights that advanced their collective interest in conserving the lobster population, without relying on governmental intervention. When Maine eventually passed lobster fishing regulations, public officials deferred to the lobstermen by codifying their long-standing conventions.

Contrast the example of lobstermen with what happened to the Atlantic cod population off the coast of Newfoundland:

ATLANTIC COD

In the mid twentieth century, large offshore fishing companies developed trawlers that could catch enormous amounts of cod. The trawlers also caught a lot of non-commercial fish, including capelin, which were a food source for cod. Because these offshore fishing companies did not have established conventions to prevent overfishing, the cod population plummeted.

Canadian officials responded to the collapse of the cod population by enforcing a wider offshore boundary for fishing and prohibiting foreign trawlers within the new boundaries. But Canadian officials, who had a poor understanding of cod life cycles, vastly overestimated the remaining cod stocks and set a high quota on total allowable catches. This policy enabled Canadian and American industrial fishing ships to further deplete the cod stock. Despite frequent warnings from inshore fishermen and scientists, Canadian officials did not revise total allowable catch quotas until the cod population was so depleted that public officials eventually banned all cod fishing from 1992 to 2024 to preserve the remaining stocks, which are still historically low.

The examples of the lobstermen and the cod trawlers demonstrate that governmental solutions are not necessary for environmental conservation, and in some cases, they can be counterproductive. The examples of the passenger pigeon and American bison show that markets can contribute to species depletion, but they can also play a role in preserving endangered species.

CLEAN AIR

The air we breathe is a public good, meaning that it is non-excludable (anyone can use it) and non-rivalrous (using it doesn't deplete it for others). If the air is clean, everyone benefits. If the air is polluted, everyone suffers. Because clean air is a public good, government officials cannot always preserve these benefits for everyone by enforcing private property rights. Unlike land or the American bison, an individual citizen cannot buy a parcel of clean air that only they can use or conserve. Though the real estate market partly enables consumers to pay for cleaner air, in a more general sense, people cannot choose the level of air quality they want to purchase in public spaces, nor can people opt out of breathing in public spaces.

So clean air is a good that everyone uses, but no one has the authority or incentive to preserve the quality of the air because private property rights in clean air are infeasible. If someone owns land, they can put up fence to prevent passing commuters from throwing litter onto their front lawn. People can't do that with the air. And air pollution causes millions of premature deaths every year:

AIR POLLUTION

Tens of thousands of commuters drive through the city every day. No one's individual car emits a perceptible amount of air pollution, but collectively they cover the city in smog.

Air pollution happens when commuters and factories undermine the quality of the air that everyone breathes because they are unwilling to sacrifice their own convenience or economic interests in order to provide a high-quality public good. Air pollution is especially harmful to people who live in developing countries that are still industrializing and dense cities where lots of people live and work.

Polluters consume the air like everyone else, and they benefit when the air is clean. But they free ride on other people's efforts to promote air quality, and worse, they even undermine the air quality. In this way, it is a negative side effect of economic growth, which is generally beneficial.

Political philosophers often claim that the moral importance of public goods like clean air provides one of the strongest justifications for taxes and regulations that could limit economic development. According to this view, public officials are entitled to coercively tax people to ensure that everyone makes a fair contribution to public goods and they also have authority to enforce laws that punish people for free riding and undermining the quality of public goods.

Yet libertarians often object to this line of argument on the grounds that a government that efficiently produces public goods is itself a public good. The same social and economic factors that cause pollution can also prevent effective clean air legislation from being passed and enforced. As noted earlier, people have little incentive to pay the cost of buying an expensive electric car to make an inconsequential contribution to clean air. But similarly, people have little incentive to pay the cost of casting an informed vote to make an inconsequential contribution to effective environmental legislation. This is not to say that public officials never pass clean air legislation—they do. Rather, libertarians raise this concern as a way of showing that the moral reasons in favor of providing public goods are not sufficient to justify state action, since that's also a public good.

Instead, libertarians favor two kinds of approaches to public goods problems like clean air provision. The first approach involves specifying the boundaries of people's bodily rights in a way that authorizes public officials to prohibit pollution by characterizing pollution as a kind of violence against people. The second approach involves enforcing property rights in a way that enables people to make mutually beneficial contracts that balance their interests in polluting against their interests in avoiding harmful pollution. In the rest of this section, we'll focus on clean air as an example of the first approach. Then we'll talk about other kinds of pollution in the next section to illustrate the second approach.

The influential libertarian Murray Rothbard argued that air pollution was a form of wrongful aggression. He argued that polluters were as liable to be prevented and punished for damaging people's lungs as any other assailant would be for physically injuring someone in a different way. Even if industrial air pollution were a consequence of economic growth and efficient travel, Rothbard argued that no one is entitled to violate another person's rights in order to improve their own, or anyone else's, well-being.

The issue with Rothbard's approach is that a world where public officials enforced everyone's rights against air pollution would be a world where public officials had the authority to prohibit an extensive range of human activity. A law that banned all pollution would require so much interference and coercion that each person's freedom to do what they wanted with their bodies would be extremely curtailed.

A more moderate version of this approach to pollution would be to say that pollution violates people's enforceable bodily rights, but that the boundaries of those rights are vague. As we mentioned in the first chapter, it is difficult to specify the boundaries of any theory of rights, and cases where people impose risks on others are also tricky cases for any normative theory. Yet the fact that it's difficult to specify and defend a consistent theory of rights and risk doesn't mean that rights do not have moral force. Rather, it suggests that public officials must enforce policies that protect the approximate boundaries of people's bodily rights, knowing that these boundaries are somewhat indeterminate.

In practice, this might mean that public officials can enforce people's rights against a certain level of air pollution by requiring all property owners to act in ways that keep air pollution below an air quality standard. Any standard is likely to define the allowable level of particulate matter in a way that is somewhat arbitrary due to uncertainty about which level of pollution would constitute a violation of people's enforceable rights. Nevertheless, an air quality standard could still approximate enforcement of people's bodily rights, in contrast to a fully unregulated approach.

Alternatively, public officials could enforce people's bodily rights against air pollution by holding polluters collectively liable for more serious rights violations. For example, officials might require polluters to pay for legal insurance so that they could then compensate anyone who could establish that they were physically injured by air pollution. This approach to pollution is also consistent with the view that people have bodily rights against being exposed to pollutants, though more trivial exposures do not constitute a violation of these rights.

POLLUTION

The second libertarian approach to pollution is more focused on finding a way to balance the welfare benefits of permitting pollution against the welfare-based reasons to prohibit pollution. To illustrate this second kind of libertarian solution to pollution, let's consider cases of noise pollution, public nuisances, and water pollution.

Like clean air, a clean, quiet, and pretty shared environment is a public good too. These are resources that we all consume, and no one can fully claim the right to control the shared environment or to exclude other people from using it. Because public spaces are shared, conflicts arise when neighbors have differing preferences about their shared environment:

LEAF BLOWERS

Doug has a gas-powered leaf blower, which he uses to maintain an orderly-looking lawn. Jen hates the sound of the leaf blower. Doug hates that Jen's lawn looks so messy.

People in Jen and Doug's position are sympathetic figures. Leaf blowers are anti-social and annoying, so to Jen, it feels like Doug is violating her property rights with his incessant landscaping. The fact that Doug owns his own house doesn't entitle him to ruin Jen's sense of serenity in her home. At the same time, Doug could say the same thing about Jen's garden full of weeds, bugs, and rodents, which makes it harder for him to enjoy the clean look of his own tidy property.

Both Doug and Jen might be tempted to head over to their town council meeting and pass a law prohibiting leaf blowers or messy lawns. But this kind of behavior is even more anti-social than leaf-blowing and lawn neglect! The mere fact that someone else's actions affect you doesn't imply that you should get a say over those actions. For example, like most people, we dislike the sight of Kansas City Chiefs gear, but that doesn't give us the right to tell Chiefs fans what they may wear. So too for anyone who dislikes the ways that their neighbors use their property.

Thankfully, public officials can enforce a win–win solution to Doug and Jen's problem by simply upholding each neighbor's property rights. Here libertarians draw on arguments that were initially formalized by the economist Ronald Coase, who describes a famous British legal case to motivate his theory:

STURGES V. BRIDGMAN

For decades, a confectioner (Bridgman) used loud machines to make candy at his shop, which he owned. A doctor (Sturges) built a consulting room on his property, right next to the confectioner. The doctor said that the noise and vibration made it difficult for him to see patients in the new consulting room, so he took the confectioner to court for being a public nuisance. The doctor claimed that the confectioner's noise and vibrations prevented him from using and enjoying his own land.

This famous case mirrors the everyday disputes that people like Doug and Jen still experience. When the doctor sued the confectioner, the English Court of Appeals held that the confectioner was liable for the noise and vibrations, just as some homeowners associations today side either with the Dougs or Jens in their community by prohibiting leaf blowers or upholding lawn care regulations.

But Coase argued that this is the wrong way to approach pollution and nuisance cases because it actually takes two parties to create a nuisance. Think of it like this. Before the doctor built his consulting room, there was no nuisance from the noise and vibrations. So it's not clear that the confectioner was entirely liable for interfering with the doctor, since the doctor's requirement that the confectioner abstain from making noise also constrains the confectioner's ability to use and enjoy his land. In this way, the case of the doctor and the confectioner is similar to Doug and Jen's dispute over neighborhood norms. They both have claimed a right to use their property in a way that diminishes the other's enjoyment and they both have a claim against their neighbor's presumptive demand that they change how they use and enjoy their own property.

Instead of appealing to authorities to shut down the confectioner's noise, we can imagine a scenario in which the doctor and the confectioner bargained over the doctor's right to stop the confectioner from using the machinery. That is, insofar as the doctor had a right to use and enjoy his property in silence, the confectioner could buy that right from the doctor or maybe just pay him to not exercise this right. According to Coase, if it wasn't too costly for them to bargain, this would have produced an efficient outcome because the confectioner could pay the doctor an amount of money that offset any financial losses the doctor suffered from having his consultation room next to the confectioner, building a new wall to dampen the sound, or from having to relocate to a quieter building. The confectioner would do this as long as the doctor's price was lower than the expense the confectioner would incur from having to change his production process or relocate.

Or, suppose that the doctor could earn an extra $20 per day if he could work undisturbed while the confectioner could earn an extra $16 per day by working in a way that disturbed the doctor. In this case, the efficient distribution of property rights in workspaces would assign a property right to the doctor so that he could work undisturbed. And if the doctor and the confectioner are able to bargain at low cost, they will arrive at this outcome whether the public officials initially grant the doctor or the confectioner the legal right to work as they please.

To see why, imagine a legal system where public officials side with the confectioner's claim that he has a right to use his candy machines on his own property, as he has for decades. This right is worth $16 per day to the confectioner, but it's worth $20 per day to the doctor. So the doctor proposes to buy this right from the confectioner for $18 per day. Why? Because the doctor would earn an extra two dollars per day if the deal goes through—the $20 from his work minus the $18 to buy the right to do the work. The confectioner realizes that he'll make two extra dollars per day under this arrangement as well—he'll get $18 per day due to the sale of the right instead of $16 per day exercising the right by making candy.

Both parties are better off, so the confectioner will sell the right to work as he pleases to the doctor, resulting in the efficient allocation of the property right.

Now imagine a legal system where the doctor starts out with the right to work undisturbed. Remember that right is worth $20 to the doctor and only $16 to the confectioner. So the doctor will only sell it for more than $20. Will the confectioner offer more than $20 for it, say $21? No! If the confectioner bought the right to work for $21, he'd lose $5, because it's only worth $16 to him. Therefore, the confectioner won't propose a sale of the right and the right will remain with the doctor.

As long as there are no transaction costs or at least sufficiently low transaction costs, it doesn't really matter how public officials enforce disputes related to noise pollution and other negative externalities as long as private property owners can make bargains that realize the most efficient distribution of the rights.

Returning to the case of Doug and Jen, both neighbors might propose a Coasean bargain, especially because they each have something to offer the other. A system of property rights that permits Doug to make noise and Jen to have a messy yard might be the efficient distribution if each party values using their property as they like more than the other neighbor is willing to pay them to stop. But the neighbors might be able to strike a bargain where they each make concessions to the other in exchange for their desired reforms. For example, Doug might agree to blow leaves before Jen returns home from work, as long as Jen permits Doug to tidy up her own yard while he's at it. Coase argues that these kinds of bargains are more likely to be effective and efficient when the costs of bargaining are low. In this case, if it is more costly for neighbors to petition a public official than to just talk to each other, then Doug and Jen can solve their pollution problems on their own without getting lawyers or legislators involved at all.

In other cases, public officials can stand in the way of Coasean bargains because they are not in a good position to balance people's interest in calm and peaceful public spaces against people's interest in using technology that makes noise. Sometimes, the loudest voices in the room are people who (ironically) support limits on noise pollution that make almost everyone else worse-off:

SUPERSONIC FLIGHT

Maris lives near the airport. She anticipates that the sound of a sonic boom would be annoying, so she opposes regulatory reforms that would permit supersonic flight.

Supersonic commercial air travel would improve countless people's lives by drastically reducing the time cost of air travel. Yet commercial airplane manufacturers have no incentive to develop safe supersonic technology because public officials prohibit non-military planes from flying faster than the speed of sound, primarily due to officials' concerns about noise pollution. These regulations are misguided for a few reasons. First, they are speed limits, not noise limits, which means that airplane manufacturers also have little reason to develop quieter supersonic technology. Second, they prevent people from judging for themselves whether they'd rather hear a sonic boom in a world with faster air travel, or whether they'd rather continue to live in a world where flights could take twice as long. And third, they foreclose the possibility that a supersonic airline could make Coasean bargains with the people who were affected by the boom, for example, by investing in communities along their flight paths or by compensating affected residents on a per-boom basis.

The Coasean approach to pollution, which gives people property rights and permits them to bargain over those rights, can also inform officials' approach to other kinds of environmental hazards. Consider the ways that public spaces are often dirtier than private property. People tend to take better care of their own property because they bear the costs of the mess and experience the benefits of investing in maintenance. Few people would stick chewed gum on their own furniture, but the bottoms of library desks and seats on the subway tell a different story. This general principle explains why environmentalists should support and encourage the privatization of land. In some cases, there are even environmentalist reasons to waive landowners' liability for the pollution that emanates from their property:

ABANDONED MINES

There are hundreds of thousands of abandoned hardrock mines in the American west. These mines pollute the surrounding land and waterways. Private actors have not attempted to claim, clean, or repair abandoned mines on public lands because then public officials could hold them legally liable for the cost of addressing spills and remediating any contamination associated with the mines.

In these cases, public officials' efforts to hold landowners accountable for pollution backfire by discouraging environmentalists and investors from purchasing abandoned mines. At the same time, public officials do not clean and repair the mines either. The way that officials enforce property rights in abandoned mines therefore discourages people from reducing pollution.

ENERGY

It's striking that many climate activists are so critical of capitalism, when market-oriented innovations are humanity's best chance for addressing climate change. We suspect that people associate climate change with free markets because the energy consumption associated with industrialization causes climate change. But it would be as much of a mistake to attribute climate change to markets as it would be to attribute climate change to the government because the largest producer of greenhouse gases in the world is the US Department of Defense.

It's true that private industry is getting rich off of climate change, but so are states. Public officials actively encourage people to extract and consume coal and oil so that they can manufacture products and provide services. Public officials then tax the sale of these products, and use the revenue to fund their other projects. Consequently, it's unclear whether we should label climate change a market failure or a government failure since both sectors produce carbon emissions and benefit from each other's energy-intensive activity.

If anything, people in the private sector often have stronger incentives to be environmentally friendly because they directly bear the costs of inefficiency, whereas public officials do not. To take one example, private sector companies have compelling incentives to adopt more fuel-efficient manufacturing processes, buildings, and vehicles because they pay for all the energy they consume and higher energy costs cut into their profits and share prices. In contrast, public officials do not profit from conserving energy, and taxpayers bear the costs of their inefficiency. This dynamic partly explains why non-market economies tend to be worse polluters than comparably developed market economies. Additionally, public officials penalize or punish state actors who degrade the environment less frequently than they tax or regulate industry actors who do the same.

Public officials also contribute to climate change by standing in the way of innovation and energy infrastructure reform. For example, public officials contribute to climate change when they enforce tariffs on solar panels and electric cars. Zoning laws that discourage residential density, which are often upheld under the pretext of environmentalism, also prevent people from transitioning to more climate-friendly living arrangements. Agricultural subsidies prop up high-emission industries. In each of these cases and more, state actors could help the environment by simply letting consumers make choices in a freer market.

This is not to discount the fact that private actors contribute to climate change, and that climate change is a consequence of industrialization. Yet going forward, it would be a mistake to view the private sector as the primary reason that climate change persists when state actors are currently the main barriers to climate solutions. Just as energy use is the primary factor that has caused the climate to warm, energy reform is the primary key to reducing climate change. Effective energy reform is possible, but public officials continue to stand in the way of clean energy infrastructure transitions worldwide.

If public officials could successfully implement energy reform then no other climate-oriented changes in behavior would be necessary. If public officials do not successfully implement energy reform then no other climate-oriented changes in behavior will effectively address the problem. And yet worldwide, public officials prevent citizens from accessing clean nuclear energy. This is the current situation in many countries:

NUCLEAR POWER

Public officials claim that they are worried about climate change. People investigate the causes and solutions to climate change and conclude that switching to nuclear power is the most effective way to reduce carbon emissions at the population level. Public officials pass a series of regulations that prohibit people from transitioning their energy infrastructure to nuclear power.

The regulations that stand in the way of reforming energy infrastructure for nuclear power provide a greatest hits of all the ways that public officials not only fail to provide public goods, but impede other people from providing these goods as well. Private energy companies are interested in selling cleaner energy to communities. Yet risk-averse public officials hold nuclear energy to a far higher safety standard than other industries and enforce strict land-use policies that prevent nuclear energy companies from building new plants or from transporting waste.

Some public officials oppose nuclear energy because their constituents work in the fossil fuel industry. But others oppose nuclear energy because their constituents falsely believe that it is more dangerous than the status quo. Voters fret over the chance of a nuclear accident while overlooking the substantial harms they suffer from the climate impact of fossil fuels.

In the absence of nuclear power, renewable energy may be a second-best part of the climate change solution. We say second-best because manufacturing some sources of renewable energy can be very energy intensive and existing limits on battery technology make it unlikely that renewables could fully replace fossil fuels today, though that might change if manufacturers develop better, more efficient batteries.

Public officials also stand in the way of energy infrastructure reform when it comes to wind, solar, and geothermal power. For example, short-sighted elected officials balk at the price of long-term energy infrastructure transition projects because they anticipate that these projects will not improve their short-term political prospects. And as noted, public officials are especially reluctant to invest in energy reform when many of their constituents work in the fossil fuel industry.

That said, public officials have recently supported some promising energy infrastructure reform policies:

ROOFTOP SOLAR

Public officials claim that they are worried about climate change. People investigate the causes and solutions to climate change and conclude that renewable energy can play a role in climate change mitigation. Officials decide to encourage people to install rooftop solar panels by passing a net energy metering policy, which requires utility companies to pay solar panel owners for the net energy they contribute to the electricity grid.

Net metering policies are popular in many states, and at first glance they are a libertarian-friendly, broadly market-oriented solution to climate change. Individual homeowners pay to modify their own property by switching to solar so that they can opt out of paying public utility companies for energy. Net metering challenges state-backed public utility monopolies and creates a more decentralized energy market, giving each homeowner the option to tailor their energy system to their unique needs. And the policy of giving solar homeowners a cut of the proceeds for their contribution to the grid uses prices to incentivize switching to renewables.

However, there are a few problems with this well-intentioned policy. First, net metering shifts the costs of non-renewable energy to low-income families who do not use rooftop solar. Rooftop solar is also an especially inefficient way to decarbonize the grid and rooftop solar programs deter larger-scale investments in solar arrays, which would be more efficient, affordable, and comprehensive. Net metering programs also overcompensate rooftop solar homes because they are not required to pay for their use of the grid and utility companies aren't free to decline to purchase energy from rooftop solar owners. And critics of net metering worry that rooftop solar households could become a politically powerful constituency that has a financial interest in the success of fossil fuel companies, since fossil fuel companies pay rooftop solar users for their contributions to the energy grid.

More generally, subsidies for renewable energy prevent manufacturers and consumers from fully internalizing the costs of producing renewable energy sources. But renewable energy technology will only become a viable solution to climate change if the sector becomes far more cost-effective and innovative. For this reason, policies that prop up less efficient renewable technologies, such as rooftop solar, may be counterproductive if they decrease incentives for innovation.

In addition to energy infrastructure reform, public officials who are concerned about climate change might also consider more radical solutions to the problem, such as geoengineering. Geoengineering refers to large-scale technological interventions that would cool the Earth without requiring people to cut emissions:

GEOENGINEERING

Bently is a billionaire who is fed up with global warming. He decides to launch giant mirrors into space to reflect solar radiation away from the Earth.

An advantage of geoengineering is that it doesn't require large-scale coordination on matters of public policy. A single private actor could provide the public good of climate change mitigation, in the way that the people who work for pharmaceutical companies invent vaccines and cures for diseases, thus providing everyone on Earth with technology that improves our health and well-being. Private citizens should not have to wait for public officials to solve problems that endanger us all.

A disadvantage of geoengineering is that it is risky, and people worry that the risks of geoengineering outweigh the risks of the status quo. To these concerns, it's worth noting that while some forms of geoengineering are riskier than others, it is unlikely that any kind of geoengineering would change the Earth in a way that is more harmful than the way that people have changed the Earth over the past three centuries through anthropogenic climate change. Additionally, radically reforming the economy to reduce emissions also carries risks. So at a minimum, geoengineering is worth considering as a short-term solution to climate change that doesn't require public officials or private actors to coordinate in order to provide a public good.

CARBON TAXES

In the absence of energy reform or geoengineering, public officials might also consider another, even less popular, libertarian solution to climate change—the carbon tax:

CARBON TAXES

Public officials enforce a tax on all economic activity that produces emissions. The tax would force producers and consumers to internalize the public cost of their choices. Officials could use the tax to fund or incentivize climate change mitigation initiatives.

Though libertarians aren't fans of taxes, lots of libertarians support the carbon tax, which preserves the benefits of a free market more than other kinds of climate change mitigation policies such as subsidies for clean energy or bans on technology.

Carbon taxes are sometimes called a Pigouvian solution to climate change, meaning that they reflect the economist Arthur Cecil Pigou's proposal that public officials should require producers to bear the full social costs of manufacturing by enforcing taxes on industry that are equal to the industry's social cost. Today, proponents of Pigouvian solutions to policy problems call themselves "the Pigou Club." Many members of this club support carbon taxes.

Coase was critical of Pigouvian taxes because he worried that they did not properly distribute the burdens affiliated with bearing the social costs of industry. For example, if public officials taxed a factory for the social costs of air pollution in proportion to the number of people who were affected by it, then the factory owners would be required to pay higher taxes if more people moved to the surrounding area, even if they only moved to the area because the air quality improved. In cases like these, Pigouvian taxes ignore Coase's point that it takes two to make a nuisance out of pollution.

On the other hand, a Pigouvian tax can also function as a way of responding to two difficulties with Coasean solutions to environmental problems. First, Coasean solutions don't really work for emissions—it would be prohibitively costly for major polluters to send representatives door to door to negotiate with each person who is negatively affected by global warming. And second, Coasean bargains might not work in cases where property owners have reason to worry that the terms of the bargain are not stable and one party might hold up negotiations when circumstances change. Economists call this the hold-up problem, and some people have argued that public officials should enforce Pigouvian taxes that approximate the terms that would result from a Cosean bargain without requiring anyone to engage in actual bilateral negotiations.

Pigouvian taxes are an especially appealing way to address climate change because all industries contribute to climate change and everyone is affected by it. A carbon tax would require everyone to offset their contribution to the social costs of climate change by paying a tax, and the tax would affect people in proportion to the social costs they imposed on others. Critics argue that a carbon tax would be regressive because taxes that apply equally to everyone are more burdensome to lower-income people. On the other hand, higher-income people consume more and emit more, and in this sense, carbon taxes would mirror a progressive consumption tax.

Another advantage of a carbon tax is that it enables government planners to use prices as a way of encouraging innovation. Public officials know that using fossil fuels as an energy source is economically beneficial but bad for the climate. Yet they cannot know the best way to balance the benefits of existing manufacturing and transportation practices against the benefits of different energy reforms. Officials don't need to figure out this balance though if they enforce a carbon tax. Instead, carbon taxes give all firms reasons to compete to produce cleaner energy in the most efficient way while still providing goods and services to consumers.

And even if government planners *did* know the most efficient way to cut carbon, they might not be motivated to subsize the most efficient ways rather than the most politically expedient ways. For instance, it's plausible that the reason why the US government subsidizes ethanol is not because it's best for the environment but because it's best for voters in Iowa, which is an especially politically powerful state. A carbon tax doesn't distort the market in favor of a particular industry or energy source; it treats all emissions equally. For this reason, carbon taxes straightforwardly address climate change whereas other energy policies are less efficient because they aim to achieve other political ends as well.

However, carbon taxes also have a few disadvantages. One problem with a carbon tax is that it could slow economic growth and deter innovation by making it more expensive for firms to produce and transport goods. Additionally, carbon taxes are politically unpopular, in part because they force producers and consumers to internalize the costs of their emissions. Another problem is that public officials could use the revenue they generate from carbon taxes in ways that are inefficient or unjust, as with any other form of taxation.

ANIMAL WELFARE

Many environmentalists are not only concerned about endangered species; they also care about animal welfare more generally. Libertarians disagree about whether public officials should protect animal welfare. Some libertarians think that animals do not have enforceable rights, so they should not have any legal rights. Other libertarians are vegans who think that factory farming is one of the greatest moral catastrophes of our time.

Some philosophical accounts of libertarianism overlook animals' interests because animals are considered property or parts of nature. Or, libertarians may discount the moral significance of animal suffering because most animals can't act autonomously, so they are not plausible rights-bearers according to many accounts of rights. Animals also do not work for wages, they have no purchasing power, and they aren't capable of rational decision-making, so the standard justifications for a market economy do not work when it comes to animals. Likewise, animals cannot advocate for their own interests in the marketplace or in the marketplace of ideas, and they lack political power. Animals are not citizens, and they can't vote or contribute to political campaigns. For all these reasons, many philosophical accounts of politics overlook animals' interests, including libertarianism.

A proponent of animal welfare might reject libertarianism on the grounds that markets don't do enough to protect animals. Factory farming is a profitable industry that is very harmful to the animals that are tortured and killed for human consumption. Critics of a market economy may point to this sad fact as proof that a libertarian society would not do enough to protect animals. On the other hand, if animals' lives are worth living, then a market in animal agriculture could be good for animal welfare, on balance, because farmers and producers have incentives to create more animals than would otherwise exist. Whether markets in animals are good for animals depends on the kind of animal that is being farmed and the conditions of the farm.

Insofar as some kinds of animal farming are so harmful to animals that it would have been better if the animals never existed, meat producers who are concerned about animal welfare have moral reasons to find new ways to produce meat and meat substitutes that do not involve large-scale suffering. However, incumbent animal farmers and public officials currently work together to pass and enforce legal barriers to ethical food innovation:

FOOD INNOVATION

Frustrated by the increasing popularity of vegetarian food, a state senator proposed a bill that would ban companies from using the term "burger" to describe plant-based foods. The senator proposed the legislation in an effort to protect animal agriculture producers.

Libertarians agree that producers have a duty to accurately describe the products they are selling, but meat producers are not entitled to exclude other food producers from using the term "burger." Legislation that prohibits manufacturers from calling their products "veggie burgers" is commercial speech censorship.

Policies that discourage alternative meat production are yet another instance of the state attempting to exercise its power to stifle innovation on behalf of entrenched market actors. An example of this kind of crony capitalism in the animal agriculture industry is proposed legislation that would ban the production and distribution of lab-grown meat. Although this meat has the potential to dramatically reduce animal suffering caused by factory farming, lawmakers are responding to their supporters in the conventional meat industry who aim to legally restrict potential competitors.

Cases like these show that threats to animal welfare don't just come from market actors; state actors interfere in the marketplace on behalf of incumbent producers, deterring innovation that would meaningfully reduce animal suffering. To make matters worse, domestic meat and dairy industries also enjoy subsidies, which are another way that public officials place their thumb on the scale in favor of conventional animal products. Here again, governments could help reduce animal suffering simply by removing the obstacles they've put in front of food innovators.

Some libertarians, such as Michael Huemer, argue that animal welfare legislation is one of the few kinds of legislation that public officials should enforce. According to Huemer, animals have moral status and people are not entitled to torture them to death.

SUMMARY

A libertarian approach to environmental justice issues from an appreciation of the positive-sum promise of markets. Whereas many people in the environmentalist movement view consumption as a form of depletion of the Earth's resources, libertarians argue that consumption is a way of incentivizing production. This is not to say that there are not cases where environmental harms are morally concerning. Libertarians are especially attentive to the ways that consumers' choices can impose costs on other people, for example, through climate change. And libertarians are also mindful that consumers can injure beings that lack market power, such as animals and future generations. Yet even in these cases, it is better if lawmakers charge prices for environmentally costly behavior and enforce property rights in ways that encourage environmental stewardship. This free market environmentalist approach is better than officials' attempts to manage resources through bans and regulations because it gives people incentives to efficiently use the Earth's resources in a way that minimizes the social costs of production.

FURTHER READING

- Bennett, Edmund H. 1880. "High Court of Justice: Court of Appeal: Sturges v. Bridgman." *The American Law Register (1852–1891)* 28 (6): 348–355.
- Christmas, Billy. 2023. "Pollution and Natural Rights." In *Climate Liberalism: Perspectives on Liberty, Property and Pollution*, edited by Jonathan H. Adler, 25–52. Cham: Springer International Publishing. https://doi.org/10.1007/978-3-031-21108-9_2.
- Coase, R. H. 2013. "The Problem of Social Cost." *The Journal of Law & Economics* 56 (4): 837–877. https://doi.org/10.1086/674872.
- Dourado, Eli. 2023. "50 Years of Silence." *Eli Durado* (blog), January 30. www.elidourado.com/p/50-years-supersonic-ban.
- Fowler-Puja, W. Briana, and Melissa Barbanell. 2025. "US Takes Important Step toward Tackling Its Massive Abandoned Mine Problem." World Resources Institute. www.wri.org/insights/us-good-samaritan-law-pilots-abandoned-mine-cleanup.
- Freiman, Christopher. 2021. "Picking Our Poison: A Conditional Defense of Geoengineering." *Social Philosophy and Policy* 38 (2): 11–28. https://doi.org/10.1017/S0265052522000024.
- Hill, P. J. 2016. "The Non-Tragedy of the Bison Commons." *PERC* (blog), June 8. www.perc.org/2016/06/08/the-non-tragedy-of-the-bison-commons-2/.
- Huemer, Michael. 2019. *Dialogues on Ethical Vegetarianism*. Routledge.
- Lomborg, Bjørn. 2001. *The Skeptical Environmentalist—Measuring the Real State of the World*. Cambridge University Press.
- Mankiw, N. Gregory. 2009. "Smart Taxes: An Open Invitation to Join the Pigou Club." *Eastern Economic Journal* 35 (1): 14–23.
- Nordhaus, Ted. 2024. "It's the Regulation, Stupid." *The Breakthrough Journal* 20. https://thebreakthrough.org/journal/no-20-spring-2024/its-the-regulation-stupid.
- Ostrom, Elinor. 1990. *Governing the Commons: The Evolution of Institutions for Collective Action*. 1st edition. Cambridge University Press.
- Rothbard, Murray N. 1982. "Law, Property Rights, and Air Pollution." *Cato Journal* 2 (1): 55–100.
- Sabin, Paul. 2013. *The Bet: Paul Ehrlich, Julian Simon, and Our Gamble over Earth's Future*. Yale University Press.
- Seal, Ben. 2024. "A Tragedy with No End." *Distillations Magazine*, September 5. www.sciencehistory.org/stories/magazine/a-tragedy-with-no-end/.
- Simon, Julian Lincoln, and Herman Kahn. 1984. *The Resourceful Earth: A Response to Global 2000*. Blackwell Publication.
- Taylor, Jerry. 2015. "The Conservative Case for a Carbon Tax." Niskanen Center. www.niskanencenter.org/new-study-the-conservative-case-for-a-carbon-tax/.

8

GLOBAL JUSTICE

Libertarian principles are not silenced at the border of a state—they extend to matters of global justice too. Libertarian principles can inform debates about the ethics of war, immigration, trade, and foreign aid. In this chapter, we outline the reasons why libertarians are skeptical of the efficacy of humanitarian military intervention and foreign aid and why the libertarian solution to global poverty is to open borders. Libertarians are uniquely well-positioned to defend free immigration, given the special priority they assign to considerations of liberty.

WAR

Libertarianism is a pacifist doctrine. Libertarians' most foundational moral commitments are to non-violence and cosmopolitanism, which is the view that all people have equal moral status regardless of the country they are in or where they were born. Nationalist wars offend against both of these commitments. Most libertarians are also fiscal conservatives, and the extraordinary financial cost of warmaking only adds insult to the far more grievous moral injuries we see in wartime.

DOI: 10.4324/9781003270720-8

Philosophically, libertarians are likely to support what is sometimes called a revisionist just war theory, in contrast to the orthodox just war theory. According to the orthodox just war theory, different moral principles apply to people who are using violence during wartime and people who are using violence in other contexts. The orthodox view holds that all combatants are morally equal, regardless of whether they are defending a just or an unjust cause, meaning that they are all equally permitted to use violence against enemy combatants and equally liable to be assaulted or killed by enemy combatants in turn. In contrast, revisionist just war theorists deny the moral equality of combatants. Revisionist theorists claim that whether a soldier is entitled to use violence or liable to be assaulted and killed depends on whether he is fighting for a just or an unjust cause. Revisionist theorists view the ethics of war in the same way that we might view the ethics of a bank robbery:

THE ETHICS OF WAR

Pat is a bank robber who has taken hostages in the bank as he collects money from the vault. Matt is a security guard who is trying to rescue the hostages and stop the robbery. Matt shoots at Pat and Pat fires back. Both are injured.

In a case like this, Pat was liable to be shot by Matt because Pat was acting unjustly. Pat was violating the hostages' and the banker's rights. In contrast, Matt was not liable to be shot by Pat because Matt was acting justly by trying to defend the rights of the hostages and the banker. When Pat shoots, he commits another injustice. When Matt shoots, he acts within his rights. The influential revisionist just war theorist Jeff McMahan argues that just and unjust combatants in wartime are not similarly situated. Just combatants are entitled to use violence against unjust combatants and just combatants are not liable to be injured or killed.

Revisionist just war theory is consistent with the libertarian conviction that the state isn't special. The fact that soldiers for an unjust cause put on uniforms and work for a government does not entitle them to injure or kill other people in the service of their unjust cause. Similarly, the fact that soldiers for a just cause represent a political entity doesn't mean that they forfeit their defensive rights. According to revisionist just war theory, the deep morality of war is the same as the morality of violence in non-political contexts. This is what libertarians say about the deep morality of all state actions.

In some cases, libertarians' commitment to pacifism conflicts with their conviction that someone who violates people's enforceable rights is liable to be interfered with. That is, libertarians generally oppose the use of military force but affirm that people have defensive rights, which anyone may permissibly uphold. These two convictions are in tension when it comes to humanitarian intervention, especially because libertarians deny that an authoritarian or repressive leader has the right to rule:

HUMANITARIAN INTERVENTION

Throughout the world, many people live under governments that systematically mistreat them. Women, religious minorities, and ethnic minorities are especially vulnerable to persecution. Public officials in rich countries could overthrow the governments that treat their people very unjustly and install new leaders.

In these cases, unjust political leaders are liable to be interfered with. They are not entitled to mistreat their people in these ways, so humanitarian intervention could in principle be justified on libertarian grounds. Yet even when humanitarian military intervention can be justified in principle, it is rarely justified in practice because military interventions are rarely the morally best option. Humanitarian military intervention often results in even more violence and fails to achieve its initial humanitarian aims. And military intervention is more morally risky than non-violent alternatives, such as refugee resettlement programs that permit the victims of repression and atrocities to migrate to safer jurisdictions.

Another libertarian objection to military intervention pertains to the cost. Public officials tax citizens to pay for national defense and other military projects, some of which are likely to be unjust, wasteful, and unnecessary. But the human cost of militarism is even more morally objectionable, especially when citizens are required to risk their lives:

CONSCRIPTION

Public officials have decided to go to war, but not enough citizens are willing to voluntarily fight. They decide to conscript men ages 18–26 to fight. Men who refuse to fight face legal penalties.

Libertarians view military conscription as one of the most unethical policies that public officials might feasibly enforce today. Military conscription involves public officials enslaving people and forcing them to potentially act immorally. It is unconscionable that public officials have historically forced so many men to endure both the physical risks of combat and the moral risk associated with potentially unjustly killing innocent people.

IMMIGRATION

Thousands of people are born on the wrong side of an invisible line. If they crossed the line, they would live longer, healthier lives and their children would have a much better future. It is difficult to cross the line, though, because if they are caught trying to cross it they could be shot or imprisoned.

The right to immigrate follows straightforwardly from basic libertarian rights like freedom of association and private property rights. If you own a business, for example, you have the right to hire a prospective employee who agrees to the terms of the job—it doesn't matter which side of the border the prospective employee arrives from. If you own property, you may sell it or rent it to an immigrant.

Letting people migrate across international borders is also one of the best ways to help the global poor. Immigration restrictions confine people to poverty and deprivation by telling them that if they cross an invisible line they will be shot or imprisoned. As an illustration of this point, consider an example inspired by Michael Huemer:

STARVIN MARVIN

Marvin is about to starve so he walks to the market. Sam draws a line between Marvin and the market and tells Marvin that he'll be shot if tries to cross the line. When Sam tries to cross the line, Sam forcibly restrains Marvin and sends him back to his home. Marvin starves.

Marvin doesn't die of starvation, though it might appear that way at first glance. Rather, Sam kills Marvin when he violates Marvin's freedom of movement and freedom of association and his right to defend and preserve his own life. Sam also violates the rights of the people who own the market and would sell Marvin some food.

Given that Sam is doing something that is seriously unjust, he is liable to be interfered with by any bystanders or immigrants who try to exercise their rights to immigrate:

BORDER GUARDS

Barry is a border guard. Diego is an immigrant. When Barry approaches Diego to detain him, Diego throws a rock at Barry and runs away.

Though libertarians generally oppose violence, in this case Barry and Diego are using violence or violent threats against each other. As in the ethics of war, it matters which side is acting for a just cause. In this case, Diego is defending his right to cross a border, while Barry is upholding an unjust immigration restriction. For this reason, Barry doesn't have a claim against Diego and Diego has the right to throw rocks at Barry or any other border guard.

For similar reasons, private citizens are under no obligation to comply with laws that aim to conscript them into enforcing unjust immigration restrictions. People should not comply with laws that require people to report undocumented migrants, for example, because to do so would be to facilitate the enforcement of an unjust law. And even though it's illegal, it's often praiseworthy when people work to subvert immigration restrictions by helping people cross borders:

PEOPLE SMUGGLING

People from South America travel to the United States to live and work. They pay people smugglers to assist them in crossing the border. If the people smugglers are caught, they are likely to be imprisoned for human trafficking.

The fact that people smugglers profit from helping people evade immigration restrictions doesn't discredit the good that they do. People smugglers who refrain from violence and uphold their agreements to safely transport migrants take substantial risks to help people move to a better life.

Free migration doesn't just save lives by letting people freely move about the Earth and associate with whomever they like; immigration has lots of good economic consequences too. For example, domestic property owners and employers benefit from immigrants who buy their property and work for them.

Of course, there are many objections to open borders. But few, if any, will persuade libertarians. Take the claim that immigrants "steal" jobs from natural-born citizens. As an economic matter, it's simply not clear that an increase in immigration brings about a decrease in the employment of natural-born citizens. Immigrants don't merely "take" jobs when they're hired, they also make jobs. Ask yourself this: why do *you* take a job? Presumably at least part of the answer is to make money. And why do you want to make money? Presumably because you want to buy things with it—like a café latte from the coffee shop down the street. And the same is true of immigrant workers—they spend the money they earn on things like café lattes, and thereby help create jobs for local baristas.

As an ethical matter, an immigrant who is hired over a natural-born citizen doesn't "steal" their job. As we've noted, an employer is a buyer of labor, just as you are a buyer of cars. When you decide to buy a Ford rather than a Chevy, you haven't stolen from Chevy. Chevy doesn't have a right to your money unless you sign a contract with them to buy one of their cars. Similarly, when an employer decides to hire an immigrant rather than a natural-born citizen, they haven't stolen from the citizen. The citizen doesn't have a right to that job unless the employer has already signed a contract with them.

Others worry that immigration will disrupt a country's culture or politics. That's certainly possible, but the exercise of many other rights can disrupt a country's culture or politics:

2030

The year is 2030. Sports bars across the United States now show hockey more often than football. Copies of The Communist Manifesto *are flying off the shelves of American bookstores. The Simpsons has been cancelled.*

In this (dystopian?) scenario, American culture and politics have been disrupted. Even so, the state couldn't forcibly interfere with the freedom of bars to show the sports of their choice, the freedom of bookstores to sell the books of their choice, or the freedom of television channels to air the shows of their choice. In the same vein, even though immigrants may change some of the food, language, media, and politics of the country they enter, that doesn't mean the state may forcibly interfere with their decision to move.

Now, the objection you're mostly likely to hear from fiscal conservatives is that "you can't have open borders and a welfare state." The concern here is that immigrants will consume government services to the detriment of taxpayers. Yet this argument overlooks that immigrants also contribute to the welfare state, both because they pay taxes and also because, insofar as increased immigration lowers the price of labor, taxpayers save on services from medical providers including home health aids and foreign-born doctors.

In any case, the objection that you can't have open borders and a welfare state has less force against libertarian theories of justice, given that a libertarian society would either not have a welfare state or at least have a scaled back one. But you might still be wondering how libertarians think about immigration within the context of the non-libertarian status quo. Given that there *are* massive entitlement systems, should states restrict immigration to protect them?

Even setting aside the empirical claim we addressed earlier, we'll offer two replies. First, people have the right to exercise their freedoms, such as the freedom to immigrate, even if doing so creates costs for taxpayers. Someone may ride a motorcycle even though there's a chance they could crash and receive treatment at a hospital that receives public funds.

Second, libertarians often propose a targeted solution to the fiscal challenge that immigration may pose. That is, if the concern is that immigrants will overconsume tax-financed services, don't restrict immigration outright, but rather restrict immigrants' access to those services:

GUEST WORKERS

Some workers in Bangladesh travel to Qatar to work. They know that the conditions are brutal but they take it to be their best option. Public officials in Qatar do not provide the Bangladeshi workers a path to citizenship or any state benefits. Bangladeshi workers are not permitted to permanently settle in Qatar.

The main objection to guest worker proposals is that they treat immigrants unfairly. But preventing immigration entirely treats prospective immigrants even *more* unfairly. Outright immigration restrictions deprive immigrants of an option they'd have if officials allowed a targeted solution, such as a guest worker program. One benefit of guest worker programs is that they can target areas of the labor market where employers struggle to hire people, thus addressing the public's concerns that immigrants will contribute to domestic unemployment. And public officials can also lower the cost of public programs, such as government-provided healthcare, if they permit nurses, doctors, and in home caregivers to come as guest workers.

Immigrants themselves are in the best position to decide whether moving to a new country without receiving its standard government benefits is better for them than remaining in their current country receiving the benefits it makes available to them. At a minimum, prospective immigrants are no worse off for having the option to move to a country without receiving its standard benefits, given that they can always decline the option—and they are potentially better off for having the option.

TRADE

The case for trade across borders is the same as the case for trade within borders. Most notably, people trade because they each expect to benefit. Though shopping at a big box store doesn't feel like an especially altruistic act, whenever someone buys something thing was made in a developing country, they helped themselves by also benefiting the global poor:

NU METAL T-SHIRT

The year is 2001. Chris Freiman is looking through a rack of nu metal merchandise when he sees a Limp Bizkit t-shirt selling for $25. He immediately buys the shirt and wears it to school. Ten years later Chris found a woman *who agreed to marry him, That's not relevant to the example, but we're just throwing it out there to give all the other Bizkitheads hope.*

In this example, Chris hands over $25 for the t-shirt because he values the shirt more than the $25. The vendor hands over the shirt for $25 because they value the $25 more than the shirt. The trade makes both Chris and the vendor better off. Indeed, both parties wouldn't agree to the trade if they *didn't* expect to benefit. This fact doesn't change when the trade occurs across borders:

NU METAL T-SHIRT, PART 2

The year is 2001. A buyer is flipping through a catalogue of nu metal merchandise and sees a Limp Bizkit t-shirt selling for $10. He mails off a check and the shirt arrives a week later from Bangladesh.

Here again, the buyer hands over $10 for the t-shirt because he values the shirt more than the $10; the manufacturer hands over the shirt for $10 because he values the $10 more than the shirt—this point stands even though the shirt arrives from Bangladesh.

One objection to open borders that we discussed earlier—namely that it will deprive domestic workers of a job—is also raised against free trade. If you buy the nu metal merchandise made by Bangladeshis, you'll put Americans out of work. Our responses to this objection to free trade are similar to the ones we gave in the context of open borders.

First, if the good Chris buys from overseas is cheaper than one made domestically, he'll have more money left over to spend on other goods and services. So buying the cheaper Bangladeshi shirt might result in fewer jobs for American garment workers, but it means Chris will have more money available to spend on expensive Philadelphia Eagles memorabilia.

Second, people generally may exercise their rights in ways that result in a loss of jobs for American workers:

ROOMBA

Claire has been employing a neighbor to clean her house every other week. She sees an ad for a Roomba and learns that it can clean her floors for significantly less money. She buys the Roomba and lets her housecleaner go.

Maybe it would be nice of Claire to continue to employ her neighbor as a greater cost to herself, but at a minimum, it shouldn't be *illegal* to replace the neighbor with the Roomba. It's Claire's money and she has the right to spend it on a machine rather than labor. We can make a similar point about occupational choice:

CHEF

Gordon is a world-class chef. Thousands of customers flock to his restaurant to taste his food. He suddenly loses his passion for cooking and retires, causing the restaurant to close and all of its employees to lose their jobs.

Even if you aren't a libertarian, you probably agree that Gordon has the right to quit his job—this decision is protected by his right of occupational choice. Here again, the mere fact that the exercise of a right can result in job loss isn't enough to justify infringing on that right.

Together, these considerations amount to a presumptive defense of free trade with manufacturers in other countries. But some critics of global trade worry that it exploits workers in poor countries. To this criticism, it's worth looking at the reasons why people in poor countries take manufacturing jobs:

SWEATSHOP

Anvi lives in a very poor country. Just about everyone in her community is a subsistence farmer. Her family cannot afford to support her, so they pressure her to marry a much older family friend when she turns sixteen. Anvi doesn't want to get married, so she travels to a nearby city and applies to work in a garment factory. The factory pays $6 per day, which is 3x what she could have earned in her hometown. She works long hours in a dangerous environment.

Sweatshops should not be banned, or even discouraged, because shutting down sweatshops simply removes an option that's available to someone who is already suffering from a lack of options. Consider an analogous case:

SALTINES

Anvi is starving. However, she has very little money and so can only afford saltines. Public officials prohibit her from buying the saltines because she really needs a full meal.

It's clear that the saltine ban is bad for Anvi. It's true that eating a full meal is better for her than eating saltines, but stopping her from buying saltines doesn't thereby give her a full meal. It just takes away the saltines, leaving her hungrier than she would be without the ban. Similarly, banning sweatshop employment doesn't thereby provide sweatshop workers with good jobs—it simply leaves them with a worse job or no job at all. (After all, if there were better jobs available, the worker wouldn't have chosen to work in the sweatshop in the first place.)

Of course, you might be thinking that the solution here is precisely to help sweatshop workers find better jobs. We agree. The most effective way of doing so is to enable them to immigrate to places where jobs with higher pay and better working conditions are available.

People also should not advocate for developing countries to enforce occupational health and safety standards, minimum wage laws, or maximum hour laws. For one thing, these kinds of laws violate the economic freedom of workers in developing countries just as they violate the economic freedom of workers in richer countries. For another, if a poor country enforced workplace regulations like these, it would be more expensive for a company to hire workers in that country. This could result in capital flight, which refers to cases where multinational companies relocate from one country to another so that they can avoid taxes or regulations that make it more expensive for them to do business. Even if a company can't find a more favorable regulatory environment by moving, they might also leave in response to regulation if they can access a more productive workforce for the same price. Poor countries attract foreign investment by offering low-cost labor. Regulations that raise the price of labor discourage economic development in these countries. Another reason to oppose regulations of sweatshops is that these regulations could send low-wage laborers to more dangerous labor markets, such as farm work, domestic services, or work in illegal industries.

Other barriers to trade are similarly misguided. Tariffs might protect domestic jobs, but they make consumer goods more expensive for everyone else and deter economic development abroad. Or, consider economic policies that punish citizens of countries whose public officials act immorally:

ECONOMIC SANCTIONS

When a large country attacked one of its neighbors, other countries enforced restrictions on trade with companies from the large country. Private businesses also closed their stores, restaurants, and factories in that country.

Public officials and private companies use sanctions to express their disapproval of immoral political regimes. Either way, they are unlikely to provoke positive political reform. Private companies are entitled to refuse to do business with people in countries whose governments they think are immoral, but they likely harm themselves by turning away potential consumers. But public officials who enforce sanctions violate the economic freedom of their own citizens by restricting their ability to trade with people abroad. And the people in an immoral state who bear the costs of sanctions aren't just the public officials; sanctions punish ordinary citizens for their government's injustices.

FOREIGN AID

Most countries don't spend much on foreign aid because public officials don't have electoral incentives to spend money on people in other countries, and because foreign aid is often ineffective or counterproductive. That said, of all the things that governments do, providing a small amount of aid to the global poor is a comparatively good use of taxpayer money.

Foreign aid is not the best way to help the poorest people in the world. The best way to help the global poor involves opening the borders to welcome refugees and economic migrants, eliminating tariffs and allowing free trade, and using the patent system to incentivize lifesaving vaccine developments. Economic development is the only long-term, sustainable solution to global poverty, and critics of foreign aid worry that aid can become a "resource curse" that people in poor countries rely on instead of building infrastructure and institutions that would facilitate economic growth.

These are legitimate criticisms of foreign aid, but aid can also save millions of people. For example:

PEPFAR

US President George W. Bush authorized a multi-billion dollar public health initiative called PEPFAR, which was designed to expand people's access to antiretroviral treatments for HIV/AIDS in Africa. To date, the PEPFAR program has prevented more than 25 million premature deaths from HIV/AIDS.

PEPFAR demonstrates that targeted aid can, in some contexts, be a force for good in the world. This point is especially salient in light of the fact that the other signature foreign policy initiatives of the George W. Bush administration were military interventions in Iraq and Afghanistan. Each war resulted in tens of thousands of premature violent deaths, even though they were defended at the time as a way of empowering Iraqi and Afghan people. Which is to say, of all the ways that a rich country could come to the assistance of people in other countries, foreign aid has a better chance of actually helping people than the standard alternatives.

Not all foreign aid is as effective as PEPFAR, though. Like any government-funded assistance program, foreign aid can be wasteful, inefficient, and counterproductive. Aid programs can inadvertently fund corrupt public officials. They can also do more harm than good when aid workers are unfamiliar with local people's needs and values. Here is a proposal for evaluating whether foreign aid program is worth funding:

THE CASH BENCHMARK

Researchers have studied cash transfers in developing countries for decades, so they have a fairly good understanding of the health and wellbeing benefits of direct payments. If proponents of a foreign aid program can establish that it benefits recipients more than giving them the cash would, then the program is worth funding.

In one sense, this standard is paternalistic because it says that public officials may choose to give people bed nets to prevent malaria instead of cash on the grounds that bed nets are likely to be more beneficial than an equivalent payment to the people affected by the program. Yet libertarians would not take issue with his kind of paternalism because they don't think that the recipients of aid have an enforceable right to assistance in the first place. Insofar as foreign aid is a pure benefit, officials in wealthy countries are entitled to decide what form that benefit takes.

A related criticism of foreign aid is that officials in rich countries can manipulate public officials in countries that rely on foreign aid. But here again, this critique of foreign aid fails to establish how providing people with an option is harmful. Though it is true that aid often comes with conditions, as long as people retain the freedom to refuse the aid, people shouldn't object to conditional aid because they do not have an enforceable entitlement to the aid in the first place.

Citizens might object to spending on foreign aid by arguing that taxpayer dollars should preferentially benefit the people who pay the taxes. One implication of this view, though, is that domestic taxation should not be progressive because that involves transfers from those who pay more in taxes to those who pay less or none at all. A critic of foreign aid might argue that transfers from the domestic rich to the domestic poor are better than transfers to the global poor because they value nationalistic solidarity. Libertarians are opposed to nationalism, but even granting that people might have an interest in prioritizing their compatriots when it comes to assisting the poor, the amount of money spent on foreign aid is typically so small that one would have to entirely discount foreigners' interests to make the case that foreign aid would be better spent at home, for example, by marginally increasing the amount of cash that states transfer to elderly citizens.

The foregoing case for (some) foreign aid is contingent. Libertarians oppose redistributive taxation. But insofar as public officials are committed to enforcing redistributive tax policies, high-quality foreign aid programs like PEPFAR are better than other uses of the revenue. A better alternative to foreign aid would be for citizens in rich countries to directly donate some of their income to the global poor:

EFFECTIVE ALTRUISM

Will gives 10% of his income to a program that provides antimalarial bed nets to people in Africa. The program is effective, and Will's contribution prevents several premature deaths every year.

Critics of effective altruism sometimes claim that it is a neoliberal or libertarian solution to problems that governments should solve. In contrast, libertarians argue that individual donations to global poverty relief are far better than foreign aid or any other governmental solution because they are freely given and because private aid organizations have stronger incentives to show their donors that they are effective.

A libertarian critic of effective altruism may argue that people in rich countries shouldn't give to the global poor because what they really need is economic development, not handouts. Yet this line of argument makes the same mistake that critics of libertarianism make when they claim that sweatshop workers really need education, not low wage jobs. Even if it's true that economic development would benefit the global poor more than bed nets or cash transfers, many people still live in places where their economic opportunities are very limited. In these contexts, effective altruism is a second-best way of helping people in theory, but it's the best available option in practice.

SECESSION

Some libertarians talk as if smaller governments are in principle morally better than larger governments. Anyone who's ever been to a school board meeting or heard stories from people regulated by homeowners associations should immediately see why that's not true. From a libertarian standpoint, what matters is whether a government is just, not whether it's big or small.

This is why libertarians are generally instrumentalists about federalism. They support state officials' rights to govern when state officials respect individual rights and uphold free markets, and they support federal legislation that limits states' authority to constrain individual rights or free markets. Likewise, libertarians should support a federal system, where power is spread across many layers of government, in cases where jurisdictions compete to provide better governance and more protections for individual rights. Libertarians should not support federalism in cases where multiple layers of government mean that there are redundant public officials who all operate as barriers to economic development and enforcers of unjust laws.

An instrumentalist view of federalism also informs libertarian perspectives on states' rights to secede:

STATES' RIGHTS

A geographically constrained group of X people try to secede from a larger country of Y people, hoping to form their own state.

In this very abstract case, we can't know whether the X people should have a right to secede from the Y people because we don't know if the X people's state would be freer and more just than the country of Y people. If the X people are southerners in the pre-civil war American South who want to enforce laws that uphold slavery, then they have no right to secede from the United States. In contrast, if the X people are free-market capitalists who want to leave a communist dictatorship, then they have a right to secede and bring about a more just state.

In other words, libertarians only acknowledge political groups' entitlements to secede from their governments when the secessionist groups would uphold more just (libertarian) institutions. The size of a government isn't morally significant; the policies that government enforce are what matters.

Libertarianism does offer a way out, of sorts, for groups of like-minded people to get away from the dominant political culture without formally seceding—people can purchase property in places that align with their values and political preferences. Throughout the nineteenth century there were hundreds of intentional political communities throughout the United States. Often, their members were motivated to move to a region where they could live with people who shared their religious zeal or utopian political ideals.

Some of these communities grew to gain substantial political power in local government, while others opted out of political life to live on their own. A few persist to this day. Mormon people in Utah took the first path and Amish people in Pennsylvania are an example of the second. These communities didn't secede from the government—they are still subject to the same laws and regulations as everyone else. But because they were able to purchase private property in an area with like-minded people, they were able to exercise a kind of self-determination within the jurisdiction of a larger state.

A more extreme version of self-determination within the boundaries of a state involves communities that attain exemptions from some of the laws that govern the rest of the area. For example, in Denmark there is a neighborhood in Copenhagen called "Fristaden Christiana" or Freetown Christiania:

FREETOWN CHRISTIANIA

The residents of Freetown initially occupied a small neighborhood as a community of squatters. Within the boundaries of the neighborhood, they permitted the sale of cannabis and mostly governed their own territory.

For decades, the Danish government did not interfere much with the Freetown Christiania residents, even passing the "Christiania law" to exempt the neighborhood from a range of laws, permitting them to self-govern as a social experiment. Eventually, after a series of violent incidents, the Christiania law was repealed and the residents were prompted to collectively purchase the land they were occupying. Yet the historical neighborhood of Freetown Christiania is an example of a libertarian alternative to secession and property ownership. In this case, public officials permitted some residents to opt out of some parts of the criminal-legal system, providing an island of liberty within the boundaries of a state.

Today, charter cities operate along a similar idea to Freetown Christiania. Many countries have geographically constrained areas where people are exempt from economic regulations or taxes. In some charter cities, there are no zoning laws or pharmaceutical regulations or licensing requirements at all. State actors may attempt to establish charter cities as a way of attracting foreign investment, tourism, and jobs. (Although this does raise the question of why government officials don't simply enforce more libertarian policies for everyone, if charter cities have such substantial economic benefits.)

The Free State Project is another way that people might collectively reshape their political environment in a more libertarian direction:

FREE STATE PROJECT

Libertarians in the United States choose to move to New Hampshire so that they can collectively influence the New Hampshire state government in support of more libertarian policies such as the abolition of zoning laws and low taxes.

As we argued in a previous chapter, most libertarians are democratic instrumentalists. People criticize libertarians because libertarians do not value political liberties or think that a law is legitimate just because a majority of citizens voted for it. But the Free State Project is a winner for both sides. Members of the Free State Project exercise their political liberties to vote for more libertarian policies and to run for office so that they can enact libertarian legislation. If it works, members of the project will advance both democratic and libertarian ideals. Who could complain?

The last way that libertarian-minded people have attempted to secede from a larger state involves abandoning the jurisdiction of the state system entirely:

SEASTEADING

Private companies manufacture floating homes, underwater habitats, cruise ships, and (eventually) floating cities in international waters, beyond the jurisdiction of any state. Seasteaders choose to live in the ocean for the political and economic freedom it brings.

There aren't many seasteaders today, but they anticipate that new technology in floating construction will make it cheaper and easier for people to relocate to international waters. Seasteading isn't necessarily libertarian—people could create a floating communist city that enforces lots of paternalistic laws. But seasteading is attractive to libertarians because it could potentially be a way for people to feasibly live in a truly stateless society.

COLONIALISM

Colonialism was a historical practice where governments would send officials to territories outside their borders and enforce laws in those territories that were often harmful to the people who lived there. Obviously, libertarians oppose the historical practice of colonialism because colonialist leaders were violent toward native populations and they enforced repressive laws. Libertarians are also critical of colonial powers' mercantilist economic ideology, wherein they extracted resources and labor from other territories to raise money for their own governments. Even when colonial powers left the territories they governed, they had changed the institutions and economies in those places so much that weak governance and ongoing ethnic and religious conflicts persist in many formerly colonized territories.

Libertarians also hold that people who violate others' property rights have duties to compensate the people they wronged and to return the property they stole. One might think that this kind of an argument could justify reparations for colonial rule:

COLONIALISM REPARATIONS

European colonists took tens of thousands of objects from colonial territories, killed, captured, enslaved, and sold people, and enriched themselves through the extraction of natural resources. Today, people in postcolonial countries argue that the taxpayers who are the descendants of European colonists should return the objects their ancestors took and compensate them for the violence, stolen labor, and stolen resources their ancestors inflicted.

Yet this case for reparations is different from the case for requiring that thieves and criminals compensate their victims. After all, people don't ordinarily hold children liable for their parents' crimes, much less their grandparents' crimes. And the case for colonial reparations is weaker than other arguments for reparations because it's difficult to justify compensation to descendants for injustices that were committed against someone's ancestors when the descendants only exist because history unfolded in the particular way that it did.

Turning to the claim that the descendants of European colonists should return the objects that their ancestors took, this claim appeals to a theory of property rights which gives people the right to reclaim unjustly acquired property on the basis of their ethnicity or national heritage. Libertarians think that a system of property rights should facilitate mutually beneficial, voluntary exchanges, not ethno-nationalist political projects. But arguments for repatriation seem to appeal to a theory of property rights that assigns rights on the basis of a person's ethnic or nationalistic identity. Libertarians deny the claim that people have rights to acquire property in virtue of their ethnic or national heritage which is why they don't support repatriation or a policy of keeping artifacts in European museums.

Instead, we might take a lesson from libertarian approaches to the protection of endangered species. In cases where it's unclear or controversial who should own a historical artifact, public officials might consider privatizing their collections. Basically no one but libertarians likes this idea. But if the people who claim an entitlement to historical artifacts are sincere when they say that their highest priority is that the artifacts be preserved and protected for all to see, privatizing the artifacts is a great way to accomplish this goal.

Two immediate problems with this plan are that, at present, it would involve European museums profiting from the sale of colonized artifacts and it would distribute artifacts to people in rich countries or rich governments. But if people in postcolonial countries object to European museums owning the actual artifacts, this solution gives them an opportunity to reclaim them. And if they object to museums owning the value of the artifacts, this solution enables the museums to return the value of the artifacts without necessarily parting with the artifact itself (e.g., if they pay the highest price in an auction.) To the second concern, it would be a mistake to assume that the privatization of artifacts is likely to distribute artifacts to wealthier people and institutions. Rather, since people pay to view historic artifacts, a private market in artifacts is likely to distribute artifacts to the places where people have a strong interest in viewing them.

If not reparations, then how should public officials today respond to the historical injustices of colonialism? Today, the term neocolonialism refers to the practice of business leaders and state actors in rich countries building factories and extracting resources from postcolonial countries. Critics of this practice argue that neocolonialism is a continuation of colonialism because, even if it benefits native people in postcolonial countries, they are placed in a position where they have less economic power than the foreign actors. Assume for a moment that economic development in postcolonial countries is voluntary, meaning that people have property rights, no one is forced to work, and no one is prevented from starting a business of their own. Libertarians point out that an economic system that perpetuates or even widens the gap between the rich and the poor can still be a good system, as long as it is voluntary and mutually beneficial to both parties. Economic development is often like this, so it would be a mistake to view economic development as an extension of colonialism, which was unfree and bad for native populations.

Land acknowledgments are another way that people acknowledge their colonial past:

LAND ACKNOWLEDGMENTS

In an area that was formerly occupied by an indigenous tribe, people preface lectures and other public events with a statement that describes the indigenous people who previously lived on the land, sometimes suggesting that they are still entitled to the territory.

One problem with land acknowledgments is that they appeal to an ethno-nationalist theory of property rights, as above, where they assume that people's enforceable rights to govern territory and extract resources are so strong that they are inalienable and enforceable for all of their descendants. The case for land acknowledgments faces some of the same challenges as the case for colonial reparations. This is also an implausible theory of property rights for a few reasons. First, a system of property rights should not give different rights to different people based on their ethnic ancestry, nor should it assign property rights to an entire political community instead of individuals. Second, some indigenous people did not recognize nationalistic property rights or territorial rights, so the practice of land acknowledgments is implicitly assuming the statist framework that it purports to critique. And third, many of the indigenous people who did recognize collective property rights or territorial rights conquered the territory they occupied, but land acknowledgments typically only recognize the most recent indigenous occupants of a territory.

FUTURE GENERATIONS

Everyone today lives in conditions of enduring injustice because the effects of historical injustices persist today. For instance, the Industrial Revolution damaged the environment in ways that are still harmful to human health. Likewise, state actors still enforce unfair policies and people act on prejudicial attitudes that they've collectively inherited from their ancestors. Officials have moral reasons to remedy these enduring injustices not because previous generations were wronged, but because they continue to harm people.

At the same time, we are also the beneficiaries of historical progress. Specifically, people today are richer, healthier, and expected to live longer than any previous generation. And the greatest gift our ancestors have given us has come from free markets. We live in times of abundance because of previous generations' productivity and innovation. And the best gift we can give future generations is the continued prosperity that a free market provides.

For this reason, some libertarians argue that the best way to help people is to support and expand free markets. If we have any reason to consider the fate of our descendants, we should invest in economic growth. Tyler Cowen, for example, is a libertarian proponent of this position. Cowen argues that it's usually a mistake to limit the rate of economic growth in order to redistribute wealth from the rich to the poor, because even if such a transfer would effectively help the poor, it imposes a much greater cost on future generations.

Longtermists are philosophers who argue that people should do more for future generations than just invest in economic growth. Longtermists are especially worried about existential risks—threats that could destroy the planet or kill all the humans on Earth. They argue that public officials should also protect future generations from threats associated with nuclear weapons and bioterrorism, and potentially enforce regulations that prevent supercomputers from harming humans.

Some longtermist causes align with libertarian values. Nuclear disarmament, for example, is consistent with libertarians' pacifism. And if a billionaire wants to fund an asteroid defense program, libertarians aren't especially opposed to the idea. But in other cases, libertarians worry that longtermist causes could backfire if public officials impose additional risks on people in an effort to prevent other risks. For example, government research into bioterrorism might introduce the risk of lab leaks or chemical warfare. Or in the case of proposals to regulate artificial intelligence for safety, libertarians worry that these proposals are actually protectionist policies that would legally entrench the market power of larger companies while shutting innovative new software companies out of the AI market.

SUMMARY

Libertarians are cosmopolitans. They think that state actors should give all people's freedom equal weight. But even people who are not cosmopolitans have compelling reasons to support libertarian foreign policies because so many military campaigns do not advance national security for the people involved and because immigration doesn't just benefit immigrants, it benefits host countries as well. And though libertarians are often skeptical of foreign aid and redistributive policies that aim to rectify historical injustices, they argue that their broader commitments to free trade and economic growth are likely to benefit the global poor and future generations more than any global redistributive policy could anyhow.

FURTHER READING

- Carens, Joseph. 2020. "9. Immigration and the Welfare State." In *Democracy and the Welfare State*, edited by Amy Gutmann, 207–230. Princeton University Press. https://doi.org/10.1515/9780691217956-012.
- Cowen, Tyler. 2018. *Stubborn Attachments: A Vision for a Society of Free, Prosperous, and Responsible Individuals*. San Francisco, CA: Stripe Press.
- El-Sadr, Wafaa M., Charles B. Holmes, Peter Mugyenyi, Harsha Thirumurthy, Tedd Ellerbrock, Robert Ferris, Ian Sanne, et al. 2012. "Scale-Up of HIV Treatment through PEPFAR: A Historic Public Health Achievement." *JAIDS Journal of Acquired Immune Deficiency Syndromes* 60 (August): S96. https://doi.org/10.1097/QAI.0b013e31825eb27b.
- Greaves, Hilary, and Theron Pummer. 2019. *Effective Altruism: Philosophical Issues*. Oxford University Press.
- Heyd, David. 2024. "Group (Non) Identity and Historical Justice." *Res Publica* 30 (4): 705–722. https://doi.org/10.1007/s11158-023-09649-5.
- Hidalgo, Javier S. 2010. "An Argument for Guest Worker Programs." *Public Affairs Quarterly* 24 (1): 21–38.
- Hidalgo, Javier S. 2018a. "The Ethics of People Smuggling." In *Refugee Crisis: The Borders of Human Mobility*. Routledge.
- Hidalgo, Javier S. 2018b. *Unjust Borders: Individuals and the Ethics of Immigration*. New York: Routledge. https://doi.org/10.4324/978131514 5235.
- MacAskill, William. 2016. *Doing Good Better: How Effective Altruism Can Help You Help Others, Do Work That Matters, and Make Smarter Choices about Giving Back*. Avery.
- McMahan, Jeff. 2009. *Killing in War*. Oxford: Oxford University Press.
- Ord, Toby. 2020. *The Precipice: Existential Risk and the Future of Humanity*. Illustrated edition. New York: Grand Central Publishing.
- Sahar, Khan. 2017. "Libertarians Shouldn't Accept the Case for Colonialism." *Cato Unbound*, October 9. www.cato-unbound.org/2017/10/09/sahar-khan/libertarians-shouldnt-accept-case-colonialism.
- Tesón, Fernando R., and Bas van der Vossen. 2017. *Debating Humanitarian Intervention: Should We Try to Save Strangers?* Oxford University Press.
- Zwolinski, Matt. 2007. "Sweatshops, Choice, and Exploitation." *Business Ethics Quarterly* 17 (4): 689–727. https://doi.org/10.5840/beq20071745.

9

CONCLUSION
Politics and Freedom

In this book, we've provided an overview of libertarian political philosophy and public policy. We focused on concrete cases in an effort to illustrate that these aren't just abstract academic debates. Theories of justice have real consequences in the political realm, and as a result, they matter for how ordinary people live their lives.

A key takeaway from the arguments in this book is that it is very difficult to justify policies that deviate from the libertarian default. Too often, political officials and citizens assume that the state has the authority to enforce most laws as long as the laws were passed according to a fair and public procedure and as long as they are not egregiously unjust. But public officials do not enjoy the presumptive right to interfere with people's self-regarding personal and economic decisions. Rather, the burden of justification lies with public officials to explain why each particular limitation on individual liberty is justified.

Suppose that there's a referendum and your fellow citizens overwhelmingly vote to cap the number of haircuts any American may receive in a year at 25. This law was passed according to a fair and public procedure and is probably not egregiously unjust. Nevertheless, it seems obviously wrong to enforce, as it violates a person's right of bodily autonomy. Now perhaps the law could be

DOI: 10.4324/9781003270720-9

justified if the haircut cap produced some great good, but this point is consistent with the libertarian claim that the burden of justification rests with public officials.

It's helpful to think of this idea in terms of moral authority. Bob doesn't have any moral authority to forcibly impose limits on your haircut choices. Nor does Cathy have any moral authority to forcibly impose limits on your haircut choices. So it would be strange to believe that Bob and Cathy somehow acquire the moral authority to forcibly impose limits on your haircut choices when they get together and vote on the issue. In other words, if each citizen lacks this authority individually, they presumably lack it collectively. Zero plus zero equals zero.

We have also argued throughout this book that theories of justice should be evaluated in comparison to each other at comparable levels of idealization. And in both ideal and non-ideal theory, libertarianism has the edge. In an ideal world, it would be morally better if everyone had the right to trade and work on their own terms, without government interference. In non-ideal contexts, markets are usually the best feasible social arrangement for generating innovation and productivity.

Another lesson of this book is that it's a mistake to treat the state as a kind of machine or agent, just as it would be a mistake to treat the market or civil society in this way. People often say things like, "The state can simply end poverty by transferring more money to the poor," when they agree that it wouldn't make sense to say "The market and civil society can simply end poverty by transferring more money to the poor." People intuitively recognize that the market isn't like a machine with a "transfer money to the poor" button on it that we can simply press. Rather, what outcome the market produces depends on how individual employers, employees, customers, and so on decide to act. But in the same vein, what outcome the state produces depends on how individual voters, politicians, bureaucrats, and so on decide to act. There's no "transfer money to the poor" button in any statehouse on Earth. So everyone should be wary of the presumption that the states are in a better position than markets when it comes to social and economic problems, because in both cases, these institutions are composed of many different individuals who are all have self-interested motivations and who all have considerable practical and epistemic limitations. This is why we've generally used terms like "public officials" or "state actors" instead of referring to "the state" as if it is a distinctive agent.

Throughout, we have also argued that ethics and politics are not separate areas of normative inquiry. People's moral rights set limits on other people's authority to interfere with them. Because well-being is morally significant, it matters whether a political ideology would promote overall well-being, and it matters whether people have stronger moral reasons to maximize overall well-being or to equalize it. Some of the trickier issues in libertarian thought arise due to controversies in normative ethics. People disagree about how the moral reasons we have to respect individual rights should weigh against the moral reasons we have to promote animal or human welfare or the well-being of future generations. They also disagree about how people should respond to moral disagreement, or risk, or uncertainty about the boundaries of a person's body, or vagueness in our everyday language.

This is not to say that libertarianism is primarily a moral theory. The case for libertarianism in this book highlights the many ways that libertarianism offers pragmatic solutions for a range of important ongoing policy problems. Yet philosophical disputes seep into debates about public policy because, as we've asserted throughout this book, the state isn't special. Insofar as any issue is morally controversial, asking public officials to resolve the issue through legislation or judicial decision-making doesn't actually resolve the issue because the same moral considerations that apply to everyday decision-making also apply to public policy.

Another practical implication of this book is that it is very morally risky to get involved in politics because public officials often enforce unjust laws or hold back economic progress. It would be great if the people who held public office and worked for the government could minimize the moral risks of their professions, but this is often difficult and individual actors are likely to struggle to meaningfully affect large governmental problems. This is why, for most people, ignoring politics is not only a good idea for their own well-being but also a way to refocus their efforts on spheres of activity that are voluntary and productive. People who want to make a difference in the world should consider starting businesses or giving to effective aid organizations.

At this point, readers might be wondering if libertarianism is so great, why aren't more people libertarians? The good news is that many people are more libertarian than a partisan vote would reveal. Pollsters find that most people in both parties endorse a range of libertarian policies. The problem is that members of each party endorse different libertarian policies alongside a package of authoritarian policies. Many people aren't more libertarian because they support policies that protect the freedoms that they personally care about, for example, guns, reproductive rights, and religious freedom, but they also support anti-libertarian policies that would benefit their favored group at the expense of an out-group.

It's also worth noting that despite the expansion of state power, increasing militarization, and the rise of welfare states, the world is nevertheless also more libertarian than it has been at any other point in human history. Markets are more open and stable than they've ever been, and the expansion of capitalism worldwide has coincided with the greatest gains in human well-being and life expectancy that humanity has ever experienced. Communism has failed everywhere it's been tried. Slavery is illegal. Women increasingly have property rights and economic freedom. Property rights are no longer assigned on the basis of hereditary privilege. There is still room for progress when it comes to protecting free markets and individual liberty, but we've already come so far.

FURTHER READING

- Brennan, Jason. 2012. *Libertarianism: What Everyone Needs to Know.* 1st edition. New York: Oxford University Press.
- Freiman, Christopher. 2020. *Why It's OK to Ignore Politics.* 1st edition. New York, NY: Routledge.
- Mack, Eric. 2018. *Libertarianism.* 1st edition. Cambridge, UK and Medord, MA: Polity.
- Pourvand, Kaveh. 2024. "Social Complexity and the Emergent State." *Politics, Philosophy, and Economics.* https://doi.org/10.1177/1470594X241264031
- Schmidtz, David, Bas van der Vossen, and Jason Brennan, eds. 2020. *The Routledge Handbook of Libertarianism.* 1st edition. Routledge.

INDEX

For Product Safety Concerns and Information please contact our EU
representative GPSR@taylorandfrancis.com
Taylor & Francis Verlag GmbH, Kaufingerstraße 24, 80331 München, Germany

www.ingramcontent.com/pod-product-compliance
Lightning Source LLC
Chambersburg PA
CBHW050646270326
41927CB00012B/2900